Becoming a parent for the fir... for both women and men, creating a complete change in the emotional and physical structure of the lives of both parents. Tony Bradman's comprehensive look at the impact of fathering responds to an essential change in attitude: that more and more men want to play an active role in parenting right from the beginning.

The wealth of literature and information available on pregnancy and childcare is primarily aimed at the mother-to-be and oriented to her needs. Previously neglected have been those aspects of pregnancy, childbirth, infant care and beyond that are pertinent to the father.

*The Essential Father* redresses the balance and covers all aspects, from the effect of pregnancy on the father-to-be to our society's attitude to fathers. Tony Bradman, father of three small children and deputy editor of *Parents* magazine, has written the book he needed when becoming a father for the first time. *The Essential Father* contains all the information and support every father will need to help him enjoy and adjust to his new role as a parent.

*Also by Tony Bradman*

So You want to Have a Baby?   (Julia MacRae)

*For children:*
A Kiss on the Nose   (Heinemann)
Night Time   (Methuen)
One Nil   (Viking Kestrel)
Rhymes With Me   (Macdonald)
John Lennon   (Hamish Hamilton)

# THE ESSENTIAL FATHER

## TONY BRADMAN

London
UNWIN PAPERBACKS
Boston   Sydney

First published in Great Britain by Unwin Paperbacks 1985

This book is copyright under the Berne Convention. No reproduction without permission. All rights reserved.

**UNWIN® PAPERPACKS**
40 Museum Street, London WC1A 1LU, UK

Unwin Paperbacks
Park Lane, Hemel Hempstead, Herts HP2 4TE, UK

George Allen & Unwin Australia Pty Ltd
8 Napier Street, North Sydney, NSW 2060, Australia

Unwin Paperbacks with the
Port Nicholson Press
PO Box 11-838 Wellington, New Zealand

Copyright © Tony Bradman 1985

ISBN 0-04-649-029-9

Set in 10 on 11 point Sabon by Columns of Reading
and printed in Great Britain by
Guernsey Press Co Ltd, Guernsey,
Channel Islands

For my father, John Arthur Bradman
  22/7/25 – 18/4/83
And for his grandson, Thomas James Bradman
  born 21/12/83


A child is sleeping:
An old man gone.
                                James Joyce

# Contents

| | page |
|---|---|
| Acknowledgements | ix |
| Preface: Mary Poppins and the new fatherhood | 1 |
| Introduction: The outsider | 9 |

| **Part one  Preparing for parenthood** | 39 |
|---|---|
| 1  Choosing to have a child | 41 |
| 2  Paving the way | 45 |
|     Your relationship, the wealth factor, making the decision, the health factor | |
| 3  What happens in conception? | 62 |
|     Infertility problems, how to deal with them | |

| **Part two  The pregnant father** | 69 |
|---|---|
| 4  What happens in pregnancy? | 71 |
|     The inside story, the outside story | |
| 5  Antenatal care | 81 |
|     Your partner's feelings | |
| 6  The brooding father | 88 |
|     Tangled emotions | |
| 7  Sharing pregnancy | 95 |
|     Sex in pregnancy, being positive, going to classes, a second pregnancy, losing a baby | |

| **Part three  Birth** | 109 |
|---|---|
| 8  What happens in labour? | 111 |
|     Getting ready for the big day, the first signs, the three stages of birth, the pain of labour, pain relief, natural childbirth | |
| 9  The father's role | 130 |
|     Feeling anxious, active support | |

| | | |
|---|---|---|
| 10 | The delivery and after<br>The crowning moment, the first feed, possible problems, coping with an emergency birth | 136 |

**Part four  Becoming a father** — 149

| | | |
|---|---|---|
| 11 | Early days<br>Coming home, making an effort | 151 |
| 12 | Back to work<br>The great divide again, outsiders at home | 162 |
| 13 | Sex – and other problems<br>Postnatal depression, positive solutions, surviving parenthood | 170 |

**Part five  Fathers, mothers and children** — 183

| | | |
|---|---|---|
| 14 | Your child's development<br>Your talented baby, walking and talking, play and potties | 185 |
| 15 | Family life<br>A mother's work..., absent fathers, boys will be boys? | 197 |
| 16 | The caring, sharing father<br>Working at fatherhood, advanced fatherhood | 209 |

**Part six  Breaking the mould** — 221

| | | |
|---|---|---|
| 17 | Parents and work<br>Working mothers, men's attitudes | 223 |
| 18 | Lone fathers<br>Swapping roles | 234 |
| 19 | The tyranny of work<br>Resistance to change | 243 |
| 20 | Changing attitudes<br>Paternity leave, financial help | 250 |

Envoi:  The love you make — 260
Useful addresses — 265
Useful books — 268
Index — 271

# Acknowledgements

Just as there are no husbands without wives, there are no fathers or sons without mothers, so here is the place to thank my mother for bringing me into the world and giving me most of whatever insight I have into much of the subject matter of this book. I owe her and my sister a great deal, and this book is theirs with love. Thanks and love also to my brother-in-law, my nephews Mark and Christopher and my niece Paula. Special thanks to Nick and Jenny, in whose house part of this book was written, and for the discussions which honed some of my arguments. Love and thanks to Martin and Deborah and Louise, too.

I would also like to thank everyone connected with *Parents* magazine in the past and present for their help and support, as well as for the insight I've gained in working with them and discussing much of what I've written about here. There are many things in this book which were first formulated in features I've written for *Parents*; this book would not exist without that background. Thanks also to *Cosmopolitan* magazine for giving me the chance to test out some of the ideas in these pages in several articles.

Special thanks must go to Mr Cyril Young and Dr Robert Dinwiddie, who have checked the pages that follow for medical accuracy. Their help and advice over the years has been more than valuable to me, and especially appreciated in the knowledge of the very hard work they do in their respective fields. Any opinions expressed are of course my own – as are the remaining errors, if any.

Special mention must also be accorded to Harriet Griffey, my editor, who believed in me enough to commission this book at a difficult time for me personally, and then to wait with almost infinite patience while I wrestled with the problems of being an involved father and an author. This book, which owes its title to her, would not have existed without Harriet, or the long conversations on the telephone during which she kept my spirits up.

Equally, it would not have existed without the help of all the fathers I've talked to over the years. I thank them all now collectively, and extend special thanks to just a few: Barry Cunningham, Richard Hill, Alan O'Kelly, Andy Seymour, Chris Bartle. Thanks also to Michel Odent, who gave me some valuable new insights into fatherhood towards the end of the writing of this book. I must also express my gratitude to Melissa Brooks for her sensitive copy-editing, which did much to make this a better and more readable book.

There is one person to whom more than thanks is due, and that's my wife, Sally. Without her constant support and encouragement, without the continual dialogue she's sustained with me, none of what follows would exist at all. Sally has made me a father three times over — and done so much more than words could ever say. This book is, therefore, above all hers.

# Preface: Mary Poppins and the new fatherhood

> It is nothing like the women's movement, and probably never will be. Each man seems to be struggling with it quietly ... It is a deceptively quiet movement, a shifting in direction, a saying 'no' to old patterns, a searching for new values, a struggling with basic questions that each man seems to be dealing with alone ...
>
> from *The Second Stage* by Betty Friedan

Not long after our third child was born, we bought a video recorder. It was a present to ourselves, a present which would enable us to catch up on all the films we'd missed because of parenthood's devastating effect on our social life. It would also mean we could record the TV programmes we didn't see, all those interesting documentaries or foreign films which were broadcast too late; we have long since found out that having children meant you tended to collapse into bed at 10 pm on most nights, however much you might want to stay up longer.

Inevitably, that present to ourselves soon turned into a present for our children. The films we got hold of were more likely to have titles such as *Pete's Dragon* and *Hansel and Gretel* than *Kramer versus Kramer*, the film I particularly wanted to see. Still, I didn't mind that much, because I quite enjoyed spending cold, wet Sunday afternoons indoors in front of a log fire with a film such as *Mary Poppins* to make us sing and laugh. The fact that I was supposed to be writing a book about fatherhood, that I was behind my deadline, that it wasn't going very well and that it felt as if I would never, ever, ever finish it did make me feel obscurely guilty.

Mind you, I felt equally guilty when I did work on this book at weekends. Writing *The Essential Father*, writing the words you're reading at this moment, actually kept me from my children and meant that I couldn't share parenthood with my wife Sally as much as I wanted to. The irony is perfect. I wanted to write this book because families need fathers and fathers need families, and although much lip service is paid to the idea of shared parenthood, the simple fact is that most men get less out of fatherhood than they could or should. What I'm trying to do in this book is to use the insight I've gained into the experience of men as fathers for two purposes: firstly, to help individual men to get the best out of their own family life, and secondly, to do my share to help along the process by which society will change to make life easier for parents of both sexes.

Society *has* changed, and is continuing to change, there can be no doubt about that. The rise of the women's movement in the last twenty years has meant that we can no longer take for granted anything about the roles of the sexes. Widespread economic and social change has affected much in the way we think about how men and women should behave. Looked at from one angle, it's obvious that we have come very far. Looked at from another — from the perspective of parenthood today — we haven't come very far at all.

Old attitudes die hard, especially when they're so deeply rooted in us and in society that much of their effect is almost unconscious. I would argue that in many ways, attitudes to parenthood *have not significantly changed at all*. I was born in 1954, and brought up by parents who were born in the 1920s. They were the children of parents who had been born in the 1890s and early 1900s. I realised not so very long ago that I was actually only separated from the Victorians by two generations, and that much of what I was doing as a father had more in common with 1900 than the 1980s.

I'm not talking about being the stern, unforgiving sort of father who never spoke to his children except to tell them how many strokes of the belt they were going to get; rather that the Victorians assumed a father's role lay in providing for his family, which in an industrial society based on the division of labour meant two things: one, that fathers in general would have to work outside the home; and two, that childcare and housework would naturally devolve on to wives, and their servants (if they were lucky enough to have them). The essential pattern was very clear: men ran the world outside the home, while women dealt with affairs inside it. Take away the servants who made upper-middle- and upper-class life possible in the England of the last century, add the fact that many women these days combine motherhood, housework *and* paid employment outside the home, and you have much the same picture. Women are still seen primarily as mothers, and men primarily as workers – and never the twain shall meet.

Of course there has been change in the last century. By far the majority of fathers are present at the births of their children, something which would probably have caused outrage when my grandfather, or even my father, was born. Men are now taking a greater share in almost every aspect of childcare and parenthood, and I know that the willingness to do even more is there. But we fathers have a problem; society is organised in such a way that it is often very hard indeed for us to share parenthood with our partners, however much we or they want us to. Society has changed to the extent that many of us – both men and women – are trying to do things differently when it comes to parenthood. Just as many women would now like to get more from life outside the home and break away from the traditional pattern of service to husband, and children, so more men would like a greater involvement with their families. The point is that society hasn't yet changed enough, and neither have our ideas. There is a tension between what many of us want out of life and what it's possible to get.

In very simple terms, as far as most families are concerned, society is still arranged along traditional economic lines. Even in those families where mothers are in some form of paid employment, most of the burden for providing the family's living rests on the father, which means he will probably have to spend five days a week or more out of the house. As I discovered, that often ensures fathers only see their children for something like an hour a day, at the most. We have the weekends and holidays, of course, but something you soon find out about parenthood is that as your children grow – and as you have more children – life tends to become ever more complicated. Weekends are often filled with essential jobs, children's parties, shopping and the hundreds of other things everyone has to do.

The result is that most fathers find themselves to be secondary parents to their children. In simple terms, when your toddler grazes her knee, she's more likely to run to the parent she sees most often, and for most families, that's the mother. So what? you might say. Isn't that the way it's always been?

Whether that't true or not I simply don't know. All I do know is that most of us suffer because families are still structured in traditional ways. Women lose out because modern motherhood can often be a lonely, isolated and isolating experience. Bringing up small children is too much of a burden for anyone to bear, especially when it's assumed that the job includes running a house with all that that entails in terms of domestic chores, shopping and cooking. But that's what we expect of mothers today. Complete financial responsibility for the support of a family is also too much for any one person to bear, especially in the early years. Fathers often lose out as well simply by not being around; we miss our children's first steps, first words, their first day at school. If that's the way it's always been, it's time we changed it and made life more equal all round.

Life today, however, is often difficult for parents because we are in a period of transition, a time when we're moving away from accepted roles and stereotypes to different sets of values and social structures. Times of transition always generate tension and anxiety, as most parents find out for themselves, because becoming a parent is in itself probably the biggest and most important transition in anyone's life. The early years of parenthood can be an anxious, unsettling time, one which changes your life totally and forever. It's a very intense experience, and under that sort of pressure, it's hardly surprising that most of us move inexorably (and often unconsciously) towards the stereotypes with which we're most familiar. At a very deep level, we tend to be happiest with the idea that women are better at being parents than men, and that men shouldn't get involved too much with the *real* business of parenthood. This inevitably clashes with what's going on elsewhere in our minds under the influence of more enlightened ideas. The tension and anxiety which ensue are sometimes very hard to deal with, not least because it's hard to work out where they're coming from.

This is the core of the book: what it's like to become a father today, and it's designed, above all, to answer all the questions you might have about pregnancy, birth, child development and family life *from a father's point of view*. When I first became a father I read through several books which purported to be about my experience; they weren't. In general, they were baby books for mothers under another name. I long ago decided that I would write the book I had wanted, looked for, and needed in those anxious days when my eldest daughter Emma was born. It's too late to help me now (so my second daughter Helen and my son Thomas have had to suffer a dad who didn't know all the answers, just as Emma did), but I hope it will help *you*.

It has been a very difficult book to write. One reason is simply that combining working at a full-time job (which I do) and trying to share the burdens of parenthood with Sally leaves me with very little time or energy for anything else. In fact this book has been written in sunny lunch hours when I'd rather be outside the office; it's been written in the evenings after I've helped put the kids to bed and read them stories (during which I nearly fall asleep); it's been written in other people's houses, in trains, on three different typewriters, in the middle of the night and when I've had 'flu, mumps (caught from the children) and fatigue-induced headaches. In short, it's been fitted in around a busy life, and I hope it hasn't suffered too much because of that. I'd like you to bear in mind as you read it that between almost every sentence and the one which follows it, between almost every paragraph and section, often between the words and even the letters of the words, I've been living the reality of what I'm writing about. Inside, around, between, underneath and all over these words that you're reading are the sounds and sights of my children: smiles and laughter, chickenpox and dirty nappies, their births, their cuddles, their achievements and love, love, love. Enough; let Emma sum it up: 'I know you have to work very hard, dad, and I know that your book's not going well. But I'm afraid you're just going to have to cope with it.' As I write, Emma is nearly six.

It's also been a difficult book to write for another reason. I discovered that although I had much to say about how fathers experience pregnancy and birth and the early months of parenthood, I couldn't really explain what I meant or give any advice until I had worked out for myself the context in which such experiences and feelings about them take place. In short, I had to sit down and analyse what it means to be a *man* today before I could write about what it means to be a *father*. The two are intimately, intricately and inextricably linked; entangled might even be a better word. The conditioning is so deep, so much part of what it means to be a man, that extracting it is like a very complex mining operation deep underground; it takes time and effort and it costs a lot, in emotional terms. I had to face up to my own chauvinism; I had to try and understand what it was that made me what I am. That's why the book begins with a lengthy chapter about my own experiences. I now see that it was a difficult thing to do because part of our conditioning as men involves encouragement *not* to look into ourselves in this way, especially where our relationships with our partners and children are concerned. That's why we stay outsiders, even when we're unhappy about not being excluded.

At any rate, to quote Gloria Steinem (from her book *Outrageous Acts and Everyday Rebellions*), 'You can't change society until you change the ideas in people's heads.' That's what I am trying to do in this book, and when it comes to fatherhood, you'll probably need to change your ideas in almost every respect. I also believe that changing your ideas must involve *changing what you do*. It's no good saying that you want to share parenthood and be a terrific father if you're then unwilling to change a nappy. I would go further and say that we men have got to be prepared to change our attitudes to work, careers, society and many larger issues if we are to show that our commitments to shared parenthood is more than lip service.

Which brings me back to *Mary Poppins*. I first saw this film years ago when my father took me to see it on a Saturday afternoon. My parents were divorced, and Saturday was 'dad's day'. At any rate, I hadn't much enjoyed it the first time round, being more interested in Westerns and war films. But it was a startling revelation to me when I watched it the second time round with my two daughters. How could I not have seen before that *Mary Poppins* summed up almost everything I wanted to say in this book about fatherhood?

For the key character in the film turns out to be Mr Banks, father to the two children looked after by the super competent nanny played by Julie Andrews. At the beginning of the film, he's one of those distant Victorian fathers, a father who expects his children to be 'seen and not heard', and indeed only when they're clean and shiny and ready for bed. He works in a bank, is punctual, a good provider, and has absolutely nothing to do with the running of the domestic side of his life or the nursery, all of which rests in the hands of his wife and female servants.

But Mary Poppins, who's on the side of children and love, artfully tricks Mr Banks into taking his children to the bank where he works; they cross the great divide from the woman's world (of home and children) to man's world of money and business. Mr Banks's son Michael wants to give his tuppence to the bird lady for her pigeons, but Mr Banks won't hear of such nonsense. He insists that Michael invest it in the bank. His son's refusal is a disaster for Mr Banks, whose employers decide to dismiss him.

What amazed me was that the main result of this is a conversion in Mr Banks as devastating – and to me as important – as St Paul's on the road to Damascus. Mr Banks realises that he hardly knows his own children, and, what's more, that both he and they are unhappy about the way their family life is organised. So he decides that he doesn't care about his job any more, and that he'd rather dedicate himself to having fun with his children and being happy. What's even more amazing is that under Mr Banks's influence and example his former employers become less money grabbing and anti-family – and the film ends with everyone gleefully flying kites.

As the closing titles of the film rolled up, I sat with my daughters trying to work out where I was going to get hold of someone like Mary Poppins. Alas, such wonderful characters seem only to exist in films; I realised that if we are to liberate ourselves as fathers – and humanise the world of work and commerce – then we are going to have to do it ourselves. That's not to say that I am excluding women; far from it. I don't believe that's possible, nor would I want to do it. When it comes to parenthood, men and women are in it together; all I would like to see is a more equitable distribution of tasks and opportunities. That's why although this book is addressed first and foremost to fathers, I'm hoping that just as many women will read it to gain insight into the way in which their partners' minds are working. Ideally, it's a book which I would like couples to read together (or one after the other, as the case may be).

But I don't want you to think that fatherhood is all unrelieved gloom, tension, anxiety and problems. It isn't; it can be a glorious experience, and one of the most rewarding and enriching things any man can do. I think that it has changed me for the better, and one of the main reasons I wanted to write this book was to show you how to make sure you get much more of the good side of parenthood and a lot less of the bad side. There are plenty of rewards fatherhood can bring, for men, for their partners, and above all, for our children. The most important thing I can do is to show you the sort of problems that can crop up – and how to overcome them.

I believe that the beginnings of a new fatherhood are evident already, and I hope that you'll find the stirrings of the new father inside you as well as inside this book, and that your reading of it will go some way to liberating him. If that happens, we'll begin to change the world.

Remember – *fathers are essential, and you can be the essential father.*

# Introduction: The outsider

'I think we are going to have an infant, Bill,' she said, from far off.

He trembled, and his fingers tightened on hers.

'Why?' he asked, his heart beating. 'You don't know?'

'I do,' she said.

They continued without saying any more, walking along opposite horizons, hand in hand across the intervening space, two separate people. And he trembled as if a wind blew on to him in strong gusts, out of the unseen. He was afraid. He was afraid to know he was alone. For she seemed fulfilled and separate and sufficient in her half of the world.

From *The Rainbow* by D. H. Lawrence

Some time during the late evening or night of 9 September 1977, a sperm from my body met an egg deep inside one of my wife's Fallopian tubes. There, assisted by several million other sperms, it finally managed to penetrate the egg's outer covering. Soon, the nucleus contained in the head of the sperm fused with the egg's nucleus, uniting 23 chromosomes from me and 23 chromosomes from Sally to make a unique combination of 23 pairs inside one fertilised cell.

Sally and I had done that most human of things; we had made love and created a brand new human being, our first child – Emma. And in doing so we had also created two other new people – a new mother and a new father. Those events, that microscopic drama, proved momentous for all three of us, as it does for the people involved every time it happens.

Of course, I can't be sure that the marvellous event did actually take place on 9 September 1977. Doctors estimate that an average, normal pregnancy lasts 40 weeks, or 280 days from the first day of the mother's last period before conception, a figure which assumes her to have a regular, 28-day menstrual cycle. I knew very well that Sally and I might have conceived Emma on 8 or 10 September, or even a whole week earlier, since throughout the pregnancy the doctors and midwives insisted that she was due to be born a week before the date on which she did arrive – 2 June 1978.

That doesn't matter. What does matter is that Emma *did* arrive on that day and promptly changed our lives forever. What matters to me is that the responsibility for her creation is half mine, something I *share* with Sally; that's why I worked out the date on which she may well have been conceived. It's a date, and a moment, which is charged with significance for me; it's a date which symbolises the beginning of the process which changed me from plain Tony Bradman, into Tony Bradman, father of Emma – and subsequently, of Helen and Thomas.

None of us, obviously enough, were really aware of that moment at the time. Sally and I may have been asleep, or even at work the next day when it happened, and Emma herself was, of course, blissfully unaware of the fact that she was being created. You may even think it strange that I should be talking about the moment of conception in such terms. Surely it's more usual to think of the day a child is born as the time when you become a 'proper' mother or father?

It goes without saying that birth is very important indeed for all concerned. But the baby who is born has been alive for many months already, and the changes which are involved in the process of becoming a parent often begin almost as soon as your child is conceived. Indeed, many of the changes you'll go through, many of the problems and anxieties which will affect your experience of parenthood for better or for worse have their roots in your life and circumstances *before* the moment of conception.

At any rate, the instant when my daughter was created grew in importance for me as I began to grapple with the realities of becoming a father during the pregnancy and after. Its significance lay in the fact that at that moment, Sally and I were equals in the creation of our child. All right, I'll admit that the entire process of fertilisation took place within Sally's body, and also that in terms of sheer size, her egg was far, far larger than any of my sperms, or even of most of them put together. But in the part where it really mattered, in the nucleus, we were absolutely equal in contributing 23 chromosomes each. My contribution was as important as Sally's, and I felt that that meant my stake in parenthood was as great as hers too. The symbolic importance of all this grew by leaps and bounds as something else began to impinge on my life – the feeling that I certainly wasn't Sally's equal when it came to childcare, the feeling that I was a second-class, useless and quite inferior parent, an outsider as far as the whole business was concerned. And all, quite simply, *because I am a man*.

In one way, of course, I am an outsider when it comes to having a baby, and couldn't possibly be anything else. The facts of human anatomy are such that it's impossible for me to be pregnant, give birth or breastfeed, and I suspect that despite all the advantages in genetic engineering and test tube baby techniques, that's the way it's going to stay. Our physical contribution to the creation of our children will remain what mine was on 9 September 1977; the delivery of a package of genetic material through the medium of sexual intercourse, although to put it in those terms says nothing about the pleasure and love which can be involved (and was on that particular occasion). At any rate, our children's mothers will still have to go through pregnancy, birth and breastfeeding, experiences which are very special and very demanding for most women. Becoming a parent for a woman is, of course, a very physical experience indeed, and one which involves an extremely close physical relationship with another human being – the child. I've seen with my own eyes just how close that relationship can be, and it's vital that it should be so. In a sense, we fathers are naturally outside that relationship to a certain extent, outsiders looking in; although as we'll see, you don't have to stay outside forever, and your role as a father can and should be a positive one from a very early stage.

But in physical terms, fathers are strange beasts. While our partners grow visibly into motherhood after conception, we appear to remain much the same throughout pregnancy and after. There are no really obvious differences between a man whose partner is expecting a child and a man whose partner isn't, at least, not in the sense that there's a difference between the two women in that equation. In fact, in terms of the history of man, it's now thought that knowledge of the male role in conceiving children is a very recent development. Anthropologists think that before the New Stone Age, we men were more or less completely unaware that sex had anything to do with pregnancy, and that women conceived either all by themselves or as a result of nocturnal visits from deities who were prepared to make house calls, or even simply by getting in the way of the right wind at the right time.

These days we do know what men's contribution to conception is, and that emotionally, for example, there is a very great difference between a man who is about to become a father and a man who isn't. Few fathers realise just how testing and demanding their partners' pregnancies can be until they're living through them. I know that I didn't, but it was only during the weeks and months after 9 September 1977 that I began to discover what it really means to be an outsider. I discovered that the commonest feelings for fathers in pregnancy are ones of exclusion and isolation. These feelings come at a time when you need above all to be involved and share what's happening to you with the woman who's carrying your child – just as she needs to share her feelings with you.

## Girls' stuff, women's talk

I did enjoy Sally's pregnancy most of the time, though, despite the fact that we hadn't planned to bring Emma into existence. It was a glorious, strange, confusing time which started with a 'half-accident', a signal lack of care in contraception when Sally was advised to come off the pill temporarily around the time we got married. Part of the reason for our lack of care was the fact that we both wanted children anyway, and once we were married it didn't seem to matter any more if we made a 'mistake'. That unstated, almost inarticulable feeling has a lot to do with the sort of assumptions society instils in us about marriage and parenthood, assumptions which in the end often coalesce into intense personal and social pressure on young couples to have a baby as soon as they can.

At any rate, in almost every way it was a mistake for us to have Emma at that time. We were too young, too broke and too totally unprepared to become parents. However, it soon became apparent that I was far more unprepared than Sally. She had something of an advantage; in fact, I began to think that she had a real head start when it came to being a parent. In the early weeks and months of her pregnancy, as I tried to cope with the shock of discovering that I was going to be a father, one phrase kept going round and round inside my head, a phrase I found silly and terrifying all at the same time: '*I've never even played with a doll!*' I suppose it was a way of telling myself that my experience of anything to do with the idea of having a baby was virtually nil. It was almost completely unknown territory for me.

It wasn't territory that Sally knew particularly well, either, but at least she *had* played with dolls as a child. She also has two younger sisters whom she'd seen brought up and, to a certain extent, helped her mother with. She had done some babysitting for relatives and friends of her parents, too, as many girls do when they're teenagers. So she had actually had *real* experience of looking after babies and young children *and* had survived to tell the tale. I had had some contact with children in the shape of my older sister's young son and daughter, Mark and Paula. With them, though, I'd always been more of the 'playful uncle' than a babysitter. The one time I'd ever looked after Paula as a baby, for example, she had reduced me to a quivering wreck inside half an hour by the simple expedient of screaming ... and screaming and screaming. Not that the experience deterred me; I enjoyed being around children, and I'd always wanted some of my own. But it was during Sally's pregnancy that I began to realise the differences between us went much, much deeper; they were differences of attitude and expectation.

At a very deep level, Sally – like most women – had always been encouraged by society to see herself as a potential mother. She had been brought up in a society imbued with the idea that women are meant to have babies and would want to spend the greater part of their lives dedicating themselves to their families, to their husbands and their children. Her upbringing wasn't at all unusual; the same could be said of almost all the women in our society today.

As we'll see further on, sexual stereotyping is so deeply embedded in us that it permeates the way we bring up our daughters right down to the level of the way we play with them and hold them, and even in the way we talk to them – and the things we say. In a way, it turns a girl's childhood into an intensive training programme for parenthood. As a child, Sally had not only played with dolls, she had played with dolls that looked like babies, she had been given toy prams, toy pushchairs, toy highchairs and all the assorted paraphernalia needed to turn her into a little mother. Don't forget that today's small girls are still being given the same sort of toys, and if anything, today's products are even more sophisticated imitations of the real thing despite the rise of feminism.

And what had I been up to while Sally had been in intensive training for motherhood? Something very different, if the toys I remember are anything to go by. I had a lot of toy soldiers, tanks, fighter planes, toy guns of all sorts, toy forts, construction sets, cars . . . need I go on? When Sally was dressing up and pretending to be a nurse or a princess or a mummy looking after her baby, I was pretending to be a cowboy, an all-action Marine or a shipwrecked sailor on a desert island (I used to drive my mother mad by tearing up old, and sometimes not-so-old clothes to look like an authentic Robinson Crusoe). Dolls, prams, babies . . . all that was girls' stuff. Real men weren't interested in any of it at all as far as I was concerned. In fact, if you were, then you were probably a little odd, to say the least; and need I add that our toy shops are packed with even more sophisticated imitation weaponry these days?

Of course, I was given little encouragement to think of myself as a potential father one day. It didn't even occur to me in any real sense until I met Sally. Like most boys in our society, I was brought up to deny the part of me that wanted children, to keep it repressed in favour of the more acceptably 'masculine' parts of my personality and life. It all came home to roost, however, during Sally's pregnancy. Of course I felt like a useless outsider as I watched Sally suffering from early pregnancy nausea, and as I watched her middle expanding. More importantly, I soon began to feel that I was a long way behind her in things like knowledge about the clothes and equipment we would need for the baby, and that I would never catch up.

Whenever we went shopping, Sally always seemed so assured, so knowledgeable about prams, nappies, baby clothes and everything else to do with babies, while I floundered in a sea of total ignorance. If she didn't know, then she could always ask her mother or mine. I didn't have anyone else other than her to talk to about it all, and my ignorance made me reluctant to ask questions. Who wants to look like a fool? Sally seemed instinctively, almost magically to have slipped into her new role as a mother-to-be without any hitches at all. I knew that she was worried, and that certain things about pregnancy and birth made her feel quite anxious. But in some indefinable way she seemed to have become a parent already, while I didn't even know where to begin.

There was something else which formed an element of this; in a sense, it was one of the main sources of Sally's apparent confidence. Almost as soon as we announced to all and sundry that we were expecting a baby, it seemed as if every female relative in our respective clans (and their neighbours and friends) started knitting tiny bootees by the dozen (blue for a boy, pink for a girl, of course) and proclaiming advice on almost every aspect of parenthood. I noticed that, all of a sudden, we were seeing a lot more of our families than we had done for quite a while. Something very strange was going on; for while Sally was disappearing with the women into the kitchen for long sessions of talk about pregnancy and birth, baby clothes and babies, I was being dragged off to the pub, 'to get away from all that women's talk'.

It's understandable that families should pull together when a baby is on the way. For many parents, finding out that a daughter or daughter-in-law is pregnant can bring back all sorts of fond memories of their own younger days. But what we were experiencing was the enormous pressure to conform that is exerted on us through our families. In fact, I would have liked to have been in those kitchen sessions asking my own questions of the people who seemed to have all the answers about parenthood – the women. But somehow, it just didn't feel right. On the few occasions I tried to infiltrate I felt slightly uncomfortable, and I knew that none of the real talking would start until I had gone. I soon began to realise that I was trespassing in an area where the mystery, the secrets of reproduction and parenthood, are passed from mother to daughter in the company of women. I was not an initiate; and I had fallen into the great divide which still separates men and women in our society. Of course this is all something of an exaggeration; but I'll bet that you recognise the truth in what I'm saying. In some senses, there's still a very great gap between men and women, and it's often during a first pregnancy that we become aware of it for the first time.

## Who does the housework?

I don't want to give you the impression that Sally and I fell into traditional roles automatically, or that there was a wilful conspiracy on the part of the women in our families to 'keep me out of it'. What I'm saying is that we both felt an intense, almost unconscious pressure to act in certain traditional, socially accepted ways. As I said, for most men, it just doesn't feel right to be very interested in pregnancy and birth. Just as it's assumed that a woman will want to spend a lot of time talking to other women — and particularly her own mother — about the experience when she becomes pregnant, so it's assumed that a man won't really want to be involved in these conversations. These assumptions are at the heart of our images of men and women, and they can have a very divisive influence.

In fact, part of our problem was that Sally and I prided ourselves on being thoroughly modern and up-to-date. We thought we were very different from our parents' generation when it came to things like assumptions about the roles of the sexes. I, in particular, was determined to be a very involved father, and already thought I was a very liberated husband. As far as I was concerned, Sally would always be a person in her own right, she would always be much, much more than 'just' a housewife, and I was going to be . . . well, I wasn't all that sure of exactly *what* I was going to be, but I knew for certain that it wouldn't be old fashioned or — horror of horrors! — *sexist* in any way. Oddly enough, I don't think we ever talked in detail about this sort of thing. We tended simply to assume that it was understood; at least, I did. Sally, like most women, probably had the good sense to see through my pretensions.

For the spirit may have been willing, but the flesh was very weak, at least when it came to putting my assumptions into action. Looking back, I simply cannot believe just how hypocritical I was. We were both working, and we commuted into the city every day from our flat in the suburbs. I was always last out of bed, and Sally usually left before me in the mornings, having made breakfast for both of us. She often came home after me at night. Yet I did very little in terms of the domestic chores, apart from taking our washing to the launderette on a Sunday, and even that I did under a certain amount of grumbling protest, I did no ironing, and virtually no cooking. Whenever I did make us a cup of coffee or burn some toast, I tended to expect extravagant praise, and certainly never tidied up after myself. I did no real housework, and wasn't even sure of where we kept things like the dusters, the furniture polish or the vacuum cleaner. Sally did almost everything with no help from me at all.

I have no defence other than, at the time, neither of us particularly thought about it. In fact, Sally has subsequently admitted to me that she felt obliged to do *all* the housework and the cooking; she felt that as my wife, it was something she should do, and that if she didn't do it, she was *failing* in some obscure way. Like many women, she had been brought up to share in the household chores. So she knew all about irons and dusters and vacuum cleaners. She grew up used to the idea that these things had to be done, that if they weren't done, life would in the end be less than pleasant for all concerned. Almost without realising it, she had grown up with the idea that the housework was, on the whole, done by women, and that men were often unlikely either to be capable of doing it properly or willing, most of the time, to do it at all. I, on the other hand, had grown up not knowing much about irons, dusters or vacuum cleaners, and at a very deep level, Sally and I unconsciously agreed on men's abilities as far as housework was concerned.

I'm not blaming our parents; in fact, my mother had always encouraged me to take some share in the chores, and Sally's dad had always done his bit around the house, job permitting. I'm simply saying that our society's image of what men and women do in terms of domestic chores is still very traditional, and it's very, very pervasive. Because of that, I had grown up believing that a whole area of daily life was 'girls' stuff', and therefore *nothing to do with me.* It just didn't occur to me that to say I was a supporter of equal rights for women, and at the same time never to do any ironing, was a contradiction, and a hypocritical one at that.

I will say that it wasn't too long before I began to realise the vague guilt I was feeling had a lot to do with that contradiction, and began to take steps to do something about it. The fact of the matter is, however, that it's only now, after three children, a fair number of rows, a lot of talking and shared experience that I think I do anywhere near enough around the home. Come to think of it, I probably still don't; deep inside me there's still a little voice which says 'don't do the washing up, Sally will do it'. That voice can be very seductive, and I know it's one many men hear all the time.

Obviously it's no longer quite so easy for us men to get away with this sort of thing. Nevertheless, recent surveys in the United Kingdom have discovered that one of the commonest causes of arguments between couples was the unwillingness of most men to do any housework. More men do help out, but as far as sharing the load is concerned, we might as well be in the Dark Ages still, even though more women go to work now than ever before. This idea will crop up again and again, but I want to make two points here. It is a very important subject, both in itself and as a symbol of that greater divide between men and women which can often make parenthood more difficult than it would otherwise be. In my own experience I found that volunteering to do more housework, and actually finding out about what needed to be done before it became necessary went a long way towards breaking down Sally's attitude that I wasn't capable of doing any of it properly because I was a man. And I think that we've found sharing the domestic chores pays a lot of dividends when it comes to coping with the stresses and strains of parenthood.

## The great divide

What is 'the great divide between men and women' in our society? It's a divide which in many ways separates us into two camps, the divide which puts us into opposite – and often opposing – corners.

In one corner – let's call it the pink one for the sake of argument – we find women. What do we find on their side of the great divide? What ideas, roles, attitudes, qualities and characteristics are generally associated with them in our society?

For a start, that's where we find everything to do with pregnancy, birth, babies, children, and everything to do with housework and home making. Women are also supposed to be more 'caring' and 'emotional' than men, qualities which are obviously associated with motherhood and transferred to the sort of jobs many women do – nursing, for example, or working with children. Women are also supposed to be less 'rational' than men, less 'business minded' or 'commercial', things which are still thought to be 'unfeminine' in a woman. It's said that women talk more than men, and there's plenty of evidence to show that women are in fact better at communicating with other people at a personal level – something which is related to the emphasis in their lives on the 'emotional'.

And what do we find in the blue corner? What characteristics do we assume that men in our society should have? We're supposed to be an unemotional bunch on our side of the great divide; big boys don't cry, after all, and they certainly don't go round telling everyone how they feel. We're supposed to keep our emotions battened down; to show them is a sign of weakness. In our corner we find the business world, money, finance, politics, power, status. You only have to look around you to see that 95 per cent of the bosses, 95 per cent of the politicians are men. It's in the blue corner that we find competition, aggression, the constant struggle to go one better than the next man in battles for power, women, status. Fatherhood comes very low down the list of the things we assume to be central to men's lives, and more often than not it's associated in a subordinate role with other, more overtly 'masculine' things. A 'steady' man, a reliable man who's going places, has a pretty wife and two good-looking, well-behaved children. But his place is out in the world, not at home, being with his family.

What I am describing is, in essence, a patriarchal society: one dominated by men, and supposedly run by men, for the benefit of men. It's a society in which women are second-class citizens, and in which the areas of life to be found on the women's side of the great divide usually have a much lower status than the areas men are said to be interested in. The link, for example, between weakness and emotion runs very deep in our ideas and language. To be soft and to yield is an admission of defeat, of being womanly. To be a masculine man means to be hard and tough and silent, a type epitomised by Clint Eastwood in the *Dirty Harry* movies or the 'Spaghetti Westerns' in which he played 'the stranger with no name'. That character in particular says little, shows virtually no emotion, is totally self-reliant and always victorious, whatever the odds.

In reality few of us are like that, we're all a mixture of the masculine and feminine; many men are very 'emotional' creatures, and I've met some very 'tough' women who could chew up most men before breakfast without any trouble at all. Yet there is pressure on all of us to deny certain parts of our selves, and that means both sides of the great divide lose out.

One fascinating – and very revealing – aspect of all this is the idea that men need 'looking after'. It's something I've heard many people say, both men and women. After all, if a man is brought up in such a way that he doesn't know how to iron his shirts or cook his own meals, then he's got to find someone to do it for him. But never fear – society makes sure that girls are brought up to see themselves as the right person for that particular job. That sort of attitude is still very deeply rooted. A very common extension of it is the idea that men are in fact little more than 'eternal babies' who need to be 'mothered' just like children.

It's another one of those paradoxes in the way we look at ourselves as men and women. Men are big, strong, tough, and big boys don't cry – but they also need to be mothered, because they're babies who can't really look after themselves. Men often find it very hard to admit anything of the sort, but it is in all of us. There's a great temptation for us to treat our wives in the way we treated our mothers, as the people who look after us and make sure our clothes are clean, the people we run home to when we're in trouble, depressed or upset. It's very easy for women to fall into that role, too, especially when they *do* become mothers. It's this sort of attitude which is at the root of many problems, such as a father's jealousy of his own children, or problems in a couple's sexual relationship.

It often seems to me that we have tended to look at all this in terms of extremes and confrontation. We say that men have the power, and women are oppressed. But most men aren't in a position of power. Like me, they're ordinary men trying to live ordinary lives. The point is that being brought up to hide our emotions makes us less effective people than we could be. Being conditioned *not* to do any housework makes us less useful as partners, less equitable when it comes to sharing in the work of living and keeping a relationship going. If in the context of our marriage Sally rapidly became a *second-class citizen*, then during her pregnancy I rapidly became a *second-class parent*, too. Remember? The whole burden of my upbringing, everything in society was saying to me that as far as parenthood was concerned, I wouldn't and shouldn't be interested, and even if I was, then I wouldn't be very good at it. The trouble was that I disagreed with the first idea, and worried about the second.

Often it's during a first pregnancy that many of us begin to think about things like this for the first time in our lives. I know that was exactly what happened to me, albeit in a very confused way. Up until then I had hardly encountered anything which made me think about these issues, with the exception of the arguments we'd had about housework. But the problem was that even when I did begin to think about them, I felt that I had no one to talk to. All of a sudden I was struggling with the feeling that I was an outsider, while Sally was discovering just how much she had in common with other women. She had, in fact, become a member of a vast club, no, a vast tribe from which I felt excluded. And my conditioning even cut me off from the people on my side of the divide, other men.

That's because men in our society are supposed to be *competitive*, and that means we sometimes tend to see other men more as potential enemies than as potential friends. We see them as people to compete with, people to be aggressive towards, to struggle against. Boys are not in general brought up to co-operate, unless it's in the form of co-operating in a team in opposition to another team, although even in sporting teams there's often intense 'competition' for places. All this is linked with the emphasis on aggression we tend to encourage in boys, and I'm using the present tense because it still goes on. Most of us tend to bring our sons up in this way even today. It's very hard not to.

I'm not totally against competition and aggression. In certain circumstances they can be good, even essential things. But the emphasis on them in terms of the male stereotype often cuts men off from each other. Yet men need to unload their feelings as much as women do. I'm not trying to suggest that all men are tight-lipped individuals with no friends, while all women are completely open about their emotions. Some women do hide their feelings and men do, of course, have friendships with other men. But these friendships are rarely as warm and supportive as female friendships. Women do have a skill in establishing networks of emotional support which are very valuable indeed at times like a pregnancy. We men often retreat and repress the tumultuous feelings we're grappling with. I know I did; and as I found out, repressed feelings have a tendency to surface in unexpected ways later on.

## Love, sex and marriage

Sally's first pregnancy was for me, therefore, something of a crisis. Many other fathers I've talked to said they felt much as I did – anxious, excluded, useless. I watched as Sally was swept into a round of antenatal appointments and family advice to which I made very little contribution. One of the most difficult things to deal with was the feeling that I no longer played a central role in her life. It was a disturbing emotion, exacerbated by the fact that it was the result of something which I had thought would bring us even closer together.

Such feelings often surface during pregnancy in the shape of sexual problems: couples suddenly discover that their sex lives have taken a nosedive. Although there are sometimes good reasons for that to happen, much of the trouble is to do with our attitudes about the differences between men and women. It's important to understand the context in which sex difficulties happen during pregnancy and in the early years of parenthood; there can be no doubt that they're very common indeed.

It is only a short step from feeling left out and excluded during pregnancy to feeling jealous, either of your partner's mother or friends, or of the baby who is quite literally coming between you. Make no mistake about it; men are often jealous of their own children, and that jealousy has a lot to do with the traditional image of the male. Men are, after all, supposed to be a possessive bunch, jealous to preserve what they see as theirs – which often means 'their' women. Men are aggressive and competitive, and compete over women as much as they compete over anything.

This sort of attitude is only strengthened by society and its emphasis on the exclusive, romantic bond between one man and one women to which we're all encouraged to commit ourselves, and which is most often seen in one form: marriage. Over and over again, the message is dinned into us; the point and purpose of life is to get married, settle down, have kids. That might sound very old fashioned, but even though the divorce rate goes up steadily, 90 per cent of us still do exactly that – we get married, we settle down and we have kids. The pressure on us to conform and do what 'everybody else' does is enormous, mostly because it's so silent and ubiquitous.

But there's a paradox here: aren't men supposed to be the promiscuous sex, the sex which spends all its time trying to get laid and, at the same time, not get tied down? The answer is yes and no, another paradox.

Our image of men does include the idea that we are naturally 'promiscuous', that there's no such thing as a 'one-woman man', while women are the opposite – or at least, should be. Men are supposed to be easily aroused and quickly satisfied, while women are supposed to take a lot longer to get going and need more to reach satisfaction. Men are also supposed to be continually interested in sex and think about it all the time. Phillip Hodson in his book *Men . . . An Investigation into the Emotional Male*, even renders this into statistical form, informing us that men think about sex 25 times an hour between the ages of 25 and 30. Women, on the other hand, are supposed to think about sex rarely, if at all. Marriage, romance, children . . . yes. But sex? No thank you, I'm a *lady*.

Oddly enough, although the definition of 'male' seems to include 'obsessed with sex', few of the men I have talked to seem to know much about women's bodies. I've lost count of the number of men I've met who don't know the facts about women's reproductive organs or menstruation, and there are still plenty of men who would be hard put to find their wives' clitorises. I've met plenty of men who wouldn't dream of going into a shop to buy sanitary towels or tampons for their wives. This ignorance and reluctance to get involved in 'women's things' is part of the great divide we've been talking about and which extends into pregnancy and birth.

It all sounds very Victorian, doesn't it? Whatever happened to the liberated couple who had no sexual inhibitions whatsoever, but simply pleasured each other from morning till night? Ask the agony columnist of our major magazines and the people who handle radio phone-in shows and the answer will be that such couples are very few and far between. Much has changed in our attitudes to sex, largely thanks to the rise of effective contraception and the (partial) enlightenment which has accompanied it. But I would argue that, in its essentials, our ideas of the differences between men and women as far as their sexuality is concerned haven't changed a great deal.

Look, for example, at the way in which we talk about those differences. Men's attitude to sex is one in which possessiveness, competition and aggression play a large part. We talk of 'conquering' the opposite sex, of 'getting' laid. We do tend to look at women as 'sex objects', not as people, but as things to have and hold and 'possess'. In all of this we're encouraged by society's attitude as expressed, for example, in the endless exploitations of the female form to sell everything, from spark plugs to beer and aftershave; vast commercial empires are based on the traditional, stereotyped idea of men's sexuality. And to keep the wheels of commerce oiled, to keep those spark plugs and bottles of aftershave and soft porn magazines selling, advertising constantly reinforces the traditional view of men's sexuality.

Women, on the other hand, are supposed to want 'romance', 'love', marriage and motherhood. There's still definitely an idea in most of us that it's not quite right for a woman to be interested in sex in the same way as a man is supposed to be; that is, in sex for its own sake. For women sex is meant to be *a means to an end*. In fact, many women have been brought up to think of sex as something 'dirty', or not quite decent, or 'rude'. Sex is something women yield up to men under pressure, something they feel they shouldn't really be quite happy in doing unless it's connected with trying for a baby.

If you find all this a great surprise, then I can only congratulate you for being one of the few truly liberated people around today. Things have changed a great deal, and there is more openness about sexual matters today, but most of the surveys I've seen, and many of the letters I've read at *Parents* reveal that large numbers of men and women are still suffering in their sex lives because of these ideas. As with attitudes to parenthood, we're not far from Victorianism – only two or three generations – and it's still very common to have a few (or perhaps even rather more than a few) sexual inhibitions. Most of the problems that couples face in their sex lives when they become parents have their roots in this fact, that *men and women are brought up to look at sex in different ways*. We enter relationships with the seeds of our problems already in us. In the first flush of physical passion which often makes the early days and months of a relationship so exciting it's easy for us to smooth over any difficulties. It's the pressure of the transition to parenthood which starts the trouble.

I believe that it's men's attitude to women and sex which causes the most difficulty and tension. The paradox is that although women are supposed to be the romantic sex, it's often men who are far more 'sentimental' and possessive. Women are far more used to the idea that you can spread your love and affection around than men. After all, if women see themselves as potential wives *and* mothers, then they've got to accept the fact that they're going to have feelings towards more than one person. And, as has already been pointed out, women often have quite wide networks of friends. Yet men aren't all that different from women; given the right encouragement, we could be much the same in this respect. The trouble is that we rarely get that encouragement, and therefore tend to focus all our emotional needs and desires on one person: the partner whom society has ordained that we should marry.

But the problem actually goes even deeper, for men's sexuality also tends to be focused on the penis and sexual intercourse. In a sense, men are brought up to consider sexual intercourse involving penetration as one of the only acceptable forms of non-aggressive physical contact between people open to us. It's rare for a man to feel comfortable with more generalised physical affection. A common complaint from many wives is that their husbands can never 'just have a cuddle', something which all human beings need from time to time; to most men, physical contact with a woman means sex. That's something which does cause problems, because non-sexual physical affection is a vital part of your relationship with your baby – and it goes a great way to improving your relationship with your partner, too, especially during pregnancy and in the stressful early months of parenthood. Learning that there are physical ways other than sexual intercourse by which you can show love to your partner is a very hard but essential lesson for men.

## The perfect father

Sex didn't in fact prove to be much of a problem for us in Sally's first pregnancy, mostly because we more or less gave up intercourse fairly soon. We had fallen under the spell of a very tenacious old wives' tale, the one that says sex in pregnancy isn't safe. And so we denied ourselves a valuable aid to making our relationship as strong as possible at a difficult time for both of us.

Looking back, I can see that part of the reason for our sexual abstinence was the terible state I got into. I was anxious about everything. I worried about the birth, and whether Sally would be able to cope with the pain. I worried about how we would cope financially after Sally gave up work to stay at home and look after the baby, something which would cut our income by more than half as she was earning slightly more than me at the time. I worried about the fact that I didn't particularly like my job, and that now I was a man with responsibilities I would have no choice but to stick it out. I worried about how Sally would manage at home with the baby. I worried about how I was going to manage as a *father*.

I felt that I had had very little real experience of fathering at first hand. My parents separated when I was five, and divorced not long after. I lived with my mother and my sister, only seeing my father on Saturdays for a few hours. My mother never remarried, and I suppose, somewhere deep inside, I had always regretted the fact that men had been conspicuous by their absence in my childhood. That feeling rose to the surface of my mind during Sally's pregnancy and soon added to the slight panic I was already experiencing. It's a feeling which has probably got a lot to do with the way I've responded to fatherhood; it's probably why I've ended up writing this book. This sort of ambivalence, these strange emotions about your own parents and childhood commonly affect many people when they become parents themselves, whatever their family situation.

What made it all worse was that I really *wanted* to make a good job of being a father. I've since wondered if that very positive wish had anything to do with not having had much fathering myself. Anyway, I did think of myself as being thoroughly modern and up-to-date when it came to marriage and relationships. I've already revealed just how deluded I was about things like the housework. Another problem was that I was determined to be an involved, caring, wonderful, perfect father, the sort of dad I thought a liberated man like me should be – but I didn't have much idea of exactly how I was going to turn myself into this paternal paragon.

I didn't seek other men's advice; I turned to books and magazines to find out about parenthood and what it means to be a father. Some of what I read did mention fathers and even offered quite sensible advice. There wasn't a *whole* book completely for fathers though, just sections, odd chapters and paragraphs which left me hungry for more. There is more emphasis on the father's role in pregnancy, birth and parenthood in today's babycare books, and the weight of informed opinion is encouraging us to play a greater part in the entire process, but, it has to be said, that sort of encouragement is only a thin veneer on the surface of our attitudes.

More men are more involved with their families. Most of us, however, still feel the impulse to achieve perfect fatherhood in the way which society seems to approve. Like me, most fathers feel they ought to spent their time being successful breadwinners. For liberated fathers (or at least, fathers who like to think they're liberated), the problem is that we want to help our partners, but we often don't know what to do or how to offer; and at the same time, we fling ourselves into our jobs and put in long hours because we're worried about money. I know that that's exactly what I was like. I did lots of overtime in a job which was already fairly demanding, something which made me even more of an outsider. I simply wasn't at home a lot of the time during the pregnancy, and when I was, I was too exhausted to be much company. However, it did make me feel a lot better; it seemed as if I was making a real contribution; it seemed as if I was doing what I should as a man. I was working hard at being the traditional good provider.

Trouble came, inevitably, when the various things I was trying to achieve clashed. For example, I wanted to be at the birth with Sally, and that was something which could be arranged quite easily. But I couldn't get any time off from work to go along to antenatal appointments with her. Not only did I know that I would be refused the time off if I asked my employers, in some deep, obscure way I felt — at least, part of me felt — that I shouldn't even want to ask for it. My place was at my desk, taking care of business, being a man, earning us a living; it wasn't sharing long waits at the antenatal clinic, although another part of me was saying that that was what I wanted and should be doing. In short I was anxious, frustrated, confused. Paradox, ambiguity, contradiction — they all feature in what it means to be a man today, and I discovered them when I was a pregnant father.

## My job, right or wrong

Work is something which plays a very large part in most men's lives, although the types of job available and the nature of much work itself has changed a great deal in this century. With the advent of microchip technology and the computer boom, it's changing even more rapidly still. But whatever the changes, we still tend to expect men to find the greater part of the meaning and value of their lives in the work they do. Much of their status is connected to their jobs, and of course, their standard of living is intimately connected to salary levels.

This image of man as breadwinner is still very deeply rooted in our society. Indeed, you could say that men tend to see themselves in terms of their jobs, rather than as people. If you're asked what you do, I'll bet you don't say, 'I'm a father who earns his living by being a plumber (or Prime Minister or football player)'. You're more likely to say you *are* a plumber, or Prime

Minister, or football player first and foremost. But the identification of men with their work has been undermined in many different ways in recent years.

Firstly, there are far fewer 'macho', men-only jobs these days. There's less call for dockers and stevedores, and more need for computer operators and office workers – jobs that need bigger brain power, not bigger biceps. It seems that we're moving towards a time when most jobs can be done by either sex. Secondly, the simple fact is that more and more women are going out to work. In Britain, for example, for every three men in employment there are two women, and a very high proportion of them are mothers. In fact it's estimated that something like two-thirds of mothers with children under five do some form of paid work, either full or part-time.

Some of these women work because they want to, because they have fulfilling careers which give meaning to their lives. Many more work out of sheer financial necessity, and a large number of families are dependent on the wages brought in by mothers. Deidre Saunders and Jane Reed, in their book *Kitchen Sink, Or Swim? Women in the Eighties*, state quite categorically that, 'There would be two and a half million more children living below the poverty line if it wasn't for women working.' It wasn't so long ago that a man was held in little regard if he couldn't earn enough to make sure his wife didn't have to go out to work. That was part of a man's social and economic status, and there's still a hangover from that today. Few men would want their wives to give up work *before* they started a family; but I know plenty who feel very unhappy about their partners going back to work while the children are small. Such a conditioned response is in me, I know, and it's linked to the idea that a woman's natural place is in the home, a man's natural place outside it, earning.

The power of such concepts can be seen in the fact that women still earn less on average than men, even when they do comparable jobs. What's more, women still do the lower paid, lower status jobs; the great divide still runs right down the middle of the working world. Even though we men can't any longer hide behind our earning power, we're only letting women into the world of work on our terms. Another problem is that often the pressure to conform produces inequality when it comes to who should give up what to start a family. In our own case, Sally gave up work to look after Emma even though she was earning more than me. Part of the reason was that we believed my potential earning power was far greater than hers; but it was mostly because we simply felt that that was the way it should be. Very often fathers put pressure on their partners to give up work and stay at home full-time when they might not want to. Although alternatives are becoming more widespread, and fewer women can stay at home as full-time housewives and mothers, the pressure on a couple to adopt this particular division of labour is enormous. It certainly pushed Sally and me into traditional roles – and I think that both of us at the least felt ambivalent about them.

As you would expect, competition inevitably plays a large part in the world of work. Just think about the way we talk of our jobs; we have to fight to keep our position, we struggle for promotion, we compete with other contenders for the plum posts. Stress and tension is an accepted part of the world of work for many men. We're also often expected to put our jobs first. There are many careers in which it's assumed a man will have no qualms about moving from one part of the country to another every couple of years, however disruptive that might prove for his family. Again, many young men are expected to put in long hours and work weekends; it often seems that it's the only way to get on. Employers – and colleagues – generally look askance at a man who says he doesn't want to work overtime because he'd rather spend time with his pregnant wife or his kids. I became aware of this sort of attitude fairly early on during Sally's pregnancy. The editor of the paper I was working for wanted me to work overtime on a Saturday; I wanted to spend it with Sally because I felt I wasn't seeing enough of her. I simply didn't want her to be alone on that weekend. It was put to me in the office that if I didn't come in, I could forget promotion. I stayed at home.

Those decisions are not easy, though. The pressure is on young fathers to get on in their jobs, and as you've seen, the pressure comes from both within and without you. This is a subject we'll be looking at in much greater detail further on, but it's enough here to say that these issues are things you may well never have considered before, but that they'll become important for you in pregnancy. You'll have to start making a lot of decisions as the effects of becoming a parent begin to impinge on almost every area of your life. Hence the tensions and anxieties; everything begins to change underneath you, and the ramifications of that one act of creation start looking endless. The tension in everyone's working life has been made worse by the fact that unemployment has returned with a vengeance. High unemployment figures in most of the developed countries make most of us feel that our jobs aren't quite as secure as they might once have been. For a man, that threat can be doubly worrying because of his conditioning, especially when a baby's on the way.

It can be even worse to be unemployed, though, if as a man virtually your entire sense of self-worth is dependent on being in a full-time job. In this case, unemployment for longer than a few weeks or months can turn into a real crisis. And there's plenty of evidence to show that men who are out of work for long periods can become very depressed for precisely this reason; they can see no value or purpose in their lives. It's certainly a sad fact that few husbands or fathers who have been out of work for a long time show a significant or sustained increase in the amount of housework or childcare that they do; in fact, the opposite appears to be true, even in those families where mothers still have full-time jobs outside the home. It seems that in adversity, men have a tendency to retreat into their stereotype like a tortoise into its shell.

But unlike the tortoise, whose carapace is part of his being, men have in recent years been trying to free themselves from their shells. In a very real sense, this book is part of what's been called 'the male revolt' and 'the retreat from the breadwinner ethic'. In simple terms, it could be said that society emerged from the second world war with the idea that adult manhood included the idea of being a breadwinner, and was indeed indistinguishable from it; what's happened since is that men have become increasingly unhappy with that idea. There's a strand of rebellion against the world of work which runs through the last twenty-five or thirty years at least, from the beatniks and drop outs of the 1950s, through the alternative cultures of the 1960s and 1970s and on into the 1980s, when writers like me talk about shared parenthood and the need for men to spend more time with their families.

It's also a simple fact that the jobs many men – and women – do are boring, repetitive, monotonous, unfulfilling, dull or perhaps even dangerous. We're not all movie stars or TV game show hosts; we're not all wealthy playboys. For most men, work is a chore that we have to put up with, while all the time the ideas in our heads (as put there by our upbringing and social influences) are telling us that we should live to work, not work to live. Is it any wonder that when we get a sniff of something better, a look at a life with more meaning in it that we might be a little unhappy and dissatisfied? Some of us get that glimpse on television or through what we read about in our coffee breaks at factory bench or office desk. Others see it in the meaning and value of family life.

Part of this retreat from breadwinnerdom is also related to discoveries about health. Apart from keeping husbands and fathers away from their families, the socially approved sort of overwork I've been talking about has been blamed for much ill-health in men. I had seen for myself how an executive life style based on high stress, high living (with plenty of boozy expense account lunches) and hard work had affected my own father; it had devastated his health. In particular, he had suffered from heart trouble from his mid-forties onwards (heavy smoking didn't help), and died from heart failure prematurely at the age of 57. It's now known that all these things – stress, bad diet, smoking, drinking, overwork, a lack of exercise – contribute to illness and premature death in men or women. Nevertheless, they are all things which we tend to associate more with men; and during Sally's pregnancy it began to occur to me that some of them were almost inevitable parts of the male breadwinner ethic. I know that I found myself smoking more, taking less exercise and eating badly, mostly because of the extra work I was doing, but also because of the generally increased level of tension and anxiety in my life. I began to feel that I was trapped in a vicious circle of anxiety which made me work harder, so that I felt more anxious ... and so on. It made me feel unhappy *and* unhealthy. But I stuck with the overtime and the feeling that I was doing the right thing. It was a case of my job, right or wrong ... even though another still, small voice inside me was saying all sorts of different things.

## Happy birth day

One thing I had certainly never heard of at the time was *paternity leave*. I knew that I wanted to be at home when Sally came out of the hospital after the birth, but I didn't realise that some unions, some other organisations and many individuals were beginning to say that fathers should have a legal right to paid time off when their children are born. Like most men, I simply put in for two weeks holiday to be taken after the baby was born. As I discovered, the first two weeks at home with your baby may involve plenty of joy; but no one in their right minds would ever call that time a holiday.

In fact, even if I had known about the idea of paternity leave, I doubt if I would have had the courage to ask for it. As with getting time off to go with Sally to antenatal visits, I wouldn't have dared and probably would have felt uneasy about the whole business of 'getting something for nothing'. These feelings were only reinforced by the comments of male colleagues and friends. About the only message I was getting from them was that I'd probably want to get back to work as soon as possible after the birth and 'leave the little woman to get on with it'. What man, it was implied, would want to spend time with a screaming baby and all those dirty nappies? 'You're better off out of it at work', was a common remark. The last thing anyone expected me to want, it seemed – other than Sally – was to be with my family at such a time. Looking back, it seems as if the pressure on me to be and to stay an outsider in the whole process by which we were becoming a family was relentless.

That pressure even played a part in my first experience of birth. Sally was a week past her due date when I finally managed to accompany her to the antenatal clinic on 2 June 1978. I had phoned in to tell my employers that I had a 'bad cold', and although I'm sure they didn't believe me and probably didn't really mind, I still felt very guilty about it all. At any rate, it didn't help me to feel any less of an outsider in the process. Indeed, if anything, I felt more excluded and alone as I sat in the waiting room while Sally was being examined by the doctor and midwife. But it wasn't a long wait; soon I was being told that labour had started. Sally and I met briefly in a corridor. She was being led off to be 'prepared' for birth, and I could see that she was more than a little nervous. I'll never forget the sight of her face; her eyes were like saucers. Neither will I forget the brusque manner of the elderly midwife who packed me off home with a 'Pop back later, dear; you'll only be in the way if you hang around'.

That was about nine o'clock in the morning of a day on which I *felt* more, and more intensely, than I had ever done before in my life. I felt every type and level of despair it's possible for a man to experience. I felt guilt and shame at the fact that Sally suffered while I didn't. I felt panic, anxiety, fear, terror. I felt seventeen types of joy, happiness and ecstasy. I felt overwhelming relief when our beautiful baby daughter was born, and, what was most surprising for me about the entire event, I felt a positively enormous surge of love and affection towards Sally and Emma. It was a wonderful, moving, beautiful experience that I wouldn't have missed for the world, or for anything in it.

But it was still an experience which was almost spoiled by the staff who helped Sally to give birth. I did feel terribly isolated and excluded when I went home from the hospital in the morning, so much so that I was back there by 11 am, only to find my wife labouring alone in a room where she had been put by the midwife. I sat with her, feeling useless, and from time to time midwives came in, asked me to leave, and examined Sally. Several times during the day they forgot to ask me to go back in again. On the last occasion that this happened, I went back into the room only to find that my wife had disappeared. I ended up wandering round the ward looking for her, poking my head into other delivery rooms, wondering where she could be. I finally found her, and only had to take one look at her position on a delivery couch to see that she was about to give birth. I angrily asked the midwife why I hadn't been told; she knew I wanted to be present at the delivery, and that Sally wanted me there too. She barely took any notice, and because I didn't want to make a scene at such a crucial time, I let it pass. The joy of that birth, the relief that flooded over me when Emma popped out of her mother at 4.21 pm, wiped the ill feeling away, but throughout the experience I got the strong impression that the medical staff wouldn't have minded very much if I hadn't been there, and that they might even have preferred it to be that way. It's not usually quite so bad as that these days, although it can be sometimes. Attitudes like that certainly didn't help to make me feel any less excluded or useless.

My isolation was only increased by what happened next. After the joy of Emma's birth, I had to face ten days in which Sally and my new daughter remained in hospital. Visiting hours were very restrictive; I was allowed only one hour in the evenings, and an extra hour in the afternoons at the weekends. I went to work, I went home, I stayed with my mother, I visited the hospital. I was a father without a family, a father who wasn't allowed to pick up his baby in the ward or change her nappy, a father who couldn't hug his wife because the room in which they found themselves together also contained large numbers of other people, strangers. I desperately wanted to get to know my child; I desperately wanted to be part of the process by which I could see Sally visibly growing into motherhood.

Eventually the day came when I arrived at the hospital to take my wife and child home. I stayed at home for two weeks with them, and that fortnight was one of total confusion, panic, fatigue, joy and pleasure, an odd mixture, which I've subsequently come to recognise as being characteristic of early parenthood. At any rate, as it does for most young parents, parenthood came as a complete surprise for us. Sally did have the advantage of ten days experience over me, and that was something I felt keenly. She could fold nappies, she seemed to know instinctively what Emma's cries meant, she seemed, in short, to be such an expert parent that I felt like an idiot. I was frightened even to pick my fragile daughter up, terrified that I'd let her heavy, warm head with its fuzz of soft hair flop back and that her neck would snap. I was rendered speechless with fear at the sight of the pulsing soft spot on the top of her skull. Most of all I was scared stiff of the cord stump on her stomach. When it eventually fell off, as all cord stumps do in the normal course of events, I almost went into shock.

It was at this time that I also first encountered a creature of legend whom I have grown to know very well indeed in my years as a father; *the cack-handed dad.* He's the dad who's all fingers and thumbs, the dad who can't be trusted with a nappy pin in case he impales his offspring on it, he's the dad who, although he's a concert pianist, a brain surgeon or a skilled carpenter, can't fold a nappy properly. I soon found out that as with the housework, I was supposed to be unable and unwilling to share the basic tasks of looking after Emma. True, I wasn't quite as good at nappy changing, for example, as Sally. True, she had been brought up to believe to a certain extent that it was her natural job to do that sort of thing. But I have since found out that to start with she was just as clumsy, just as afraid as I was. Only her conditioning and the encouragement of the traditional stereotypes which we were being forced into made her persevere, and me give up – more or less. Everyone seemed to be telling me that I was hopeless at changing nappies, that I wouldn't get up in the night . . . and so I began gradually to do less and less. Even Sally helped in the process. She often 'took over' from me when I got into a mess, partly because it was simpler and quicker for her to do so, but also partly because she felt vaguely guilty at the sight of me doing things her conditioning told her *she* should have been doing. It's all a two-way process, but it ends up with men being on the outside, yet again – which is where I didn't want to be.

The fact is, if you give a dog a bad name, it sticks. If you tell a father often enough that he's cack-handed when it comes to childcare, he'll believe you – especially when statements like that agree with the sort of conditioning he's likely to have had. But there is no reason to believe that childcare is something only women can do; it needn't necessarily stay on the woman's side of the great divide. As I'll show further on, men are perfectly capable of doing almost everything for their children, with the exception of breastfeeding. We even have a role to play in that, though; our support can make it much easier for our partners to breastfeed successfully. The point is that we need to be encouraged, we need to be aware both of what we can do and what the benefits of sharing childcare can be. It's always tempting for men to pull back into the shells of their traditional masculinity under the pressure of early parenthood. My problem was that I could feel myself slipping in exactly that direction – and as I've said, part of me at least inarticulately wanted something different, something better. I loved that fortnight at home with my new family, and I did fight to stay involved. I had had my glimpse of the sort of value and meaning I wanted in my life. From then on, I looked at everything in a changed light.

## Back to work

On a sunny Monday morning – Monday, 26 June 1978 to be exact – I opened the front door of our flat and stood on the threshold of the outside world, the world of work. At that moment I stood poised in the middle of the great divide, my wife and new baby daughter behind me, my job and the responsibilities of a breadwinning man in front of me. Sally, at the age of 21, was about to be plunged into the role of suburban housewife and mother, with all that it entailed – isolation, boredom, and almost inevitably, depression. I was going out to take on the world for the sake of my wife and child.

It was during the months which followed that both of us discovered many unpleasant things about the new roles we had undertaken so lightly. Sally found herself totally responsible for everything to do with the day-to-day care of Emma and all the housework and shopping. Her new role united enormous responsibility – she was, after all, now completely responsible for the welfare and survival of another human being, our daughter – with enormous drudgery, for which she got about the same amount of help from me as she had already grown to expect; that is, very little at all. It wasn't entirely my fault, though; I'd discovered in those months that it was possible to be a parent and hardly see your child from week to week. Because I was still stuck in the 'good-providers-work-hard-syndrome', I was leaving home early in the morning, virtually before Emma was awake, and getting home late in the evening, usually after she was tucked up in bed. I felt as if she hardly knew me, and I hardly knew her; and of course the gap between Sally and I as far as childcare skills was concerned only grew wider with every day that went past.

But childcare wasn't the only area in which a gap between Sally and I appeared. In fact our relationship was under enormous pressure, both within our home and from outside it. Emma formed part of the problem; she, like many babies, decided that she didn't particularly want to sleep at night very much for most of her first year. Our inexperience combined with our anxiety to make a perfect, and very common, recipe for disaster. Emma cried, so we tried to get her off to sleep. We were anxious about it; she picked up our anxiety and became even more anxious herself, which made her cry more and us more anxious . . . and so on, in a vicious circle which many parents have found themselves trapped in at one time or another. It's no surprise to me that torturers use sleep deprivation to break their victims' will to resist. After a month of broken sleep, late nights and early mornings and the time between spent pacing the flat (and even sometimes the streets) with our baby daughter, both Sally and I would probably have agreed to anything for the sake of an uninterrupted eight hours sleep.

The result was, inevitably, a lot of irritation which sometimes developed into arguments. We found ourselves resenting each other and not really prepared to admit the fact to each other. Sally resented me for the simple fact that I wasn't really helping her very much in any area; but more importantly, I wasn't even aware of the sort of pressure she was under. I didn't realise that she was depressed, or that she felt lonely, isolated, and was frightened of becoming a 'dull little housewife'. I didn't realise that she felt unattractive and that she'd lost her confidence, and that her sudden loss of financial independence had come quite hard, too. Of course, I knew that something was wrong, and that made me feel very uncomfortable. But I resented the fact that Sally seemed to expect me to do much more than I felt I possibly could; somewhere inside me I felt that just doing my job should have been enough for her, and that she shouldn't have been expecting me to get up in the night and change dirty nappies, too. I also resented the fact that she didn't seem to understand or even want to know about the problems I was having at work, the pressure I was under. In short, we weren't communicating at almost any level, and our resentments festered. Our rows grew more frequent, and even violent. It seemed at one stage that we were almost at breaking point. Something that had started so brightly, something so full of the joy that we had felt on the day Emma was born, seemed about to die.

The world of work wasn't exactly doing much to help, either. I was bewildered by the extent to which my new status as a father was ignored by my employers. It was as if I hadn't had a baby daughter; nothing changed. Their demands on me in terms of time and energy were as great as ever, and even now, as I write this sentence, part of me wants to know why I should have expected them to make any allowances for the fact that I was now a father. I was discovering just how hard it is to reconcile the worlds of work and family, something many fathers find out in the early months of parenthood. No matter how tired I was after another night of Emma's crying, I still had to be at work the next morning. No matter how fed up Sally might feel, no matter how much she might have needed some help and comfort, I had to be at my desk, earning our living. And it wasn't long before I began to resent my job for another reason – it made sure that I missed out on unique parts of Emma's childhood. As a working father, I wasn't there when she smiled for the first time, when she rolled over, crawled, stood up, took her first steps or said 'dadda'. It dawned on me one day when Sally rang me at the office to tell me about some new achievement of our daughter's that *I had missed something which would never be repeated* – I had been deprived of something which I was beginning to feel should have been mine by right. I sat at my desk, with an unpleasant vision of the future in my head; a future in which I missed every single important event of my child's life because I was out at work. It wasn't a vision I particularly enjoyed.

But it wasn't something I could do that much about. And that was the worst feeling of all, for both Sally and me; we both felt trapped in roles for which we were unprepared, roles which were keeping us apart and making us unhappy. I channelled all these feelings into looking for another job, and eventually I found one which I thought would help to make our problems a little easier to bear. I went to work for *Parents* magazine, a publication which deals with every aspect of pregnancy, birth, child development and family life. I reasoned that so long as I couldn't spend as much time with my family as I wanted to – and in the end, that's what our problem seemed to boil down to – I thought that I could at least work for a magazine which was connected to that part of my life. It was a way of bridging the great divide; and there's no doubt that it did help, and that the change of job came at crucial time.

From then on things did begin to improve. Our expectations became more realistic, and we didn't set ourselves – or Emma – such impossibly high standards. We began to communicate again, and we simply became more experienced parents. But what helped me more – as a father – was the discovery that many other men felt the same way as me, and that many couples were struggling towards a different idea of parenthood, an idea that ran counter to much that was in their upbringing. I discovered that Sally and I were not unusual or abnormal, and that our experiences and feelings about parenthood today were the common property of very many couples. I interviewed many mothers and fathers, I read hundreds of the letters that came into *Parents*, I read up on the research that has been done into fatherhood. My own personal experience united with what I saw in all those hundreds of words to give me the ideas that I've been writing about in this chapter. My own personal Odyssey through fatherhood took me right back to the beginning, to 9 September 1977. My glimpses of the rewards of parenthood made me want to achieve the equality Sally and I had had at that moment of conception.

That meant coming back in from the outside, and that's what the rest of this book is about. It's about turning you from an outsider into an insider when it comes to parenthood, so that you, your partner and your children can all get the best out of the experience. And to make that more likely to happen you'll need to go back to the beginning – and beyond.

PART ONE

# PREPARING FOR PARENTHOOD

There seemed to be no use in waiting by the little door, so she went back to the table, half hoping she might find another key on it, or at any rate, a book of rules ... this time she found a little bottle on it ... and round its neck a paper label, with the words 'DRINK ME' beautifully printed on it in large letters.

It was all very well to say 'Drink me,' but the wise little Alice was not going to do *that* in a hurry. 'No, I'll look first,' she said, 'and see whether it's marked "poison" or not ...'

from *Alice's Adventures in Wonderland* by Lewis Carroll

# 1 Choosing to have a child

If you were asked what you thought was the most revolutionary development of this century, then you might well come up with all sorts of answers, from antibiotics to computers. Yet the one thing which has changed people's lives most dramatically has been the development of cheap, effective contraception. Unlike our ancestors, we have almost complete control over our fertility with a wide variety of methods, ranging from the condom or sheath, through the cap and the intra-uterine devices like the coil and the loop, to the contraceptive pill.

Admittedly, some of these methods have their problems: they're not all completely effective; some are less pleasant than others to use, and some have been associated with risks to health. Disturbing facts have come to light about the pill especially, although IUDs have been linked with health problems too. Nevertheless there can be no doubt that generally reliable methods of contraception have changed people's lives – and therefore society – beyond recognition. Some commentators have even ascribed the rise of feminism to the new control over their fertility that women have gained, and there must be some link between the two. It is no longer inevitable that a woman should spend her life having a baby every two years and succumbing to the enormous strain that such an existence entails. Who could doubt that this is a good thing?

What's more important is that we now have a choice in an area where there was no choice before. We can choose whether or not to become parents at all, and that's a choice which some couples and individuals are now making. They're choosing to remain childless voluntarily, and I believe that it's a choice which should be respected. Having children is a big step in anyone's life, and if you decide that it's one you don't want to take, then that's up to you. The sort of pressure which comes from our traditional stereotyped ideas often makes it a very hard choice to carry through.

Nevertheless, most people do still end up becoming parents, and for a variety of reasons. In *So You Want to Have a Baby* I devoted the larger part of a chapter to analysing those reasons, but I think they boiled down to one thing. Human beings have a very powerful, instinctive, biological urge to reproduce, an urge which is encouraged in a very intense way by the attitudes in our society which impinge on us all the time. What I'm saying is that somewhere deep inside most of us we want to have children, and pressure is put on us from all around to go along with that urge. After all, that's what our conditioning is all about; girls are brought up to see themselves as mothers, and boys as workers to provide for their partners. It's all very neat.

The problem is that those pressures can often combine to make you succumb to the urge to reproduce at inappropriate – or even disastrously wrong – times in your life. Part of the reason I went to such length describing my personal experience in the last chapter was to give you some idea of what it means to be pitched into parenthood before you're ready. The important thing to remember is that parenthood is such a major change in your life that you can in fact, never really be entirely ready for its total effect; *but the more unprepared you are, the worse that effect is going to be*. The research evidence that I've seen backs this up. It's been found, for example, that those couples who marry very young and start their families straight away are those who are likely to have more problems. The mother is more likely to have problems during her pregnancy and a difficult birth; she's also more likely to suffer from postnatal depression too. Couples like this also feature prominently in the divorce statistics eventually, so it's reasonable to assume that relationship problems could be a major part of their experience.

Of course, just getting married young and having a baby quickly doesn't mean that you'll inevitably have problems, but it often means that you'll have a less than auspicious start to marriage and family life. It probably means you haven't got a lot of money, that you're struggling to get a foothold in the world of work, that you have had little experience of living and all its problems. I know that both Sally and I found that we had an awful lot of growing up to do in the first year or so of Emma's life, and that there was much between us which we hadn't even worked out properly before Emma was born. In short, it's vital to remember that parenthood can come as a shock, and it's worth trying to minimise its impact by taking some preparatory measures beforehand – just as Sally and I didn't.

What I'm saying is that as most of us become parents anyway, it's worth making sure that we have our children when the time is right, or as near to that time as is possible, given the fact that we're all human and therefore fallible. That means taking into consideration some of the factors that come out of what I wrote about in the last chapter. Becoming a parent will affect your emotions, your relationship, your material circumstances, your job. Your health and your sex life are all involved too; all of these things exist before your child, they form a context into which your child is born. There are certain things to look out for and ways in which you can prepare, ways which will help make your experience of parenthood more rewarding than it might otherwise have been.

I'm not talking about planning your child's birth date to coincide with a public holiday so that you won't have to sacrifice too much of your annual leave. I'm talking about fitting a major transition into the pattern of your life and taking your needs, wishes, plans and desires into account. Of course, that applies to both of you, to potential mothers as well as fathers. But it's something which may even pay more dividends for fathers, and that's because of the great divide between the sexes. If you remember, I said that we men tend to start off as 'second-class parents' simply because that's what society expects us to be. Any preparation we do is going to be a help in that context. Another point is that there is plenty of evidence to show that by making a positive commitment to parenthood you'll be doing both yourself and your partner a favour. It's been shown that those couples who are positive about parenthood and do some preparation in the sense that I'm talking about in this chapter usually experience fewer problems in pregnancy, birth and afterwards. What's more, fathers who positively support their partners at every stage help them to manage better – they actually tend to have shorter and easier labours, for example.

It's also very important to realise that if you don't make this sort of positive commitment, then you're far more likely to feel excluded and left out of the whole process of becoming a parent. It seems fairly clear from various research studies that those fathers who feel most jealous of their children, who feel excluded and unhappy about the impact of parenthood on their lives are often those men who have made little effort to take an active part at any stage after the moment of conception. It's easy to see why; if you're ambivalent about the idea of becoming a parent, if at heart you're not really sure that it's something you meant to do, then you're likely to retreat from the whole business when it actually starts to happen in reality. But at the same time, you won't be able to escape it entirely – and that can lead to resentment.

Of course, it must seem to those of you who have children or whose partners are already pregnant that this chapter is something of a waste of time. Admittedly, it may have less relevance for you, so you'd be justified in skimming the next few pages at least, if not in leaving them out altogether. But I hope that you'll read them, none the less. Much of what I'm talking about here has relevance to all fathers at every stage of parenthood; all I'm doing at this stage is examining the foundations of what's to come.

# 2 Paving the way

## Your relationship

Perhaps one of the most important aspects of parenthood is the fact that having a child can have a tremendous impact on your relationship with your partner. In some ways, the decision to create a new human being is one that will bind you together more permanently than anything else can. Even if you separate and divorce later on, the child you and your partner created will always be a link between you.

Even couples who feel that their relationships are very strong before they become parents often report a deterioration after the baby arrives. It therefore seems logical to assume that if you want your relationship to survive the test of parenthood, let alone prosper and thrive, it's essential that it should be in the best possible shape to start with. It is, of course, very difficult to say what it means for a relationship to be in 'good shape'. Each of us has different reasons for sharing our lives with particular people. We're all looking for different qualities, characteristics, abilities and gifts in our partner, and in most cases, much of what we want operates on an unconscious level. Few of us *really* know why we choose the partners we do — or why they choose us.

However, I'm sure many of us would agree that one major point of spending your life with someone is to achieve some sort of happiness or fulfillment. Again, this is something which varies from person to person; one man's happiness may well be another man's poison, and the wise little Alices among us are very wise indeed if they truly know what they want in life. But it is possible to point to specific things which, according to the research evidence, at least, can contribute to making a relationship more stable and secure — and perhaps even happier. Chief among these factors seems to be good *communication* between partners. In fact it's been shown that those couples who rate themselves highly for communication before they have a baby are the ones who consistently report the *least* deterioration in their relationships after the birth. For those couples, good communication means being able to talk openly about their feelings with each other, even when the feelings they're talking about might be less than positive.

As I've already said, it is far better to get any bad feelings out in the open and to sort them out, or try to get rid of the problem that's causing the trouble, rather than to suppress the emotions. Of course none of us is perfect, and every relationship is likely to have its problem areas, just as we all have the odd fault (some more than others, as I would be the first to admit). These things might appear to be very trivial. Sally and I, for example, soon found out certain things about each other. She's like her father, and methodically tidy. I'm just untidy by nature. Before Emma was born, my habit of leaving clothes scattered on the bedroom floor was an irritation to her. As a brand new young mum and housewife, it began to drive her crazy. As she quite rightly said, it showed a callous thoughtlessness. My male conditioning told me not to worry about being tidy because some female would come round after me and pick up my discarded clothes. Sally soon found herself tidying up after everybody in our house all the time – and I still slip into my old bad habits occasionally, even now. The point is that what might appear to be a trivial problem can often reveal a fault line in a relationship which, under the strains of early parenthood could turn into a real crack. And don't forget the great divide; many problem areas in relationships do centre on things which are affected by our traditional views of the differing roles of the sexes, things like tidying up, housework, jobs, sex.

That's why it's important to try and isolate the potential areas of disagreement in your relationship and sort them out – if you can – before you become parents. Obviously, it's not always possible. But the more effort you make in that direction, the better. It often seems to me, in fact, that one of the biggest difficulties in many relationships – and in the broader sense of how the sexes relate – is that we often simply don't know how to talk to each other, and that's a pity because talking is good for you.

But it's also important to remember that talking isn't enough by itself. It's all very well to clear the air, but if there is a problem it's not going to go away if all you do is talk at it. Actions do speak louder than words, and if you discover that your partner resents the fact that you're untidy, or that you never do the dishes, or that you don't do any housework, then that resentment isn't going to go away unless you do something to remove its cause. What I'm saying is that you can't expect everything to be perfect in your relationship under the stresses and strains of parenthood if you're not prepared to meet your partner half way on at least some things. I'm not saying that you should divide all the household chores down the middle, or that you should set up rigid schedules and schemes to make sure you both do the same and no more than each other. What's important is that you should come to an agreement in sharing as much of your life together as possible, and that means sharing the unpleasant, dull and boring things as much as the more exciting stuff.

I have a strong feeling that in most couples this sort of approach will pay real dividends – and that it will usually mean the men doing more than they did before. The point is that a little willingness, a little volunteering goes a long, long way in a relationship. If you don't know where the toilet cleaner is kept, then it's time you found out. If you leave your clothes scattered all over the bedroom and never put them away, then it's time you did. If you don't put as much into that side of living together as your partner, then it really is something for you to think about. Women do appreciate men who make the effort – usually. It has to be said that your partner may have to get used to this idea, too; she may even feel guilty about you doing any extra household chores because of the way she's been brought up. But both of you need to overcome that conditioning if you're going to get the best out of parenthood – and the time to start is as soon as possible.

I've already said that sex can be a problem area in a relationship, and it's surprising just how widespread sexual problems can be. One major area of tension between men and women lies in the fact that our conditioning tends to result in women feeling that they shouldn't take the initiative in sex. This is something which might be blurred by the 'honeymoon effect' – the well-known tendency of couples to make love more often at the beginning of a relationship. There may well be other areas of your sexual relationship with which you're unhappy; your partner might like doing things you don't, or seem unwilling to do something you would like to try. At any rate, we're often afraid to talk about sexual matters of this nature for fear of hurting or upsetting the people we love; and if you add to this the prudery and reserve many of us still feel about sex, then you'll understand how unhappiness in this area can persist for a long time.

That's why it's important to try and be frank about your sex life with your partner, and to do something about any problems that might exist. What happens in bed between you (or wherever else you might enjoy making love) is often a good indication of the general health of your relationship. Again, men have got a lot to learn here; it's often hard to see that our partners might find it difficult to come half way, as it were, in sex by taking the initiative when we're not going half way towards them in things like sharing household chores. It's also important to realise that women often don't talk about what they don't like in their sex lives because they know very well that a man's sense of his own masculinity and virility is a very sensitive plant. We men can take almost any slightly negative comment about our sexual performance as a criticism – and that's because of the heavy emphasis in our upbringing on the link between 'manhood' and 'performance' – the *superstud syndrome*.

The key is to strengthen your relationship so that it can weather the storms ahead. It doesn't take much to see that an unstable, unhappy relationship doesn't provide a good foundation on which to build a family. Indeed, the evidence shows that bringing a baby into the world in that sort of context is enough to finish off the relationship altogether. The quality of your relationship is also very important as far as your children are concerned. The research shows that children whose parents are in general happy and secure with each other tend to have fewer developmental or emotional problems than children from homes where the parents don't get on. I'm not saying that every child whose parents have a rough patch in their relationship is going to turn out to be a juvenile delinquent. Nor am I saying that your children are likely to turn out to be a disaster unless you're perfectly happy all the time. I'm not even saying that children have to grow up in happy two parent families to be normal or well adjusted.

Children need security; they need love and affection. These things are harder to provide if your relationship isn't going well and your emotional energy is being siphoned off into rows, tension, resentment and anxiety. I also happen to believe that the two parent family is a very good working arrangement for bringing up children, and that it could be made even better. Mothers and fathers can provide different and complementary skills in the job of bringing up their children, and as I'll show further on, it's often in the interplay of these differing skills that children benefit. But in the end nothing works right unless the context is right, and that means sorting out your relationship before it has to grow to accommodate the new person – or new people – who are coming into it. Parenthood is something of an 'emergency', with all sorts of new things to be taken into account and dealt with very suddenly. What you need is a relationship strong enough and flexible enough to take the strain and bounce back – and it's bound to be stronger if you make the effort to prepare yourselves for what's coming.

## The wealth factor

Whether you like it or not, an important part of your life, your relationship and becoming a parent is your financial situation. The simple fact is that babies do cost a lot of money. Exactly how much is something many surveys have tried to discover. Why anyone should bother to make the attempt is, quite frankly, beyond me. Like most parents, I long ago gave up trying to tot it all up. Just bear in mind that having children is not going to make you rich. In fact it's probably going to take all your money – and a bit more.

Obviously this isn't a point which stops most people from becoming parents. But few of us realise just how much of a financial impact our children are going to make on us – and the expenditure begins almost immediately. For starters, your partner is going to need maternity clothes and underwear during pregnancy, and it won't be long before you're out there buying baby clothes, too. If you're lucky, your family may well help you out with some of the major items like a cot, or a pram. You may even be fortunate enough to have relatives or friends who can pass on big pieces of baby equipment and plenty of clothes (be careful always to check for safety, though, in any hand-me-down equipment). But you can't rely on it, and anyway, many parents – especially first time parents – like the idea of their brand new baby having all brand new things. And once you start spending, it doesn't stop.

That's because children grow ... and grow and grow. A small all-in-one suit for a tiny baby may not cost you very much. But he'll outgrow it in a couple of months, and then he'll outgrow the next size clothes, and the next. Meanwhile, you've got to keep his clothes clean, so you'll probably have to invest in a washing machine if you haven't already got one, and you'll use it constantly. It sometimes seems to me that our washing machine with its peculiar noises (plenty of clunks and bangs) is on duty permanently, its porthole like a glimpse into the continually whirling centre of all the galaxies where activity never stops. That means bigger washing bills, more washing powder. Oh yes, and don't forget the bedding you'll have to buy, the extra heating bills for keeping your house or flat warm for baby, the shoes, the books, the toys, school meals, school visits, musical instruments, dancing classes, sports activities, holidays, a bigger house to accommodate your growing family. Few parents settle for just one child, either, so it's all doubled if you have another (or trebled if you're lunatics like us). You may start off as the proud dad buying his new baby a rattle for a few pennies (although they can be quite expensive); you'll end up like me, a harrassed, hardworking dad who's disappearing under a storm of bills.

It isn't all that gloomy, though. For most of us, making a living and paying our way is tough enough before we have children, and anyway, the expense grows gradually over the years; you can get used to it. What's more, we all have different levels of income and different expectations, different wants in terms of our life styles. And, I hasten to add, I don't know of any parents who'd swap their children for any amount of wealth. They are, in the end, worth every penny and more. But equally, I don't know many parents who could say that they haven't had to think fairly carefully about money since they've had children. What you spend is up to you, obviously enough, and like most people, we live up to (and slightly beyond) what we earn, and any increase in our income is soon gobbled up. But it's important for you to remember that even just providing the basics of life for your children is going to cost you quite a lot.

The point is that the impact of all this on your life might be worse at certain times. If you're only just starting out in your career and you aren't earning very much, then having a baby can put an almost intolerable strain on your finances. It's almost inevitable that starting a family will at the very least reduce your partner's earning power either temporarily or permanently. Many women do still give up work late in their first pregnancy and stay at home as full-time housewives and mothers until their youngest child goes to school. It's true that more women do combine paid employment and motherhood these days, but several factors combine to operate against them. Firstly, because in most families women do take the role of primary parent – fathers, remember, are likely to be the ones whose jobs come first, and whose jobs are in the traditional nine-to-five, five-day-week mould – they're more likely to look for jobs around which they can fit being a mother and looking after the home. That often means low-paid, part-time work near where they live. So even women with real skills or strings of qualifications may find themselves lowering their sights when it comes to returning to work after they've had children.

There are also problems for those mothers who keep their sights on their career and try to combine ambition, job satisfaction or dedication to their field with motherhood. In very simple terms, it's unlikely that they'll be able to go back to work full-time and leave their husbands holding the baby. A few couples have managed to swap their roles in this way, and I hope that it's something which will grow. But for most of us it's impossible for a variety of reasons, ranging from our own inbuilt prejudices about what men should and shouldn't do (it's hard to think of a man as a housewife), to the fact that most industries aren't geared to the idea at all. They simply don't think of mothers as people who might be reluctant to lose out in their careers. That's why it is still very difficult for women to get to the top unless they deny themselves the chance to have children. Another very basic point is that if a woman does have a baby and go back to work, she's likely to have to find and pay someone to look after her child for her, and that can be a complicated, difficult and expensive business.

Whatever your partner does, whether she gives up work for years or takes her maternity leave and goes back to her job a matter of months after the birth, you have to accept that fact that she's either going to earn less or you'll have to pay out for childcare. In Britain few mothers go back to work straight after the birth of a baby – the figure is something like 10 per cent for those women who take up their maternity leave option. So for most couples, at least in the early months and years of parenthood, having a baby represents a straightforward drop in income. We do have one thing to be grateful for in Britain, though; you can have your baby privately and pay for the medical care involved, but whatever you think of the National

Health Service, it means that you can have your baby without the spectre of an enormous medical bill haunting you. In other countries birth can work out to be very expensive.

In this context it's also well worth your while to start thinking about your priorities, both as individuals and as a couple. As you can see, becoming a parent can be very disruptive for a woman; it can, in fact, set her life off in a completely new direction and one which, moreover, it's very difficult to change once she's stuck in it. But it can – and probably will – be just as disruptive for you. I talked in the last chapter about society's attitudes to work and the fact that men's jobs are usually expected to take precedence over women's. Your partner may well give up her job to look after your baby, but you and she are likely to experience a few problems if you think that you'll be able to continue to throw all your energies into your career. The simple fact is that you won't – parenthood is going to make its demands on you too.

In the early months of parenthood it's often simply a question of broken sleep, tiredness and getting used to a completely new, exciting and confusing role. But there's a lot of pressure on many men to put in extra hours or to bring work home, or to finish a particular, important piece of work, however long it takes. The problem is that the years of your fatherhood also often coincide with the years when you have to work hard – and be seen to be working hard – to get on in your chosen career. The result can be that you find yourself stretched on a rack between two things, both of whose demands cannot possibly be entirely satisfied; at one end is your family and at the other, your job. You often can't have one without the other; your family is probably dependent on what you earn, and you may also get lots of satisfaction out of the job you do. But if you put everything into your job, you lose out – as does your family – at home; if you put everything into your family, you lose out in the world of work.

Of course, for many of us the problem isn't quite so intractable. But it is something you would do well to think about. Whatever you do, having a baby is going to add new demands to your life, it's going to increase the number of things you have to do. The time to start thinking about the priorities in your life should be before your options have closed down. Again, I'm not saying that you should sit down with your partner and work out a rigid plan for your lives and follow it to the letter. It's simply that it seems a good idea to think about some of the areas which may prove difficult and try to come up with some joint decisions about how you're going to handle them.

Society is structured in a way that puts us all under a lot of pressure to follow the conventional pattern. But just because most people do something one way, it doesn't mean to say that you have to. It is possible to arrange your lives differently, and some couples have achieved a much greater measure of sharing. Many men have decided that their priority is their family, and have either eased off in the career struggle, or opted for part-time work. Some have even swapped roles entirely. None of the alternative ways of organising family life are easy options, though, and if you and your partner are interested in doing something different, the sooner you start thinking about it – and even planning for it – the better. Remember that financial matters, careers, work, all these are things which operate over long time spans. To make sure that you get what you want in a couple of years, you may need to take action *now*.

## Making the decision

Whatever you decide, it's vital that you should come to that decision together. If it's at all possible you should feel that you've both thought it through and agree on the plan of action you're going to follow. If one of you feels that you've been over-ruled or bulldozed into parenthood, then there could be trouble ahead. Becoming a parent is a very big step for anyone at any time of life; that's why you need to go into it very positively, knowing as much about what you're letting yourself in for as possible.

One major problem in this area is that at certain times of life we can find ourselves under pressure from society and the people around us to conform in the business of starting a family. You may well have some idea of what I'm talking about already. The pressure comes in the form of your aunt telling you at your wedding that she expects to be knitting baby clothes for you very soon; or in the shape of television commercials which tend to assume that everyone over 20 in a steady relationship is either a parent already or desperate to become one. The idea that parenthood is a natural, normal – and therefore inevitable – stage in your life is part of our consciousness. The longer you leave it before you become parents, the heavier the pressure is likely to become, especially for your partner. Although it is now more accepted that it's sometimes sensible to wait, we've still got a very long way to go before we escape from this sort of thinking entirely.

Of course, part of the traditional, stereotyped idea of the differences between the sexes is that we men are always bulldozed into marriage and parenthood by the women in our lives. Firstly, we're caught by our brides (and I suppose the idea is that like some wild beast we're tempted into handing over our 'freedom' for the sexual carrot that's dangled in front of us), and then we're hoodwinked into becoming fathers. Have you ever seen those Hollywood movies where a wife says to her husband something like this: 'Sit down dear, I've got some news for you'? What she's about to announce to the poor, dumbfounded schmuck is that she's expecting a baby. I must confess that I haven't actually seen a film in which hubby then replies: 'But how did that happen?', although that's the general idea. When it comes to conception, there's still a strong feeling in most of us that women are the ones who will be making the decision – or at least have the greater say in when it happens.

To a certain extent it's right that a woman should have a greater say in this matter. Even if you are able to share parenthood more than the average couple, it's still likely that your partner's life is going to be more affected than yours. But remember that you are *both* going to be affected, that you're going to be affected together, and that deciding to have a baby could be the first of a multitude of joint decisions you're going to have to make about that child's future, from what to call him to what present to buy for his child when he becomes a parent himself. So start as you mean to go on, talk over whether you want to become a parent and when, get everything out in the open; don't forget that the decision you're making is a life and death one for your child. He doesn't ask to be called into existence. It is only right and fitting, therefore, that you should – if you can – make that decision a real one.

I say 'if you can' because it isn't likely that you'll be able to get exactly what you want without making some concessions and coming to some compromises. But then that's what life is all about, for most of us at least. In fact, as most couples realise, when it comes to deciding whether to have a baby, the time is never right. You can always think of reasons not to – you're not far enough up the career ladder, you haven't got a big enough house and can't afford to move yet and so on – and there's always that impulse to go ahead and do it in the back of your mind (or elsewhere). I knew one couple who spent several years trying to decide whether to have a baby or just buy a dog, instead. In the end, they bought the dog – and had a baby almost exactly nine months later.

The point is that simply making the effort to think – and talk – about the issues involved in becoming parents can pay dividends. It can help to raise the level of communication in your relationship, and it will certainly help to make you aware of some of the things in your life which might be affected by bringing a baby into it. It's a particularly good exercise for men; it's one way of bridging the great divide between the sexes at a time when the pressure isn't on. It does actually help to make you feel more a part of what's happening in your life; and your partner will appreciate your concern and interest in this major area of your lives, too. It's a time to start thinking about priorities, about job versus family, about who does the housework and how much, about all the issues I've talked about so far. It's also a time to take action wherever it's appropriate.

In fact this sort of decision-making process about parenthood is becoming more common, even though one survey I saw estimated that at least 50 per cent of first pregnancies could be classified as accidents. I'm sure that a similar survey done twenty-five or even ten years ago would have come up with a much higher figure than that for 'slip-ups' of the sort that changed life for Sally and me so dramatically. It seems that slowly but surely, our awareness of the choice made possible by contraception is growing. Other surveys have shown that the average age at which couples have their first child is rising slowly, and that more and more couples are waiting until their mid-20s or even later before starting a family. It's easy to see why; you may well be physically at your most fertile in your late teens or early 20s, but you're more likely to have a better financial, material and even emotional base on which to build your family life when you're a bit older. I know that I wasn't really ready emotionally or financially to start a family at the age of just 24; more and more people would agree with me now. Indeed, it's no longer uncommon for a woman to put off having a first baby until she's well into her 30s.

Obviously, this decision is a very personal one, perhaps one of the most personal decisions you'll ever make in your life. There are good reasons for waiting until you start a family. You're likely to be better off in your 30s than you were in your late teens or early 20s. You're also likely to have a much better idea of what you want out of life, and both of you may well be so established in your careers that it might be easier to minimise the impact of parenthood on your working lives. At the same time, having children when you're younger means that you'll get the early parenthood stage of your life over more quickly, and that you'll also be correspondingly younger when your children grow up; they won't have older parents. You may also not be quite so settled in life as older parents might be. However old or well prepared you are, the impact of a first baby on your life still comes as something of a surprise, and that surprise may be greater if you've got used to a pleasant way of existence in which you can do much what you want.

I could go on forever talking about making the decision. In the end, the choice is yours and yours alone, and all I would try to stress is that you should remember that you do have a choice, not only about when you have your first child, but when you have your second or subsequent children. The process of deciding when and how to have your children is a very important part of preparing for their arrival. If it does nothing else but make you think about the miracle of having a baby, then that in itself is a good thing, for it is a micracle, a miracle which happens every day. When I see a small baby I marvel that something so beautiful and so full of potential should have been created out of no more than love between two people. That tiny scrap of humanity will grow to love and feel many things herself. She may have children of her own, she may live a hundred years or more and see and hear things her own parents could never even have imagined. That baby's parents are hostages to her health and happiness, but they're also the immensely privileged spectators of and participants in the most important process in the human experience, the growth and fostering of the future generations of humanity. Our babies and children are the link between today and tomorrow, the past and the future. That's why the decision you make is so important.

## The health factor

There's still one more factor – or at least, a set of connected factors – which you'd do well to take into account before you and your partner start trying to conceive your baby. At its most basic level, the process of becoming a parent is a very physical one, so it makes sense to try and make sure that the ingredients which go into the making of your children are of the best possible. The simple fact is that healthy parents make healthy babies, and that's something which is backed up by research.

At any rate, there are four main areas which you need to look at, all of which can have an effect on the physical process of becoming a parent, your child herself, or your experience of parenthood. These areas are *genetics*, *diet*, *exercise* and *stress*.

## Genetics

Huge strides have been made in the science of genetics in recent years, and we now know far more about what we inherit from our parents – and what we pass on to our children – than ever before. It's known, for example, that certain diseases are passed on from generation to generation, some of which are very serious indeed. People whose families originally came from the Mediterranean (Greece and Italy in particular) are at a higher risk of inheriting a blood disorder called *thalassaemia*. It's well known that *haemophilia* (a disease in which the blood doesn't clot properly after wounds or bruising) is passed on genetically. *Cystic fibrosis*, a disease in which various important glands in the body don't work properly, is another such disease.

Fortunately, most of these illnesses are quite rare, but the problem is that it's often the combination of specific genes from *both* parents that causes the disease to occur in a child. If you carry the gene for cystic fibrosis and marry someone who also carries the gene, then each of your children has something like a one in four chance of developing the condition. You therefore have a harsh choice to make; should you take the risk or not? It is possible to go to a *genetic counselling clinic* for testing, though. These clinics are growing in number, and if you are worried about potential problems like this, or know that there have been health problems of this nature in your family or your partner's, it's worth asking your doctor for a referral. These clinics can't guarantee that your child will not have any sort of health problem, but they are likely to put your mind at rest over specific, genetic illnesses.

## Diet

'You are what you eat' is a phrase which has been used so much in recent years that it's become something of a cliché. Nevertheless, it does express an important truth which more and more people are coming to accept and act on in their lives. The food you eat *is* vital to your health, and you should aim to do two things in your diet – eat the things you need, and avoid the things which can harm you.

In simple terms, we all need a balanced diet which includes certain things in the right proportions – vitamins, minerals (like iron and zinc), carbohydrates, proteins and so on. I haven't got the space to go into much detail here. But remember that you're only likely to achieve this if you eat a wide variety of fresh and natural foods. Processed foods – the ones that come in tins, packets, bottles and over the counters of some fast-food restaurants – often have a lot of the goodness taken out of them by the refining processes to which they're subjected. They may also contain chemical additives and colourants, many of which have been implicated in cases of allergy. Of course, opinions among the experts vary, but it would seem that if your diet includes plenty of *fresh* fruit and vegetables, wholemeal bread, lean meats (and not too much meat at that), plenty of fibre (to keep your bowels moving and help you to avoid constipation and haemorrhoids or piles), then you shouldn't go too far wrong.

It also seems to be very wise to avoid having too much animal fat in your diet, a substance which has been heavily implicated in the very high figures for heart disease in the western world. Fried food is a major culprit, as is refined sugar and the products made from it in that other widespread curse of the developed nations, obesity. Many of us are overweight, and that's something which can also put strain on your health in general, and your heart in particular. It hardly needs saying either that cigarette smoking will add to the strain imposed on your heart by any other bad habits while it's ruining your lungs, and that heavy drinking will do the same. Another common problem in western societies is the number and variety of drugs we take, many of which are either freely prescibed by our doctors or available over the counter from chemists and pharmacists. I'm not talking about obviously harmful drugs like heroin which are illegal in most countries because of their known, damaging effects; I'm talking about the fact that millions of us take billions of pills and potions of all sorts, and now more and more doctors are saying that this is a growing problem.

There are two points to make here. The first is that you will actually be healthier – and feel it – if you do eat a good, balanced diet of fresh, natural foods. You'll feel even better if you don't smoke or drink too heavily, and the fewer drugs you take, the better, too. Obviously, you should be guided in this by your doctor, especially if you need certain types of medication for specific health problems. But it's important to be aware of these things. Your partner, as you'll see, will be advised along these lines by her doctor during pregnancy, and as I'll explain further on, there is thought to be a link between fertility problems and your diet, smoking, drinking and the sort of drugs you take. The time to start thinking about these areas of your life is as soon as possible, and if you can sort them out to your satisfaction before the conception of your child, so much the better. Try to be like the wise little Alice: every time you lift anything to your lips, look at the label and find out whether it's poison or not.

*Exercise*

Another problem for many of us is a lack of exercise. Our bodies need to be used, and if they're not, they don't work as well as they should in any department. At a very simple level, if you're unfit, then everything you do – walking, climbing stairs, running for that bus – is harder and leaves you more out of breath and tired than it should. In the long term a lack of exercise isn't going to do your heart or circulation any good either, especially if your diet's bad and you smoke. Unfortunately, these habits often come together as a package, with the bad diet not giving you enough energy to take any exercise and the smoking destroying your wind if you do.

I gave up smoking very soon after I saw my father die of coronary heart disease brought on by years of sedentary living and 40 king size cigarettes a day. I also took up squash and generally tried to take more exercise. I was surprised to discover that the benefits of both actions were almost immediate. Where before I'd had to have a rest half-way up the four flights of stairs to my office, I was now finding that I could walk straight up without stopping, and the day soon came when I ran all the way. I felt better, I felt happier, I slept better. Taking exercise isn't a cure-all, but it certainly can help to make life more pleasant. Remember that the early months and years of parenthood are often a strain on your whole being. You'll cope much better with all of it – the broken nights, the worries, the extra demands on both your body and your spirit – if you're fit to start with. You don't have to take up marathon running, and again, it's important to take it easy if you haven't done much exercise before. Don't strain yourself, build up slowly, and see your doctor if you're at all worried.

*Stress*

A certain amount of stress is a normal part of anyone's life. Indeed, without it and its attendant emotions, tension, anxiety and relief when the stress is satisfied or overcome, life would sometimes be very dull indeed. If you didn't feel a little tense, then you probably wouldn't perform quite so well when it comes to taking that important exam or doing that vital piece of work. But the key point about stress is that too much of it can be a very bad thing.

We live in a stressful society in stressful times. In many ways, unacceptable levels of stress are built into our very existence. I know that I feel under a lot of stress when I take Emma to school then race off to the station to make sure that I'm not late at the office, for example. But stress and tension is part of the very structure of the job I do when I get there. The same is true for many men (and women); much of the work we do is in a context of competition and pressure. There are tensions, rows, arguments, deadlines to be met, apart from the simple, physical pressures of the working day with its travel in crowded buses or trains or traffic jams, its noisy, smoke-filled offices or factories.

Stress makes you tense and anxious; tension and anxiety have their physical sides, too. In fact your body reacts to a problem at work much as it would do to a physical threat, such as being attacked, for example. If your job's on the line, you may well tremble, go pale, your blood pressure will probably go up and your heart will race. You'll want to fight back or simply run away from the problem, just as you would if threatened by an attacker. This sort of tension needs to be discharged. If it goes on for a long time – if, for example, you feel that your job is permanently insecure – then the effects of being continually wound up and tense will begin to show. Like a spring that's coiled tight for years under pressure, or an engine kept running too high for too long, something eventually gives.

Much research has been done in recent years into the effects of long-term, continual stress, and it seems fairly clear that it does you no good at all. There is evidence which shows a link between high levels of stress and heart disease, for example, but the simple fact is that too much tension for too long can make for a very uncomfortable life. The important point to remember is that parenthood is in itself a very stressful experience; even the good things about it, the positive emotions you feel, can be disturbing. In order to cope with all this properly you're going to need to keep the stress in other areas of your life down to a minimum if you possibly can.

It's here that you can see the paradoxes inherent in fatherhood raising their ugly heads again. Competition, aggression, the world of work – all these things are an essential part of our idea of maleness, and as you'll see, you'll find yourself increasingly pushed towards them even more when you become a parent, both by your own conditioning and the attitudes of people around you. That's why pregnancy and the early months of parenthood can be so stressful for men. This combination of stresses may leave you feeling crushed between two opposing and irreconcilable forces, almost like the clashing rocks of Greek mythology.

What I've been talking about in this section comes down to achieving a good base on which to start a family. An essential part of that is cutting out as much unnecessary stress from your lives as possible. Sorting out your relationship, thinking about the relative priorities of work, your partner's needs, family needs and so on will also help. Making sure you get enough relaxation and time to yourself, making sure you eat properly and get plenty of exercise, all these things will help to cut down the harmful stress in your life. Change one thing in your life, and there's likely to be a spillover effect into other areas, too.

# 3 What happens in conception?

All this preparation, of course, focuses on one thing eventually – the conception of your child. Something few of us realise until we reach this stage is that making a baby isn't always quite so straightforward as it might appear. In fact for quite large numbers of people it can actually be very difficult, perhaps even impossible.

The figures speak for themselves. It's estimated that 25 per cent of couples who make love using no contraception achieve a pregnancy within a month of trying. Between 80 and 90 per cent of couples will have conceived a baby within a year to 18 months of trying. But that still leaves over 10 per cent of couples who haven't achieved success. In his book, *Why Us?*, Dr Andrew Stanway says that it's likely something like 15 per cent of the adult population could be said to have fertility problems – which in a country like Britain, where there are 16 million people in their so-called fertile years, means that there are something like $2\frac{1}{2}$ *million* people who may not be able to have a baby when they want to, if at all.

This isn't really very surprising when you understand just how complicated our bodies are, and how many things can go wrong when it comes to bringing the various ingredients together. At any rate, to understand conception and fertility problems we need to know something about the way in which the reproductive systems of our bodies work.

A woman has two *ovaries*, one on either side of her womb. At puberty, these ovaries become active, and in a system which involves the pituitary gland in the brain, hormones like oestrogen and other hormone producing glands, one ovary a month is stimulated to produce an egg or *ovum*. This contains 23 chromosomes, one half of each of the 23 pairs in each of the mother's cells. When it's fully ripe, this egg is released to be picked up by the end of the Fallopian tube, of which there are two, connecting the ovaries to the womb. This process is called ovulation. At the same time, the levels of various hormones in the woman's system go up, and these stimulate the womb's lining to become thicker and more 'nutritious'. This is so that if the egg is fertilised, it will be able to embed itself into the wall of the womb and grow properly.

If it isn't fertilised, the egg dies, breaks down and is shed together with the thicker lining of the womb in the process called *menstruation* – your partner's period. The entire cycle then begins again. An average mestrual cycle is 28 days. Day 1 of the cycle is said to be the first day of the period, and for many women ovulation usually occurs on or around day 14, at the mid point. However, many women have longer or shorter cycles, and the length of the cycle in an individual woman can be affected by all sorts of things, like illness or stress. Nevertheless, ovulation almost always happens 13 to 16 days *before* a period.

It's always seemed to me that the production of eggs is a very sensible, economical and efficient arrangement. Men, on the other hand, tend to be profligate when it comes to reproduction. We don't have anything that could be described as a cycle, either; in sexual and fertility terms, our motto really should be 'we never close'. What we produce is sperms, and we produce them in vast numbers, millions at a time. We start producing them at puberty and go on making them until old age, perhaps even death, while our partners' reproductive life comes to a definite end when their periods stop, at the *menopause*.

Sperms are produced in the male equivalent of the ovaries, the *testicles* or *testes*. These are in the scrotum, a bag of skin outside the body, for a very simple reason: sperms can only develop normally at a temperature lower than that inside the body. Inside each testis there are several hundred *lobes*, and inside each lobe there are many tiny tubes tightly packed. These are called the *seminiferous tubules*, and that's where sperms are made. These tubules get larger and larger, finally uniting in one large tube, the *epididymis*, of which there are two, one from each testis. Each of these feeds the sperms into a *vas deferens*, of which there are also two. These take the sperms out of the scrotum and into the body itself.

Each sperm is about 0.05 of a millimetre long, which makes it invisible to the naked eye. It consists of a head, which contains a nucleus with its 23 single chromosomes waiting to be matched up with those inside an egg, a neck and a long tail, making them look very much like elegant tadpoles. The tail is designed specifically to enable the sperm to swim under its own power through the cervix (the neck of the womb), the womb itself and up the Fallopian tubes in search of the egg.

It takes about three months to make one sperm, from the time it starts its life inside the seminiferous tubules to the day it's ready to be ejaculated into the big, wide world. Ejaculation itself is quite a complicated matter, too. When the erect penis is stimulated, it sets in train an intricate process. The vasa deferentia begin to send more sperms onwards towards the *seminal vesicles*. They go on to the *prostate gland*, which is near the bladder, where they pick up some more fluid which provides essential nutrients to enable them to get through the womb – it's a sort of pit stop for fuel. Then there's another pick up of fluid from two small glands called *Cowper's glands*. While all this is going on, a valve shuts in the bladder so that urine can't go down the penis – there's only one tube, after all. And finally it's lift off, with the sperms shooting forth in their liquid vehicle. You might ejaculate anything between 150 and 400 *million* or more sperms at once, propelled outwards by automatic muscular contractions.

Once they've been ejaculated, your sperms swim forward into the womb. It's thought that they might be assisted in their progress if the woman has an orgasm, which makes the womb contract and therefore 'suck' the sperms in. This isn't essential for conception, though, as many women could tell you. At any rate, within a fairly short time – a matter of hours – a much smaller number of sperms who have survived an arduous, mammoth journey will start to swim up the Fallopian tubes, where, if some of them are lucky, an egg will be waiting. During their journey, apart from losing most of their companions, the remaining sperms will have undergone a subtle chemical change known as *capacitation*. Without this they would be unable to penetrate the egg's outer surface. Even so, it's thought that the single sperm out of all those millions which does finally achieve that penetration needs the chemical assistance of the many other surviving sperms which cluster around the egg to make that entry possible. Once the head of the sperm is inside the egg, the tail is shed and the egg manages to make itself impenetrable to any other sperms. (Twins occur when two eggs are released and both are fertilised by single sperms, or when one egg is fertilised by one sperm and for some reason divides into two identical fertilised cells early on. The former are *fraternal twins*, who are no more alike than ordinary brothers or sisters, the latter *identical twins*, who are exactly alike in every respect. Triplets, quads, quins and sextuplets and so on are caused in either of the same ways.)

It's not long before the two nuclei – the head of the sperm and the nucleus already inside the egg – approach each other and fuse. That moment of fusion, the one I described earlier on as taking place on 9 September 1977, when my daughter Emma was created – that is the moment of true miracle, and it's one about which we still know very little. Soon that fertilised cell in which there is now a unique, new combination of chromosome pairs, begins to divide. First it divides into two cells; those two divide into four, then eight, then sixteen. Each new cell carries that same chromosome pattern, which is, in fact, the blueprint for the future development of your child. As it divides, this new living being continues to move down towards the womb where it will embed itself and begin to grow into a person.

## Infertility problems

This whole process is very complicated and, as with any complicated process, problems can occur at any stage to prevent conception. One major problem is that your partner's egg only survives for a day at the most, and probably only really lives for 12 hours. Your sperms usually survive for up to 48 hours, so that means that there's probably only one or two days at the most during your partner's cycle on which she can actually get pregnant. Much research has been done in this field, and we now know that a common cause of infertility is problems in a woman's hormone system which might affect her ovulation adversely, or the quality of the lining of her womb, for example. But the causes of fertility problems are many and varied, and it's important to remember that in about 40 per cent of couples with this sort of problem, it's thought to be the man who is the cause.

Of course, in such a complicated process, it's often impossible to sort out exactly who is *not* contributing what to the final result, and it's often the case that the problem is caused by a combination of factors. However, some men are found to be unable to produce any sperms, for example. Other men produce sperms which are abnormal or dead, while in some men there's some missing tubing in that intricate pattern which joins the inside of the testicle to the penis. A common male cause of infertility which may people have heard about is a *low sperm count*; it seems that quite high numbers of sperms are required for conception, and that less than, say, 20 million in any one ejaculation may not be enough to do the job.

Anyway, this book is not meant to be a treatise on infertility, male or female. There are two points to be made here; you should bear in mind that you could have fertility problems which might mean it takes you much longer to conceive a child than you might have hoped. The second is that if this happens, there is no need to despair or give up hope. Research into this area continues to make new discoveries almost every day; in recent years we've seen all sorts of developments, from new drug treatments for women to the use of the test tube baby techniques to overcome the problem of damaged Fallopian tubes. It's now estimated that up to 60 per cent of those who suffer from fertility problems can be helped to have the baby they want – in time.

I don't want to be glib about this subject, though. It can cause endless heartache not to have the baby you want. That instinct to reproduce is enormously powerful, and you only have to think about the sort of conditioning and pressures I've been talking about so far to see why a fertility problem can have such a devastating effect on a woman. Remember, though, it can affect you in much the same way. In fact, it's often much more difficult for a man to cope with the idea that there's something 'wrong' with him. Men are very sensitive creatures when it comes to thinking about their sexuality or their reproductive equipment. We often associate fertility with virility, although there's no real connection between 'performance' and results in this field, just as it's not essential for a woman to have an orgasm to conceive. I've met men who have been absolutely devastated by the discovery that they can't have children, either because their partner has a problem or they find that the cause is in themselves. The latter is probably a lot worse for a male ego; as one man said to me, 'It was like being told I was only half a man.' That man's partner may well have felt like only 'half a woman', too, and we all need to understand that these feelings are very difficult to cope with, especially in a society which apparently sets such a high value on having children and family life.

## How to deal with them

If you find that it's taking you and your partner longer to conceive than you had hoped, there are several things you can do to help yourself.

*Don't panic* – remember that couples of perfectly normal fertility may take up to a year to conceive. Certain factors can play a part in this. If your partner has been taking the pill, for example, it may take several months for her menstrual system to settle down and for her to start ovulating properly after she gives it up. Good health based on a good diet and a lack of stress will also be important. The evidence is by no means clear as yet, but it doesn't seem too unreasonable to assume that if you over indulge in some of the unhealthy habits I've looked at in this chapter it may well have an effect on your fertility. So that's another good reason for eating well, giving up smoking, cutting down your alcohol intake, getting fit and keeping stress to a minimum. There's some pretty good evidence to show that anxiety can have an adverse effect on your fertility, in fact.

*Making sure you're doing the right thing* – I'm not saying that you don't know how to have sexual intercourse, even though doctors who work in the field of infertility still meet couples who have exactly that problem and don't realise it. Nevertheless, even if you're completely *au fait* with everything you need to know about sex, there are still a few tips worth keeping in mind. First, it's important to concentrate your efforts round the time of ovulation, obviously enough. You can either work this out on the basis of calendar calculations of your partner's monthly cycle, or use one of the other indicators – some women feel a slight pain in the abdomen, but most experience a slight rise in temperature on the day of ovulation. It's probably worth seeking your doctor's advice on this, or reading about it in one of the excellent books on the subject (see the booklist). Second, it's important that the sperms should be delivered as far up inside the vagina as possible, so positions for intercourse which afford deeper penetration are probably best. It's also a good idea for your partner to lie fairly still for a while after you've ejaculated. But most of all enjoy making your baby to the full!

*Seek help for your problem* – don't be afraid to seek help if you are at all worried about conceiving. There's no need to visit your doctor if your partner isn't pregnant within a month or two, but you'd be fully justified in asking your GP's advice if you've been trying for six months to a year without success. He may be able to help you immediately, and if he can't, he'll probably refer you to a doctor who specialises in fertility problems, of whom there are now many. Don't despair if he does – a specialist may be able to give you some simple advice or a simple treatment which will sort out the problem. For example, he might discover that you wear tight trousers and that in your job you spend a lot of time sitting down, which means the average temperature of your crutch will be high, and as we've seen, sperms can only be produced at lower temperatures than those inside the body. The simple answer is to give your scrotum some room! From this point it's apparent that one thing is essential above all in dealing with fertility problems; any doctor you consult will need to talk – and probably even examine – both you *and* your partner.

And what your doctor is bound to advise you at any stage during his treatment is to *keep trying*. For most of us, that's something that doesn't need too much encouragement.

PART TWO

# THE PREGNANT FATHER

During his wife's first pregnancy... he suffered from morning sickness. Curiously enough his wife never had this complaint. He also complained of severe toothache which lasted 3 weeks and led him to demand multiple extractions from a dentist, as a result of which all but 8 molars were removed. During the day the child was born he was seized while at work by severe stomach ache which forced him to sit on the lavatory for an hour or so. This suddenly left him at 11 am. He subsequently discovered that it was about this time that his son was born.

From *Uncommon Psychiatric Syndromes* by M. David Enoch and W. H. Trethowan

# 4 What happens in pregnancy?

For a man, pregnancy can be a very odd experience indeed. As I've already said, we are excluded from it in a very real, physical way, simply because we're men. Everything to do with the growth and development of the child you and your partner conceived together will actually take place inside *her* body, and sometimes it seems that all you can do is to watch her expand as your baby grows within her. Sylvia Plath in one of her poems uses the image of winding a timepiece to describe conception: 'Love set you going,' she wrote to her child, 'like a fat, gold watch.' The problem for fathers is that it can seem as if after a certain amount of winding, all we have to do thereafter is to sit and listen to the ticking.

It doesn't have to be like that, though. You *can* make a positive contribution to your partner's pregnancy, and by doing so you'll help to ensure that you don't feel any more excluded or left out than you have to. The sort of exclusion I talked about in chapter one can start very soon in pregnancy. You can begin to feel left out and left behind, and as you'll see, you may actually have to make a real effort to stay involved right from the very beginning, whether it's by making sure you stay informed, or by taking on the might of the medical profession or your employers to maintain your foothold in parenthood.

At any rate, the benefits of sharing the experience of pregnancy as much as you can with your partner are very great indeed. I've already explained that women whose partners do help and support them through pregnancy are less likely to have problems in pregnancy, labour, birth or in the early months afterwards. It's also been shown that those fathers who make the effort to be involved are the ones who enjoy pregnancy and birth more – and fare better as parents in general. There's a very strong connection between your attitude and the results you get as a father. The research evidence shows over and over again that positive thinking, positive commitment, positive sharing with you, the father, making an effort, pays real dividends. It's a strand which runs through parenthood, just as you'll find it running through this book.

I quoted the case of the long-suffering 'pregnant' father for two very good, very positive reasons. Firstly, you should remember that pregnancy can have a very direct effect both on your body and your emotions. Few men are affected as seriously as that particular father, but we all experience a number of feelings, some of which can even be translated into physical effects serious enough to send some fathers to their doctors for help and advice. Secondly, although your partner's pregnancy can be a very anxious, testing time for you, it's not all gloom and doom. In fact it's a unique experience which you can – and very probably will – enjoy most of the time. It has its own problems and stresses, but with the right approach you can keep these to a minimum and make a positive contribution. Remember as you read what follows the father in our chapter heading had such a bad time during that pregnancy that he went on to have another *five* children, and probably suffered even more. Your author is another multiple-pregnancy lunatic, and I discovered that one of the best ways of handling anxiety in pregnancy is to find out as much as possible about it.

## The inside story

The journey of the fertilised egg down the Fallopian tube to the womb usually takes between five and seven days, and while it's moving, the tiny piece of living tissue which will be your child, is dividing all the time. By the time this tissue emerges into the womb it's quite a big collection of cells – and it's ready to embed itself into the thick, nutritious lining of the womb. Once embedded, the pregnancy has truly begun. And bear in mind that this has all happened *before* your partner even misses her first period, long before you're even aware that she might be pregnant.

When talking about pregnancy, doctors usually divide it up into three parts of roughly three months each, or three *trimesters*. In many ways, the most important trimester is the first one, for by the end of the first three months, the foundations of all your baby's major organs will have been laid. After that it's more or less a question of your child developing towards the

## WHAT HAPPENS IN PREGNANCY?

level of physical maturity he'll need to survive in the outside world. The important point to remember is that your child is most vulnerable to outside influences during that first trimester. If your partner smokes, drinks a lot, takes harmful drugs or comes into contact with any dangerous substances or illnesses (like German measles) during that time, then there's a real risk that the baby will be damaged in some way.

At any rate, the first thing the *embryo* (that's the medical term for the baby at this early stage) has to do after it's embedded itself in the wall of the womb is to set up its own life-support system. At about the time your partner's period would have been due, a space begins to appear inside the collection of dividing cells which is your child. This space later becomes the *amniotic sac*, the membrane which surrounds the baby throughout the pregnancy. That membrane is also known as the 'bag of waters', because it's filled with amniotic fluid. This is the baby's suspension system, a way of making sure that she gets a smooth ride inside her mother's body; it absorbs much of the impact of any knocks and bumps.

At the same time another group of cells begins the phenomenal growth which produces a complete human being in the space of 280 days. This *inner cell mass* begins to burrow into the wall of the womb (doctors call it the *uterus*, by the way) with root-like pieces of itself called *chorionic villii*, which take the nutrients the cell mass needs. Eventually these 'roots' grow into the *placenta*, which is connected to your child at her navel by the *umbilical cord* (the navel is the *umbilicus*). The system of which the placenta forms the main part is a marvel of economical efficiency. Your partner's bloodstream brings oxygen and nutrients to the placenta, where they are transferred to the baby's blood which comes along the cord to meet it. They're then carried back to the baby along the cord, and enter her bloodstream direct. Waste products from the baby's bloodstream are brought back to the placenta, where they're transferred to your partner's for disposal. The two bloodstreams never actually meet or mix; the closest they get is the very thin cell walls inside the placenta where transfer takes place.

The placenta works in this complicated way to make sure that nothing harmful gets from the mother's bloodstream into the baby's. The problem is that it's not 100 per cent secure. Some things to which a baby is vulnerable can get through the placenta to harm him – things like nicotine, alcohol and the German measles virus (rubella). Certain drugs can also do the same, and it's well known that one particular drug given to some women in the 1960s who suffered from anxiety – Thalidomide – caused terrible handicaps in their babies. The point is that babies in the womb are at their most vulnerable in the first three months of their existence. That's because their major organs are being formed in that time. By the end of the first month in the womb, for example, the head and body are differentiated and some of the major internal organs – like the heart, brain and nervous system – have already developed to a rudimentary level. By the end of the second month, recognisable arms and legs have appeared, the fingers and toes are beginning to develop, and the eyes are completely formed, although still closed in under eyelids which haven't separated yet from the surrounding skin.

Although the foundations are laid in the first trimester, your baby needs the rest of pregnancy to develop to a stage where she'll be able to survive in the outside world. Growth and development continues ceaselessly throughout the 280 days of pregnancy, right up to the moment of birth; it's thought that the brain does most of its growth in the last month or so, though the finishing touches aren't applied to that vital organ until after the birth.

The *foetus*, as doctors call your baby after the first few weeks, can even make a few movements by the end of the second month. Your partner won't feel these until much later on, however. Early on in pregnancy, she may feel something like 'butterflies in the tummy', but it's unlikely that she'll feel a definite kick until she's somewhere between 18 and 22 weeks pregnant, with most first-time mothers feeling it later, rather than sooner. This moment – a real highlight in a woman's pregnancy – is called *quickening*. These days there are several highly sophisticated ways of looking into the womb, techniques like *ultrasound scanning*, for example. These have, to a certain extent, reduced the significance of the moment of quickening. Nevertheless, it's still a very important piece of evidence; your partner now knows, in a very direct way, that the child you created together is alive and kicking. That kicking will become even more noticeable as the pregnancy progresses.

It's also thought now that the baby is *responsive* to what happens around her. In fact we now know that your child is aware of a lot while she's still in the womb, and that's hardly surprising. It's not that long before all her senses are working to one extent or another. By the middle of the pregnancy, the foetus can see, and if you think that there's nothing to see inside the womb, you'd be wrong. Strong light shines through your partner's skin, giving the interior a warm, orange-red glow, the colour caused by the light passing through blood vessels. At the very least, it's likely that your child can tell the difference between day and night before she's born. She can also hear, and it's been shown that babies in the womb respond very definitely to noise. A loud bang, or a clap near the womb, will make the baby jump, a reaction your partner will be able to confirm. Towards the end of pregnancy, when your baby probably fills the womb, it's a reaction you might be able to see for yourself; I've seen my children's movements distort their mother's bulging stomach from within many times. Your child will also spend a lot of time listening to the internal sounds of your partner's body, recordings of which reveal the interior to be a very noisy place indeed. Blood whooshes round the circulation, the heart pounds away, the stomach gurgles and rumbles. It's also known that your child can hear voices – her mother's most of the time, and it probably resonates throughout the womb as yours does in your own head when you put your fingers in your ears and talk loudly. But your baby can also hear *your* voice – especially when you're close to your partner.

## The outside story

Although pregnancy is a normal condition for a healthy woman – that is, one with which her body is basically designed to deal – it still represents a massive physical change. For example, her womb will grow to forty times its original size to accommodate your growing baby, whose needs will be supplied by means of an increase in the amount of blood in your partner's circulation – something like 40 per cent, in fact. Your partner will even take in more air with each breath during pregnancy, some of which is for the baby.

All these changes are brought about – and, more importantly, sustained throughout the pregnancy – by means of hormones produced by a complicated system. In early pregnancy they come from the ovary, but later on, the placenta takes over as their main source. But it's the fact that the levels of hormone in the system change very suddenly at the beginning of pregnancy which has been blamed for one of the most common early signs that a baby is on the way, pregnancy *nausea*. Most people, including male film directors and popular novelists, seem to think of it as something which only ever happens in the morning. Although it is true to say that some women do feel sick (and sometimes even vomit) in the mornings early on in pregnancy, many feel nauseous at other times of the day. Some women never actually vomit at all, while some feel sick all day, every day for a time. Other women are unlucky enough to feel sick all through their pregnancies.

Another common problem of early pregnancy, and one which few people are even aware of until they have to cope with it, is simple tiredness. Many pregnant women find that the early months leave them feeling very tired indeed, and doctors have ascribed this symptom to raised hormone levels in the system, although it seems to me that all the extra work your partner's body is doing to maintain the pregnancy is quite enough reason to feel tired. Most first-time mothers are still doing a full day's work every day in early pregnancy too, and women who already have an older child or children (and maybe a full-time or part-time job, as well) also have plenty on their plates. It all adds up to one thing, something which is going to become a very familiar part of parenthood: fatigue.

Those hormones in your partner's system are also helping to bring about other changes in her body, changes which are noticeable quite early on. For example, it's the hormones which suppress ovulation, and therefore put a stop to your partner's periods while the pregnancy lasts. They also stimulate the milk-producing glands in her breasts to start the process by which they'll be able to supply your child with the milk she'll need after she's born. One early sign of pregnancy for some women is in fact a tingling feeling in the breasts, perhaps even some slight discomfort. Your partner's breasts will also probably get much larger quickly; it's surprising just how big some women's breasts become. One woman I interviewed went from a 36B bra to a 44DD in a couple of months!

Of course, one of the most striking outside signs of pregnancy is the change of shape it wreaks upon a woman's body. You're unlikely to notice much change in your partner's figure in the first three months of pregnancy, but it won't be all that long before her waist begins to thicken up. By the middle of her pregnancy she will probably have outgrown many of her clothes.

## WHAT HAPPENS IN PREGNANCY?

Obviously, it's her growing womb that pushes out her waist measurement, but that's not the only place she'll be putting on some weight. Most women find that they put on a few pounds round their hips, buttocks and thighs, too, and the extra inches on your partner's bust will also mean some extra weight there.

The growth of the womb also puts pressure on the other organs inside your partner's body. This can cause problems quite early on in pregnancy. Pressure on the bladder might mean that your partner finds she has to go to the lavatory a lot more often than usual; she may even have to get up several times in the night to do so. Later on, her bladder may settle down, although towards the end of the pregnancy the problem may be acute. Not only will she have to pass water more often, she'll be less mobile because of her sheer bulk – getting out of bed two or three times in the night with that big lump on her front is no joke! The pressure of the growing womb goes upwards as well as down, too. In the last couple of months your partner may well feel a little breathless sometimes, something which is the result of the growing womb pressing upwards on the diaphragm and the lungs above it. This isn't usually a serious problem; it's more an inconvenient discomfort than anything else.

Another change you'll probably both notice is in the pigmentation of your partner's skin. She won't change colour, but it's likely that certain areas of her skin will become darker, areas such as her nipples and the darker skin surrounding them (the *areolae*). Some women also develop a line of dark pigment running down from the navel to the pubic hair. This is called a *linea negra* (Latin for 'black line'). Some mothers also find that faint brown patches appear over their cheeks and forehead. It's rarely very noticeable, and the phenomenon derives its name from its shape – it's called a *butterfly mask*.

Many women positively glow in pregnancy, and there's a lot of truth in the idea that women can 'bloom' while they're pregnant. Some, indeed, look at their most beautiful and their most feminine at certain stages of pregnancy. One beneficial side effect of those hormones in your partner's system is that they may well give her a lovely soft complexion and glowing, beautiful hair. If things are going right, your partner may well feel happier, more fulfilled and more relaxed than she ever has done before – all of which makes for a pretty winning combination. The best time of all for most women seems to be the middle trimester. In those middle three months, many mothers have got over the worst of the nausea and the fatigue, and have 'settled' into being pregnant. Their bumps aren't too large and awkward yet and birth is still far enough off not to be too much of a worry.

The last trimester of pregnancy is often the most uncomfortable time, with the discomfort growing as the day of birth approaches. The growth of your partner's abdomen will reach a peak at this stage, and many women say that they feel like a 'beached whale'. Obviously, the extra weight does make almost everything in your partner's life a little harder. Simple things like carrying the shopping, walking up stairs, even walking itself can be very much more tiring towards the end of pregnancy, and your partner will need plenty of rest. Most mothers also find that they just can't bend in the middle any more, which makes getting in and out of chairs – or in and out of bed – very difficult.

This is one of the reasons why *insomnia* is a common problem of later pregnancy. However tired your partner gets, she's still likely to have a few problems getting to sleep – and staying asleep once she dozes off. Don't forget that the sheer size of her bump will make it difficult for her to turn over or even move very easily in bed, and she certainly won't be able to sleep on her stomach for a while! Many babies also seem to wait until their mothers lie down quietly in bed before they start their most vigorous kicking of the day. I can vouch for this myself; I've almost been kicked out of bed several times by my children while they were still in their mother's womb. Add to all this the fact that many women understandably feel a little nervous and find that their minds are often full of worries, plans, and anxieties during pregnancy and you can understand why your partner finds sleeping a problem sometimes.

Her problems won't end there, though. She's likely to suffer from various aches and pains, the commonest of which is *backache*. This is usually caused by a combination of factors, the main two being those hormones again, and the purely structural strain of the baby growing in the womb. One side effect of pregnancy hormones is to soften and loosen ligaments throughout the body; the growing baby puts an increasing strain on the ligaments and muscles of the lower back, and the result is backache. It's a problem which can be made worse by bad posture and wearing shoes with high heels, both of which tend to put more strain on the same area in any case.

Another common hormonal side effect in pregnancy is *consti-*

*pation*. The hormones have a tendency to make the bowel more sluggish, something which can be made worse by a diet low in fibre. This is related to another problem which, although not all that common in pregnancy, is one which many mothers worry about: *varicose veins*. The blood in your system returns to the heart through your veins, which help it along by muscular action. To make sure it doesn't slip back – a real possibility in areas like the legs, if you think about it – there are one-way valves at intervals along their length. If the valves don't work properly or are under too much pressure, the blood may seep back and cause the veins to become swollen and twisted.

The connection with constipation is that there is a very strong link between straining during bowel movements and varicose veins. It's thought that our western habit of sitting on a lavatory increases the amount of pressure on the veins anyway, and that with our low-fibre diet leading to constipation we're at greater risk of damaging our veins. Unnecessary straining certainly appears to be a key factor in causing *piles* (their more medical, and more gruesome sounding name is *haemorrhoids*). Piles are simply varicose veins of the anus. It's fairly easy to see why piles might be a problem in pregnancy if constipation is common. Other factors in varicose veins as well as piles are thought to be standing too much and the simple fact that there's a greatly enlarged volume of blood in a pregnant woman's system which puts a strain on her circulation.

Obviously these are problems to try and avoid, if at all possible. It's important for your partner to bear in mind that the strain of birth can itself lead to temporary piles, and if she's already got some, they may turn into a long-lasting complaint. The answer is very simple: a fibre-rich diet based on plenty of whole, fresh foods such as wholemeal bread, fruit and vegetables should keep constipation at bay, and therefore mean that she won't have to strain.

Part of the reason your partner will want to avoid varicose veins is the simple fact that they can look very unsightly. Many women are extremely worried about what effects pregnancy will have on their bodies in general. A common concern in this context are *stretch marks*. These are scars in the skin caused by the stretching and tearing of layers of muscle under the surface. During pregnancy they may appear in areas where there has been a lot of expansion and therefore stretching of the skin, such as around the abdomen, breasts, hips or buttocks. They'll appear as pinkish-red stripes and turn silvery white (just like an ordinary scar) after the birth when a woman's body goes back into shape. Unfortunately there's very little a woman can do about stretch marks. It's now thought that dietary deficiencies in childhood – particularly the lack of the mineral *zinc* during the crucial growing periods of adolescence – leaves some women with skin which simply isn't supple or elastic enough to deal with the sudden expansion of pregnancy. And it's known that there isn't a cream or potion in the world which will get rid of them once they've appeared, despite the claims of manufacturers.

# 5 Antenatal care

It's important for your partner to go to the doctor as soon as she thinks she might be pregnant. He'll probably ask her for a urine sample which he'll send for testing, and you'll have the result fairly quickly. The sooner the pregnancy is confirmed, the sooner your partner can start making sure that she's doing the right things and not taking any chances with her health or the baby's. Remember, your baby is at his most vulnerable in the early weeks and months of pregnancy, so it's important for your partner to avoid certain things even if she only suspects that she might be pregnant. For example, it's been shown that embryos can be damaged by exposure to too many X-rays; that's why doctors and dentists often only give young women X-rays in the first two weeks *after* a period.

At any rate, an early visit to the doctor will also mean that your partner's *antenatal care* can start sooner. How this care is handled varies from country to country, and even within countries from area to area. Its point is simple and straightforward: doctors now know a great deal about what sort of things can go wrong in pregnancy and through regular check-ups during pregnancy, they can ensure that any problems can be spotted early and the correct solutions applied before they become too serious. At the same time, regular meetings with a doctor or a *midwife* (a nurse who has had a long extra training to enable her to deal with normal antenatal care and birth) will give them an opportunity to advise your partner about such things as diet and exercise. It's also a good chance for your partner to meet and get to know the people who are likely to be present at the birth.

In Britain – and the same is true of most of the developed countries – the vast majority of mothers give birth in hospital. That's why many mothers go to the hospital in which they're going to deliver their babies for antenatal care, where they'll usually see a midwife and (occasionally) a doctor. He's likely to be an *obstetrician and gynaecologist*, that is, a doctor who specialises in pregnancy, birth and treating women in general. Oddly enough, most obstetricians and gynaecologists are men.

Your partner may be able to obtain antenatal care from your family doctor for most of the pregnancy, or get what's called *shared care* between your GP and the hospital, something which speaks for itself. Whatever system applies to you, your partner is likely to see a doctor or midwife every four weeks or so up to 28 weeks of pregnancy, and then every two weeks up to about 36 weeks. After that, she's likely to have a weekly check-up until she gives birth.

The first of those check-ups is called a *booking-in appointment*, and its main purpose is to find out all about your partner. That's why she'll be asked all sorts of questions about her medical history – and even some about yours. The answers she gives will help the doctor to work out if there are any particular risks involved in your partner's pregnancy. A blood sample will be taken which will be sent to a laboratory and tested for various things, such as whether your partner has any diseases which might cause problems. It's also tested to see if she's *anaemic* – that is, whether she's got enough of the mineral *iron* in her system, of which she needs plenty during pregnancy – and also whether she's immune to *German measles* (*rubella*) or not. This infection is almost completely harmless when caught in childhood, but if it gets across the placenta and attacks the baby in the early part of pregnancy, its effects can be devastating, involving severe handicap. Most women are aware of this problem, and there's been a campaign running for several years to get teenage girls immunised against rubella while they're still at school.

Your partner will also be given a full physical examination, her blood pressure taken, and asked for another urine sample for more tests. She'll also be weighed and measured, and all for very good purpose. Her weight is the starting point by which her weight gain during pregnancy can be measured. Most experts say that a weight gain of between 20-28 lbs by the end of pregnancy is about right, depending on a woman's size before conception. It might sound a lot, but a large proportion of that includes the baby (the average baby weighs $7\frac{1}{2}$ lbs at birth), the placenta and the amniotic fluid, for example. The weight should also be gained fairly steadily, and to keep a watch on it your partner will be weighed at every subsequent check-up. She's measured because it's been found that short women, or women with small or narrow pelvises sometimes have difficulty during birth.

Much the same sort of thing happens at subsequent check-ups, and the point is simply to build up a detailed picture of how the pregnancy is going in every department. The doctor or midwife will also occasionally feel your partner's abdomen; this is called *palpation*, and it's a special way of checking the size of the womb and the position of the baby, a method which needs special training and experience. This will happen more towards the end of pregnancy. Doctors and midwives also use an *ear trumpet* which they press into your partner's abdomen to listen to the baby's heartbeat.

These days, however, medical staff have at their disposal much more sophisticated methods of looking into the womb, techniques which, in a sense, actually produce a real picture of what's going on inside. I'm talking about *ultrasound*, of course, which uses sound waves to look at the baby. Sound waves from a special machine are passed through the womb and bounce off the baby, in much the same way as sound waves are used to detect submarines under water. The signals which come back are fed into a television and produce a picture which, although at first it looks strange, eventually reveals all sorts of details about the baby growing in the womb. In some hospitals ultrasound is offered to all pregnant women as a matter of routine. Ultrasound has become very widespread in the last few years, and until recently it has been considered by almost everyone to be a completely safe technique. Some researchers have written recently of risks associated with it, although the BMA has declared it to be safe for the vast majority of women and most doctors feel it is an enormously valuable aid.

## Your partner's feelings

Although there are very positive reasons for all these regular check-ups, it's sometimes easy for your partner to lose sight of them. It is important for her to keep all her antenatal appointments, even if she has a completely normal, trouble-free pregnancy, but sometimes the attitudes of the staff who are looking after her can be offputting. 'I finally got very fed up with waiting rooms and being poked and prodded by people who had forgotten my name,' one mother told me. 'I felt as if I was losing control of my body and my life, almost as if I was being taken over by the pregnancy.' This is a very common feeling for many mothers. Not all doctors and midwives are good at making women feel at ease, and it has to be said that in big city hospitals medicine – and antenatal care – can be a very impersonal business. That's the last thing it should be; having a baby is a deeply personal, vitally important experience for a woman, and what she needs is plenty of tender loving care and reassurance. Happily, criticism levelled at poor communication between medical staff and pregnant mothers seems slowly to be producing results in making antenatal care a more human affair. Nevertheless, your partner may well feel less than happy with the treatment she receives from the hands of those in whose care she finds herself.

But however unsatisfactory her meetings with midwives and doctors might be, she does at least meet them. Fathers, as you'll find out very early on, are almost totally excluded from their partners' antenatal care. You simply won't be invited along to the booking-in appointment or any of the other check-ups during pregnancy. What's more, it's highly unlikely that you'll be able to get any time off from your job to go along. As I said in chapter one, most of us are so conditioned into our masculine roles that we don't even feel justified in asking for time off to accompany our partners on their antenatal appointments. The result is that we can begin to feel very left out of the whole process; we begin to feel like outsiders. 'It was as if I wasn't supposed to have anything to do with Sarah any more,' one father said to me. 'She was swept off into a round of check-ups which had nothing to do with me. I felt useless, and worse, I didn't understand what was happening to her.' These feelings can be compounded by the fact that your partner may obviously be suffering as a result of becoming pregnant. I knew that I began to feel quite guilty that I wasn't feeling sick and exhausted as Sally was at the beginning of her first pregnancy; nothing was happening to me, while everything was happening to her.

Your partner's feelings may also be something of a problem. Nausea, fatigue, insomnia, constipation, feeling like a 'beached whale' . . . with all these things, it's hardly surprising that your partner might feel a little less than positive about being pregnant at some times. Obviously, if your partner suffers a great deal from the sort of discomforts I've talked about, then she's going to need a lot of help and support. But even those mothers who don't suffer very much – and there are quite a few who sail through the whole experience without much bother – may have a few emotional problems to work through.

These can start very early in pregnancy. In fact, it's very common for both men and women to react with a sense of shock to the news that they're going to become parents – and this can happen even to those couples who might have been trying to conceive a baby for months, perhaps years. *Mixed feelings* is the key phrase in this context. 'It's all very well wanting to have a baby – that can be a very abstract feeling,' one father said to me, 'But it's all a bit more daunting when you're faced with that desire becoming reality.'

This is a perfectly natural and normal way to react. We may not know very much about the details before we actually start to live the reality of parenthood, but we are usually very aware that it's going to mean a major transition in our lives. Any period of change is likely to generate a certain amount of anxiety, exactly how much depending on the extent of the upheaval. As I've said, parenthood is probably the biggest upheaval any of us is ever likely to face, and the shadow of what's coming spreads backwards over pregnancy, which is the way it should be. In fact, if you or your partner didn't feel a little worried about what you're taking on – at the very *least* – then that in itself would be something to worry about.

The problem is often that you can't admit any negative feelings to yourself, something which may even be more of a problem for your partner than it is for you. Remember, your partner has probably been conditioned into implicitly believing two things about pregnancy. The first is that, because motherhood is seen to be the only means by which women can – or should – gain fulfillment, she should now be overjoyed that she's expecting a baby. The second is that motherhood is all deeply instinctive and comes naturally, and that now she's pregnant, she should begin to adapt to her new role without any problems. Obviously this sort of thing isn't said directly by anybody, but it is a part of our belief system, part of the atmosphere which we breathe. 'I couldn't believe it,' one woman said to me, 'everyone kept saying to me "You must be so pleased!" when I told them that the pregnancy had been confirmed. There seemed no room for doubt, and although part of me was delighted, another part inside was practically screaming with fright.'

For many women it's an intractable problem. Your partner may well worry about many things to do with pregnancy and birth, and she needs to be able to get these fears out into the open. That same woman went on to say that she was 'scared of lots of different things. I was frightened that my figure would be ruined forever, I was frightened that my breasts would sag and that my vagina would become loose and floppy after the birth. I was scared of the birth itself, although I found that hard to admit. Most of all I was simply scared that I would make a mess of being a mother, that I would be completely hopeless when it came to looking after my baby and loving her.'

All these fears are very common, very real – and very understandable. Your partner is bound to worry about what pregnancy and birth are going to do to her body; another part of her conditioning tells her that women have to look beautiful at all times, and that to look beautiful they must be young, sexy, slim and immaculately coiffed and attired. Call it the 'Playmate syndrome' if you like; it's there in most women, to one degree or another, and it's constantly being reinforced by the promotion multi-million dollar industries – cosmetics companies and the world of fashion – use to keep their profits high. It's these attitudes which can often make pregnancy a nightmare for beauty-conscious women. Can you imagine anything less like our current image of female pulchritude than being a 'beached whale' with stretch marks and constipation?

It's also perfectly natural for your partner to be apprehensive about birth. One problem of pregnancy can be that it sometimes seems that as soon as everyone knows you're expecting a baby, you become a focus for all the nightmare stories about childbirth they can remember. It also seems to me that birth still gets a very bad press; on films and in television plays, it's still more likely to be portrayed as an affair of screaming and hanging on to one end of the bed like grim death, with unnamable horrors going on at the other to the sound of squelching, tearing and blood splashing in buckets. For such a normal, everyday event it still seems to be surrounded by an awful lot of mythology. However, it is true that birth does hurt; so your partner's perfectly justified in being a little afraid, although as we'll also see, how much it hurts is to a large extent dependent on keeping fear to a minimum.

Another common fear many women experience is that the baby they're carrying might be handicapped. I've even known women who have had nightmares about the baby in their wombs, and with all these fears to keep her mind active, it's not surprising that many mothers report an increase in disturbing dreams of all kinds during pregnancy. In fact, very, very few

## ANTENATAL CARE

babies are born with major handicaps.

With all this in mind, you won't be astonished to hear that a common symptom of pregnancy is for a woman to exhibit strange changes of mood. One minute she may be feeling on top of the world, brimfull of confidence about the future and her abilities to cope with birth and motherhood. The next she may well be terribly depressed, a prey to all sorts of morbid imaginings and thoughts. She may become irritable from time to time, and may even snap at you for no reason. Again, doctors have ascribed these mood swings to the raised – and changing – levels of hormones in your partner's system. Again it is also important to remember that pregnancy is a very emotional time for a woman and that problems of temperament are, in many ways, a natural reaction. Whatever the cause, you'll find that you're the person who's likely to take the brunt of your partner's moods – and you'll be going through some similar experiences yourself at the same time.

# 6 The brooding father

The strength of some men's feelings about pregnancy can be gauged from the results of a survey conducted in Britain in 1965 which discovered that something like 10 per cent of prospective fathers in the study suffered from physical or emotional symptoms serious enough to make them think about consulting their doctors. Oddly enough, most of these problems were related to the stomachs of the fathers in question. They included loss of appetite, nausea, vomiting – often in the form of morning sickness – indigestion, stomach pains, constipation, and diarrhoea. There were other complaints, too – headaches, bad nerves, general weakness, tiredness, depression, irritability, insomnia, tension, not to mention food cravings and toothache. A control group of similar men whose partners were not pregnant suffered from any or all of these ailments significantly less than the pregnant fathers.

The quote at the beginning of Part Two, about the father who ended up having multiple tooth extractions, comes from the book in which I first came across this fascinating study. More specifically, it comes in a chapter called 'The Couvade Syndrome', in which the authors describe what happened to the rare fathers who became psychiatric cases during their partners' pregnancies. Men whose abdomens became swollen – that is, cases of 'sympathetic pregnancy' – are very, very rare indeed, although the authors do cite the case of an Australian who did suffer in this way. His stomach became as large as that of a woman at about eight months pregnant, and subsided completely when he was put under general anaesthetic, only to re-inflate itself eerily as he awoke. Needless to say, there was nothing inside it except plenty of wind.

The word *couvade* is derived from the French word *couver*, which means to brood or to hatch. Anthropologists have used the word to describe a fairly widespread ritual in primitive societies in which a man actually imitates his wife's labour pains and generally behaves as if he was giving birth, and not her. All sorts of motives have been ascribed to the labouring father. Some experts maintain that by making a fuss, he is attempting to ensure that any unwanted attention from the Evil Eye or harmful spirits will be drawn his way, rather than towards his wife and baby. Others have said that it's a way of staking a paternity claim in societies where the ladies rule the roost and call upon the services of several men to help them conceive. Still others have said that it can all be put down to straightforward jealousy of women's ability to create life in such a dramatically visible way, making it a sort of theatrical wish on the part of fathers to hog all the creative limelight.

There are probably a number of motives behind the ritual. What's clear is that the ritual is related to the anxieties most human beings feel at these times of transition in life, especially one in which so much is at stake. In short, the *couvade* is a rite of passage, a means of marking a point of no return and a way of making the passage between one stage of life and another a little easier by acting it out. These rites of passage are very important indeed in many cultures; they're used at different stages in life, and vary from tattooing at adolescence in certain tribes to Barmitzvahs in Jewish families and white weddings. Although we advanced beings in our developed, industrialised nations pay less attention to such rituals we still need these outward signs of inward changes, and by not having a *couvade* ritual we end up having a *couvade* syndrome.

Those symptoms listed above are the classic signs of anxiety; even things like toothache can be related to high levels of tension. When we're anxious we often focus our feelings on one particular area of the body or on small, annoying physical complaints which become major problems under the pressure of our tensions. And anxiety is a key feature of most men's experience of pregnancy. Interestingly enough, that same survey revealed that many more than 10 per cent of pregnant fathers suffered from odd aches and twinges or symptoms of tension. It shouldn't really be surprising; after all, the anxieties generated by the transition from being a childless male to being a father can be very hard to cope with.

Many fathers worry about the physical and medical aspects of pregnancy and birth. 'I realised that Jane was going to have to go through a lot of discomfort and pain to have our baby,' one father told me, 'and I was scared of it all for her.' This sort of feeling is often strongly linked with a man's own fears of being at the birth itself. These days, with eight or nine out of ten fathers being present throughout labour, the pressure is on men to say they'll be there. But it has to be said that it isn't an easy decision. 'I wanted to be there,' the same father said, 'but I was scared of the idea. I had no experience of anything like it to go by.' The problem can be that a man feels reluctant to talk about his fears of birth, especially if his partner wants him to be there. You may also feel that it's unfair of you to want to avoid something which your partner can't get out of, however much she might want to!

It also has to be said that some men are afraid of what pregnancy and birth are going to do to their partners' bodies, although that's something we're even less likely to want to admit. Part of the reason is that in today's climate it's increasingly hard to be seen to be so overtly chauvinist (and quite right, too); a bigger part though is that most of us are very aware of just how important their bodies – and our attitudes to them – can be to our partners because of their conditioning. Again, these fears are coloured by the sorts of myths perpetuated in locker room conversations, myths which grow out of men's habitual ignorance of the true facts of women's anatomy and childbearing – all of which is due to our conditioning and the sexual stereotypes which still dominate our society.

You may well also worry about the baby and the possibility that he might be born handicapped or abnormal in some way, although from my experience, this sort of anxiety seems to be less common in men than it is in women. You'll probably be a little more concerned about how you're going to cope with fatherhood itself. It's very disconcerting for most men to realise suddenly that soon they're going to be called upon to be parents. This is where the problems in our conditioning become apparent. It's all very well to be brought up thinking that everything to do with pregnancy and children is on the woman's side of the great divide; pregnancy is the time when you begin to realise that however much you think you might be able to avoid it all, the experience is going to impinge on you in very many ways.

The roots of the anxiety most men feel lie in the fact that they're fundamentally very unprepared for parenthood at a deep level. When they become 'pregnant fathers', the turmoil of their emotions and feelings can be very disturbing indeed. What makes it all worse is that your conditioning will also have had the effect of making you uneasy about any form of emotion, especially when it's to do with things which have traditionally been thought of as lying on the woman's side of the great divide – like pregnancy and childbirth. It's Catch 22; you feel strangely upset by pregnancy, but you can't admit the feelings to yourself. Like your partner, you feel that you shouldn't be feeling anything but delighted, with the added problem that as a man, you're supposed to defer to your partner in all matters concerning *her* pregnancy.

And make no mistake, that can be a very real problem. It's the beginning of something I've come to call the 'you-never-can-win syndrome'. In early pregnancy, for example, your partner may suffer from mood swings and irritability. At any other time you'd probably feel justified in getting a little irritable yourself and expecting her to take your feelings into account, too, but in pregnancy, she's the one who's suffering, so you're more likely to swallow your resentment at her moods (which you're bound to feel sometimes; none of us are angels, after all) on the grounds that you're not the one who's feeling nauseous or tired and so on. Some men try sympathy, which sometimes works and sometimes doesn't; others try a policy of carrying on as normal, which isn't always a great success. Whatever you do you're likely to feel that you can't win, that you're fading into the background, that you'd better keep your negative feelings and worries to yourself because you don't want to bother your partner, and that in some way it's wrong even to want to express your worries and anxieties.

## Tangled emotions

In short, your emotions and anxieties in pregnancy may become very tangled indeed. 'I just didn't know which way to turn,' said one father. 'Part of me was saying that this was all terrific, and another part was saying that it was all terrifying – and that was the part I couldn't admit even to myself.' It's very easy for a father simply to feel completely out of his depth. Another problem is that our conditioning exerts more pressure on us of a different sort. Pregnancy is the time when we prospective fathers begin to feel that we should be fulfilling our traditional male roles and be good breadwinners and providers for our families.

This was something I felt very keenly, at least. During Sally's first pregnancy we had come to the inescapable conclusion that our only choice was for her to give up work and look after the baby, and for me to become our family's sole source of income, and as a consequence I immediately began to take my job a lot more seriously – a common reaction among fathers-to-be. You begin to realise that your family will now be totally dependent on you financially, that unless you earn enough money, your wife and child will suffer. In a way, it can seem like the final end of the carefree days of bachelorhood and freedom. You can't buy what you want any more, you can't throw caution to the winds, you feel you can't be extravagant. Now you're a responsible man with a family to support – and that can seem very burdensome.

Given the combination of various factors – namely your conditioning, your tangled emotions and your new feeling of responsibility – it's hardly surprising that a common reaction among fathers is to fling yourself into your work with renewed vigour. It's a way of escaping from the problem of facing up to your feelings about the transition you're going through by taking the easy way out, the socially conditioned and approved way. It's a way of saying to yourself that you're a good father because you're a good provider. It was something I did. I did lots of overtime in a job I wasn't particularly keen on, and I even took on as much freelance work as I could, too, during Sally's pregnancies. It wasn't long before I seemed to be working all the time.

It's also common for men to fling themselves into other traditional masculine pursuits and occupations during pregnancy, and for much the same reason. Some men suddenly take to decorating the house or building things, and often set themselves deadlines for having a nursery ready for the baby, for example. Of course, the most usual deadline is the baby's estimated date of birth. 'I decorated every room in the house,' said one man, 'and the closer to the birth I got, the more frantic I became. I didn't realise it until after Paul was born, but that day had been hanging over me throughout pregnancy.' In fact *deadlinitis*, an anxiety-based tendency to feel frantically under pressure to get all sorts of things completed by a certain date, is an extremely common part of men's experience of pregnancy.

Of course the main problem that this presents is that it's another way in which men's exclusion from the process of becoming a parent is perpetuated. What happens is that you're so busy proving you're a good provider, so intent on not

## THE BROODING FATHER

burdening your partner with your feelings, that you can begin to feel very left out. Remember what I said in chapter one about all those friends and relatives who'll keep telling you that you won't be all that interested in pregnancy and birth? Add to that the fact that you are excluded from antenatal care, and that you probably do feel a combination of anxiety and guilt at the sight of what your partner's going through to have your baby, and you've probably got quite a problem, especially if you try and repress all this, as we men often do. The result is that the repressed emotions get channelled into something else – which can be work, or playing football, or going out for a drink with the boys.

This can sometimes mean that you and your partner begin to drift apart at a time when you should be drawing together. It's that old great divide coming between you, but because it's often hard to see just what society, circumstance and our conditioning are doing to us, we tend to blame something – anything – else. In pregnancy it's easy to blame what's literally coming between you – the baby. And it's true to say that many fathers often do feel quite jealous towards their own babies in the womb. It's the baby who's making their partners feel sick and put on weight; it's the baby who's wreaking such havoc on their lives. It's important to remember that it's perfectly normal to feel this way about our children, and that most of us do, at least occasionally. We'll see that women often resent their children, too.

The end result for many men is that they feel left out, excluded and unhappy during pregnancy. These feelings can often be made worse by the fact that a couple's sex life becomes the first casualty of family life – even before the baby is born. For women aren't the only ones to suffer from mood swings and irritability in pregnancy; these are also common symptoms of the male experience. Your partner will probably pick up your anxieties, your jealousy, your worries, and may even feel hurt if you don't talk about them. So if you're both on edge, both anxious, and both feeling that you're not exactly going into parenthood hand in hand, then it's easy to see that your sex life might not be too terrific.

There's an awful lot of mythology related to sex in pregnancy too. Both Sally and I felt during her first pregnancy that sex was wrong, and I was particularly worried that intercourse might bring on a miscarriage or even hurt the baby in some way. 'It was very strange,' one man told me, 'it felt really weird to be making love knowing that there was a third person present. I worried about it quite a lot, and I even got to the stage where I fantasised that a tiny hand would come down and grab my penis at a vital moment. I was also very concerned that my penis might actually damage the baby or disturb the pregnancy.' These fears are related to our jealousies and concerns, and even though few of us would admit to them in public, ideas like these are very common. And of course, the result is that you can become quite reluctant to make love.

'We were making love when all of a sudden the baby moved inside Linda,' another father said. 'She just laughed and said something like "Junior doesn't like what his father's up to." But I couldn't carry on after that. It just turned me right off.'

# 7 Sharing pregnancy

Of course I've drawn something of an exaggerated picture so far. Few father experience *all* the negative feelings I've been talking about, or feel so excluded that they become desperately jealous of the baby. But it's important to bear in mind that much of what I've described is very common, and that you'll need to take some positive action to ensure that the negative aspects of pregnancy don't take over and spoil the experience for you and your partner.

Perhaps the most valuable thing that you can do right from the beginning of pregnancy is to remember that you're both in it together. You both need to understand that you're under pressure and that you both might be feeling anxious about what's happening to you and your lives and your relationship. If you can communicate with each other about your feelings – even when they're apparently less than positive – then you'll be doing yourselves and each other a real favour.

Many couples do in fact find that pregnancy brings them closer together, at least to start with. I've already said that many fathers do worry a great deal about their partners, and it has been said that the sort of symptoms I described when talking about the couvade syndrome could be the result of simple sympathy in the sense of its original Greek roots, that of 'suffering with' your partner. That's what lies behind the idea of a 'sympathetic pregnancy'. 'I was surprised at just how much my feelings for Jane seemed to deepen when she became pregnant,' said one man. 'I wouldn't have believed that it could happen, but it did.'

The important thing is, of course, *not* to hide your feelings. Like steam from a pressure cooker, repressed feelings find their way out in some way eventually, and when they do, irritability and arguments often follow. Tell her how you feel, and make sure that she has her chance to tell you how *she* feels about what's happening to her. You really need to try and spend some time together exploring the impact of becoming a parent with each other. You will find that developing a greater understanding of what your partner's going through will help her to understand more of your feelings, too.

## Sex in pregnancy

A greater depth of understanding between the two of you will also help to keep any problems in your sex life to a minimum. The first point is that almost all of the myths about sex in pregnancy are untrue. It's now known that sex is safe throughout pregnancy (with an exception which I'll be explaining a little further on). Your baby is sealed in tight, with a plug of mucus firmly in the cervix (the neck of the womb) which stays in place until just before birth. It's there specifically to keep infection and foreign bodies *out*, and your baby *in* – so there's no chance that your penis can bash your baby or dislodge him, or even that he'll grab you while you're in the throes of passion. In fact, the full range of sexual activity should be available to you both, although doctors warn that you shouldn't blow into your partner's vagina during oral intercourse because there's an increased risk of creating an air bubble in her circulation in this way.

Nevertheless, you should bear in mind that now your partner is expecting a baby, sex is more than likely to be a little different. One good thing about it is that there's no need to worry about contraception – it's too late for that! The absence of periods can also mean that you feel relaxed and easy about sex, with nothing to worry about and no interruptions. For some couples expecting a first child all this adds up to a real renaissance in their sex life. 'It was better than when we first knew each other,' said one man. 'We made love more often and enjoyed it more, too.' But remember that there will probably be times when your partner isn't going to feel much like having energetic intercourse. At the beginning of pregnancy, for example, she's hardly likely to feel amorous if she's feeling nauseous and tired. Towards the end of pregnancy the sheer size of her bump, the breathlessness, the backache and all the other minor niggles to which she may well be subject aren't going to make her feel much like a sex goddess, either.

None of this means that she doesn't love you any more, nor

that she is going off sex with you, nor that your sex life is over for ever. What it does mean is that you need to show some understanding, and perhaps even get used to a broader idea of sexuality which includes more cuddles and less penetration. Our conditioning tends to make us equate sex with intercourse, while at the same time making it difficult for us to respond in any other way to other forms of touching or physical contact with our partners. Your pregnant partner may not, at times, feel like having intercourse, but she may well feel very physical, very erotic. Carrying a baby in your body is a deeply physical experience for a woman, one which many mothers find almost disturbing in its ability to make them feel more at one with their bodies and its physical rhythms. It's a time when physical contact can be very important to her, and if you can tap into this sensual physicality you'll help yourself to feel that you're a greater part of what's happening to both of you in a very deep and fundamental way.

Your partner will certainly appreciate it if you are as tender and gentle as possible in your lovemaking at this time. Don't forget that she may well be feeling quite delicate at times, and her breasts, for example, will certainly need careful handling. Towards the end of pregnancy they may be full of the early milk, a fluid called by doctors *colostrum*, your baby will be dependent on in the first few days after birth. Some couples discover that even the lightest pressure on the breasts can start this milk flowing, while hard squeezing, biting and sucking is only likely to make your partner do a lot of wincing.

You'll also need to experiment with different positions for intercourse as the pregnancy progresses. It is possible to continue to enjoy sex in the man-on-top missionary position throughout pregnancy if you take more of the weight on your arms and knees, although most couples find that they stop using it once the bump begins to get too big. Woman-on-top positions (either with you on your back or sitting, with your partner's back towards you) are usually very popular, as are rear entry positions, either lying down or standing up. In fact pregnancy can be quite an exciting time sexually, as you discover new areas of interest which will become permanent parts of your sexual repertoire in years to come.

At the same time, it's important to be *sensual* in pregnancy to match the increased sensuality in your partner's life. By this I mean that you shouldn't be afraid of non-sexual touching, as men so often are. Towards the end of all her pregnancies, Sally found that she could no longer cut her toenails; she simply couldn't bend in the middle any more. So I did it for her, and although I would never have believed it beforehand, it was a delightful experience and gave us both some fun. But at a deeper level it's important to try and enjoy pregnancy in a physical way. 'As we got closer to the day of birth,' one father told me, 'I spent more and more time caressing my wife's body. I used to spend ages lying there, listening, feeling my child rippling underneath the skin separating us.' It is an amazing experience, and one which you don't get that many chances in your life to enjoy. So make the most of it. Watch your partner's stomach move as your child kicks and does somersaults. Put your ear against her warm flesh and listen, and better still, *talk* to your child in the womb. That's not as silly as it sounds; remember what I said about your child being able to hear sounds outside the womb? He will certainly therefore be able to hear your voice, and there are some experts who believe that by talking to your child in the womb you'll help him get to know your voice, and that he'll recognise it more quickly after the birth. It all adds up to delighting in your joint fertility, enjoying and sharing pregnancy at its most basic, physical level.

By doing this you'll also be helping to make sure that your partner stays relaxed and happy, and that will help to make labour and birth easier for her. In fact positive support from you at this time is going to make a real contribution in other areas, too. For example, if your partner wants to breastfeed, then she needs to start thinking about it and preparing before the birth. There's not much needed in the way of physical preparation, although some experts say that it helps to massage the breasts and nipples, and even to 'express' some milk by hand. What does matter is that her attitude is right, and it's been shown that *your* attitude counts here. Women whose partners are positively in favour of breastfeeding and who actively support the idea breastfeed more successfully, for longer, and with fewer problems. Your support should start in pregnancy, and it can begin with you changing your attitude to your partner's breasts. Too many of us seem to think of breasts as useful sexual aids which come attached to our partners, and in this we're encouraged by the way in which newspapers, advertisements and magazines (to name but a few) use women's bodies to promote all sorts of products and ideas, or simply for the sake of exploitation. Of course none of this has anything to do with the purpose for which breasts are basically designed – feeding babies. The ridiculous thing is that there's still something of a taboo about breastfeeding a baby in public, although naked (non milk-producing) breasts on huge advertisement hoardings hardly even raise middle-aged eyebrows these days.

This is where you can really help your partner. Understand what's happening to your partner's breasts, and don't recoil in horror if they happen to 'leak' occasionally. Some men even help to massage their partner's breasts and express some milk. Others help their partners in and out of the bath, and turn bathtime into a time for fun and relaxation. You can oil and massage your partner's body to help her relax and keep her skin supple, for example – all of which will add to the sensuality of pregnancy.

## Being positive

Sharing and helping each other on this simple, physical level can – and should – be extended into other areas of your lives together. Now is the time, for instance, to start taking a greater share in the domestic chores, if you haven't done so already. It was estimated from a recent survey that less than one-third of women who were asked about their husband's contribution were anywhere near satisfied with the amount of help they received. Other surveys have shown that very few men do much housework at all. What's more, many women begin to experience the first glimmerings of resentment about this during pregnancy, especially if they have to cope with a full-time job, nausea, tiredness *and* a moody, anxious husband. Some men actually help less around the house during pregnancy, perhaps because they're flinging themselves into their work and aren't around as much. Some unconsciously retreat into the masculine stereotype where they feel more comfortable rather than make the effort to grapple with their feelings.

The point is that your partner does need help in pregnancy, especially when it comes to things which are going to make her more tired. She's also going to need a lot of help after the baby is born. Help is never so sweet when you have to ask for it, and you can raise your stock in your partner's estimation very easily by *volunteering* to do the ironing or the weekly shopping, or the cooking or the tidying up and generally sharing the chores. In the short term this will make life much easier for your partner at a difficult time, and will probably contribute to making pregnancy a better experience for her. In the long term it will put your relationship on a more equal footing and mean that you'll develop a base on which you can be fully involved as a parent in the new family that the two of you are creating.

You may have discovered that taking positive steps to share the experience of pregnancy with your partner may not be as easy as you would have hoped. In fact to share it properly, you're probably going to have to take on officialdom in two of its most imposing manifestations — the medical profession and the world of work, which probably boils down to your partner's doctor (or midwife) and your boss.

To take the medical profession first: it's very important to establish your presence early on in the minds of the people who are going to be looking after your partner during her pregnancy and delivering your baby. This means going along to the antenatal clinic and meeting them if it's at all possible, although if you do you'll probably discover that you're quite unusual. On the occasions when I've been along to an antenatal clinic with Sally I was generally a minority of one in the waiting room and found it virtually impossible to breach the barrier that stopped non-medical males gaining entrance to the consulting and examination rooms. It's at this point that you're likely to feel at your most excluded.

In an ideal world, medical staff would see both parents together at antenatal check-ups; it's only sensible, after all, that the two people who made the baby should both be present when decisions are made about the pregnancy and birth. However there's a large barrier to break down in that many medical staff — especially male obstetricians, and most obstetricians *are* male — don't like the idea of having a woman's partner around. I've always had the impression that it can cramp their style and makes them feel embarrassed, uneasy, perhaps even less authoritative, although such unmedical emotions are often rationalised away with various excuses. However some progressive doctors do make the effort to meet fathers in early pregnancy. The important point is that even simply by being in the waiting room to talk to your partner directly after her check-up you'll be giving her just the sort of support she needs. She'll find it much easier to get the best out of her antenatal care if she knows she's got your complete understanding and support. If she feels that the midwife and doctor aren't being particularly sympathetic or answering her questions to her satisfaction, it's easier for her to tackle them if she knows she's got you behind her. Also be sure she asks the medical staff any questions that *you* might want answered. It's a good idea to write down all the questions you both want answered before going to the clinic.

Remember that you have certain rights as far as medical treatment in pregnancy is concerned. I've talked so far about giving birth in hospital, and although that's where something like 97 per cent of all births take place in Britain, you can choose to have your baby at home, although it might be quite difficult to organise, depending on where exactly you live and what facilities there are in your area. (The 'home versus hospital' debate is discussed more fully in the next chapter, but it is something you should bear in mind.) At the very least, you have a right to choose the hospital where your baby is born, although again, your choice in the matter may be restricted, depending on the area in which you live. If there is only one hospital within 40 or 50 miles, for example, then you won't have much choice at all.

Why should you choose a hospital, anyway? Aren't they all the same? The answer is simply No. Hospitals vary in their facilities, and more importantly, the staff vary in their attitudes and approach to handling labour and birth. This is where we begin to enter the territory of debate and controversy, and cross the battle-lines drawn up between campaigners for natural birth and their opponents. Briefly, in recent years, many individuals, experts and groups have criticised the so-called 'medicalisation' of birth, and point to the fact that most women give birth in hospital, many are given powerful painkilling drugs and have their babies delivered with the aid of all sorts of mechanical devices. The campaigners maintain that this is wrong because birth is a natural, normal event for which the human female body is perfectly designed. They say that in most labours, all that women need is to be allowed – with expert help available – to do very much what they want to do. They say that women should be in control of their labours, not doctors with their technology, and that although birth is much safer than it used to be for both mother and baby, it has become an experience which can be a great disappointment to mothers.

Of our three children, two were born in hospital and one at home, and although all three experiences were wonderful, the home birth was best, mostly because it was completely natural and we were in control. I have to declare my bias at this point, and say that I believe it is vital to 'humanise' birth in our hospitals as much as possible. It should be said, however, that there is growing evidence that doctors and midwives are coming to the same conclusions, and that the worst excesses of hospital control and manipulation of births may well be a thing of the past. But it is important to try and decide as early as possible what you both want as far as the style of birth is concerned – and there are alternatives. You'll have to decide whether or not you want to be there, for a start. Your partner will have to decide whether or not she wants to have a 'technological' birth, with plenty of painkilling drugs, or a 'natural' birth in which she's free to move around without any or only limited use of drugs. Obviously, these are matters which will affect your choice of hospital, and some hospitals favour one style rather than another, and as antenatal care is linked sometimes to the hospital where the delivery will take place, these are things you'll have to try and sort out early on. Remember, the choice is yours, and that the important thing is for the two of you to make the decisions together to your own satisfaction. Try not to let anybody pressure you into doing one thing or the other, but on the other hand, do at least listen to good advice. It's your experience, so do it in the way which will make it good for *you*.

I'm not preaching confrontation with your doctor and midwife; that's the last thing I'd want. Bear in mind that they are as concerned as you to make sure that everything goes well and that a healthy baby is born to a healthy mother. You should also remember that their advice is based on specialised training and a great fund of experience in handling pregnancy, labour and birth. What you should do is to try and establish a spirit of harmony and co-operation with the medical staff involved in your case if it's at all possible. You should make them aware of your wishes early on, and ensure that they've understood what you want. To make doubly sure, your partner should have anything you're particularly concerned about inserted in her notes so that even if different staff actually handle her delivery, they'll know what you want; I'm talking about things like not having any drugs during the birth, or ensuring that your presence at the delivery is guaranteed by having it inscribed for all to see.

You'll probably also find out that the other arm of officialdom – your boss – may make it very difficult for you to share in your partner's antenatal care. Even if your boss or your company is

## SHARING PREGNANCY

enormously sympathetic, they're still unlikely to be very keen on you actually taking time off to accompany your partner to the clinic. Some enlightened employers are beginning to grant this sort of time off, and one or two are even making it a right (usually under union pressure), but they're very few and far between, and most fathers find that, if they want to do it, they have to take paid holiday, unpaid leave, or simply develop a very sudden cold or bad stomach. I don't suppose I should admit it, but I've done all three, with the emphasis being on the latter (like most fathers).

At the same time I've gone out of my way to campaign for the right to paid time off for men to go to antenatal clinics with their wives. I've also campaigned for the right to paid time off after the birth – paternity leave – and that's a subject I'll be looking at in more detail in chapter 20. But if you want to get something out of your company, then it's worth starting your campaign early. Talk to your boss, and talk to your union too, to see what they advise. Find out what your rights are, and if they're not very good, try and get a better deal. It's not a purely selfish exercise; every concession that we get makes life easier for fathers and families in the future.

Don't forget, either, that you and your partner need to start thinking about financial matters. If she's worked for her company for at least two years she's probably entitled to maternity pay, which means that she'll get a percentage of her full pay for six weeks after she gives up work. She'll also be entitled to her old job back at the same salary if she returns to work within a certain period after the birth and fulfills certain conditions. You're also entitled to a Maternity Grant from the government and a weekly child allowance; the grant stands at £25 at the time of writing. It's not very much, but as you'll soon find out, every little bit helps. You and your partner need to decide whether she's going to go back to work or not, and if she is, you'll have to start thinking about child care and so on. Again, these are things that we'll be looking at in greater detail in later chapters, but you should be aware of them now.

One last point about money here; remember that it will help you to feel more involved in the pregnancy if you share at least some of the shopping for your new baby. Try and go out together to choose a pram or your baby's first clothes rather than allowing your partner to do it all herself. Remember too that pregnancy is nine months long, which allows you plenty of time to prepare for what's coming, so your bank balance might look healthier if you spread out the essential purchases over a period of time rather than doing it all at once. It's also a good idea to do things like decorating a room for the baby's nursery together if you can, and to do it early rather than late – don't get carried away by all that 'deadlinitis'.

## Going to classes

One of the best things for helping you to feel more involved with your partner's pregnancy is going to *antenatal classes* with her if you can. Your partner will probably be told at the booking appointment about the different types of classes available to her. The hospital is almost certain to offer classes run by a midwife. Your local health clinic may also offer classes which are handled by a health visitor in conjunction with a community midwife. There are also classes offered by an organisation called the National Childbirth Trust, a charity whose aim is to improve birth in every way. Hospital or health clinic classes are free, while NCT classes have to be paid for. They don't cost very much though, usually only enough to cover the teacher's expenses, although the charge isn't standard and varies from area to area and teacher to teacher.

Classes usually begin in late pregnancy, at around the sixth or seventh month, and their purpose is simply to back up your partner's antenatal care in various ways and to prepare her for labour and birth. In hospital-based classes your partner will probably get the chance to have a look round the labour wards and delivery rooms; the equipment and procedures for labour will also be explained to her. A large part of all classes is preparation for birth, and that usually involves learning how to relax the body and how to do some special breathing exercises which will help your partner to cope with the pain. Your partner will also probably see a film of a birth, and be shown how to bath the baby. If she's really lucky, a new mother might come along to one class to show pregnant mothers how to change a nappy and feed the baby. Feeding also usually plays a part in classes; these days mothers are almost certain to be encouraged to breastfeed, although bottle feeding is also discussed.

Classes are good because they give your partner the chance to meet other women facing the same experience and the same problems, and the emphasis throughout is on finding out about what's happening to her. The whole process of labour and birth will be explained to her in detail so that she can learn how to relax through it; the idea being that once labour starts it's sensible to relax all the other muscles in the body so that effort is concentrated in the muscle that's doing all the work – the womb. The breathing exercises are taught specifically to help your partner through each contraction and through labour as a whole.

Hospital and health clinic classes usually include a 'fathers' night' to which you can go, and some hospitals actually show potential fathers round the labour wards and delivery rooms too. But real involvement is possible with a course of NCT classes, because these often take couples rather than mothers on their own. If you do a course of classes together, you'll learn a lot about labour and birth and something about what you're letting yourselves in for as parents. At the same time you'll be able to learn the relaxation and breathing exercises with your partner. Indeed, some NCT teachers encourage fathers to play a very active role and to remind their partners during labour what to do as far as their breathing is concerned. Many women find this sort of help and support absolutely invaluable.

## Second pregnancy

For many women, a second pregnancy is easier and more pleasant than a first. Even if your partner gets all the unpleasant symptoms she had first time round, at least she'll know that they don't last forever! Fathers too often find a second pregnancy easier to cope with, mostly because it's a familiar experience – although don't be surprised if you do feel just as anxious. One major difference for you both is that there is another person to take into account when you think about preparation, and that's your first child. (You'll see in chapter 16 just how important a father's role is in that.)

Some fathers feel that it's not so important to be involved in a second pregnancy as it was in the first. There's even a feeling in some men (perhaps unconscious) that seeing as their partners have survived the experience once, they don't need much help at all. Obviously that sort of thinking isn't going to do your relationship very much good, and it certainly won't help when it comes to coping with second time parenthood. In fact you need to be just as involved in a second pregnancy as you were first time round. The experience changes, because life changes; your circumstances, feelings, your situation, all will be different. What's constant is that you both need to share the experience as much as you can, as positively as you can. And from my own personal experience I can say that the same applies to a third pregnancy – and should also apply in any more after that!

## Losing a baby

Nowadays, regular antenatal check-ups and the high level of medical knowledge and expertise in the developed countries mean that most women go through their pregnancies without any problems and give birth to healthy babies after a safe labour. Sadly, however, some women – and I must emphasise that it's quite a small number – suffer from serious problems which can affect either them or their babies or both.

Your partner's blood pressure is taken regularly at the clinic, for example, to make sure that it isn't too high for too long. Consistently high blood pressure can be a serious problem in pregnancy. It can be a sign that a woman is suffering from a dangerous illness called *pre-eclampsia*, which can lead to her having a fit and her baby suffering serious harm or even dying. Other signs of this illness are swelling of the hands and feet (due to the retention of fluid in the tissues) and protein in the urine, which is why your partner will be asked for regular urine samples.

Although it's very rare for things to become so serious these days, it's a sad fact that a pregnancy can end prematurely in a *miscarriage*, or *spontaneous abortion* as doctors call it. It's thought that a very high proportion of first pregnancies end in this way, perhaps as many as one in three or four of all conceptions. Very often a woman doesn't even know she's pregnant before the pregnancy is over, the embryo being lost in what appears to be a heavier period than usual. A small consolation in these cases of very early miscarriage is that it's now thought the miscarried embryos are likely to have had something wrong with them, and that a miscarriage is nature's way of making sure a handicapped baby isn't born.

Doctors usually don't know for sure why a particular miscarriage should have occurred, especially if it happens early in pregnancy. The first sign of a threatened miscarriage is usually some bleeding from the vagina and perhaps some pain, probably in the lower back. If this should happen to your partner – and remember that bleeding from the vagina at any time in pregnancy is something to be taken very seriously indeed – she should go to bed immediately and you should inform your doctor, the midwife or the hospital. The only treatment is bed rest, which is often successful in preventing the loss of the baby. Your doctor will also probably recommend that you abstain from intercourse for a while, at least until it seems that the pregnancy has settled down.

A miscarriage shouldn't affect your partner's fertility in any way. She may be advised to have her womb cleared out (in a procedure called a D & C, or *dilatation and curettage*) to make sure that none of the pregnancy remains to become infected; but there shouldn't be any problem in conceiving again simply because one pregnancy hasn't been successful.

Later miscarriages (and any miscarriage after 13 weeks is said to be a *late* one) are often caused by a weak or 'incompetent' cervix which cannot hold the contents of the womb. Women with this problem can have repeated miscarriages until it's sorted out, which it can be these days with a technique known as the *Shirodkar suture*. In this method, a stitch is inserted into the cervix to keep it closed during the pregnancy, and removed just before birth to allow the passage of the baby in the normal way.

Like many of the unpleasant things in life, miscarriage is something few of us even think about until we actually experience it ourselves. I know that after having had two children normally both Sally and I were completely unprepared for the miscarriage which ended her third pregnancy prematurely at seven weeks. It was a great shock, and left us both feeling more depressed than either of us would have thought possible. Even though it was very early on, both Sally and I felt that we had lost a child, and there can be nothing more distressing than that. Medical staff and other people can sometimes be quite unthinking and even brutal about miscarriage, partly because it's very difficult for anyone to know what to say in such circumstances, and partly because it's something few of us seem to think of as being particularly upsetting. So you're bound to get your quota of comments like 'buck up' and 'better luck next time' if it happens to you, although some people can be marvellous at such times.

Your partner will certainly need plenty of love and care and lots of support and reassurance, and it will come best from you, her partner. The more loving and understanding you are in such circumstances, the better. Remember too that you need time to get over the upset of the miscarriage, time to work through all the emotions involved – so don't rush to conceive another child too quickly. But while you're being understanding, don't forget that you'll need some love and care and support yourself. If women are supposed to 'buck up' and 'put on a brave face', men are often supposed to play down their feelings almost entirely after a miscarriage. But most men are deeply upset by such a sad event; I know I was. Part of the reason I'm writing about it here is that I would like that lost child to have some sort of memorial; I still think quite often about him or her and what he or she would have been like. I'd also like to think that my experience will help those of you who go through it to understand and cope with it a little better. Remember that you have feelings and that you need to express them too, even though you're a man.

PART THREE

# BIRTH

Joyce wrote the details of the birth to Stanislaus and asked him to borrow a pound from Curran to help pay expenses. The child would be named Giorgio... on July 29, he noted with pleased amusement, 'The child appears to have inherited his grandfather's and father's voices.' There was a resemblance to early pictures of himself... The event staggered and delighted him; a few years later he said to his sister Eva, 'The most important thing that can happen to a man is the birth of a child.'

from *James Joyce* by Richard Ellmann

# 8 What happens in labour?

I was present – and, I like to think, a participant – at the births of all three of my children, and I have subsequently written about the experiences several times. I have always known that whatever I wrote would inevitably fall far short of what I had seen and heard and felt. Like me, when your child is born you will go through almost the entire range of human emotions in less time than you would believe possible. You will feel despair and joy, hope and fear, love, wonder and a thousand other things. Like most mothers and fathers, you will emerge from the experience a slightly different person, and you will probably say that birth is 'overwhelming' and 'indescribable'. I know that words have literally failed me each time I've witnessed a child of mine entering the world.

Your experience of birth is central to your experience of fatherhood. If you and your partner can make sure that your child's arrival is a positive, enjoyable event for all concerned, you'll help yourselves get off to a tremendous start as parents. That's why it's important to know what's happening, and also to be as prepared as you can be before the big day.

## Getting ready for the big day

Your partner's body will have been getting ready for quite some time before the birth. Her womb will probably have been undergoing contractions throughout the pregnancy, but these may become more noticeable, and perhaps involve discomfort or even pain, in the last few weeks. Some women know they're having the contractions and aren't particularly bothered by them, while others can find them quite uncomfortable. Doctors call them *Braxton-Hicks contractions*, and it's thought that they are the womb's means of rehearsing for the big day when contractions will serve to open the cervix and push the baby out.

We've all heard of false labours, those embarrassing trips to the maternity hospital made by couples convinced that baby is on the way and who are sent home. Braxton-Hicks contractions can sometimes be the cause of such a scare, because they can be quite strong. It's important to remember though that you should never be afraid to ring the hospital for advice, or even to go there towards the end of the pregnancy. They would far rather be safe than sorry just as you would, and no one is going to laugh at you for being careful.

You will be relieved to know that there are definite signs to look out for that your baby is on the way, signs that your partner's doctor and midwife will be checking for in the last weeks before the birth. We've seen that your partner is likely to feel very uncomfortable at that time because of her 'bump' and the internal pressure that it causes on her other organs. That pressure may be lessened six or so weeks before the birth when the baby's head *engages* in the pelvis. To me, that phrase produces an image of a shell being loaded into a cannon ready for firing, and, in some ways, that is what happens. The baby drops down into the pelvis so that your partner may well feel a little lighter round the midde; that's why it's called *lightening*. You'll probably notice a real change in her shape at this time as a consequence; her bump will look much lower, much more imminent.

However, it doesn't always happen in this way. First time mothers are likely to experience lightening, but women having second or subsequent babies might find that they don't engage at all until just before birth. Some women are told at one check-up that the baby is engaged, only to be told at the next a week later that he isn't any more. Indeed, some women are quite upset to hear from the midwife or doctor that the baby is in quite the wrong position for birth – in the *breech* position. All that means is that your baby hasn't turned round yet, and that his head is up and legs pointing down. Birth in this position is more difficult than in *vertex* positions (with the head down), but you shouldn't worry too much. Many babies turn several times before they settle down in the vertex position; breech births are quite rare, and these days they're not so risky as they used to be. We'll see a little further on that there can be variations in head down positions which can have an effect on birth, too.

You and your partner may also be feeling a little impatient and fed up with pregnancy in the last weeks. 'It just seemed to go on and on,' said one father. 'It never seemed to get any closer.' The second 'it' he was talking about, of course, was the *EDD* or *Estimated Date of Delivery*, which will have been worked out for you at your partner's booking-in appointment all those months ago. It is an actual date, and the problem is that nature works on a much looser time scale than we expect with our clocks and calendars. The statistics show that only one in 20 babies arrive on the exact day predicted. Most are born any time between the 38th and 42nd week of pregnancy, some earlier, some even later. You can be mesmerised by that date before it comes; it can become the focus of all your nervousness and fears and hopes and anticipations. Once it slips by and your partner still hasn't gone into labour, you can begin to feel very disappointed, even cheated. 'I just wanted to get on and get it over,' one father told me. 'It seemed that we were living on borrowed time. The waiting was agony.'

These last few weeks *can* be particularly difficult for men. Your partner will probably have given up work at around 30 weeks (perhaps a little later in some cases), but you'll still be going to your job every day. The closer you get to the day of birth, the more likely you are to spend a lot of time waiting for a telephone call to summon you home. It can be very nerve-wracking, and add to any feelings you might already have of being excluded. 'Part of me did resent very much being at work at that time,' another man told me. 'All I really wanted was to be with Kate. I couldn't think of much else anyway, so I wasn't much use in the office.'

Doing some rehearsal of your own might help to ease these feelings a little. It's the traditional role of fathers to get their partners to the hospital on time, which usually means these days making sure that the car is in full working order, has a full tank of petrol, and knowing where the hospital is. It's worth taking steps to ensure your transport arrangments are tied up – and with no loose ends. Try the journey to the hospital at least once or twice and at different times of the day and night so that you know exactly how long it will take you, when the streets are empty (Sundays are good days for testing 'small-hours' conditions) and when they're full. Then you'll have a good idea of how long you need to allow to get there in time. It's also worth making sure you have a set of useful telephone numbers with you wherever you are, numbers such as the doctor's, the midwife's and the hospital's, and perhaps even of friends and neighbours who could – and are willing – to help out in an emergency. Your partner will already have been advised what to take into hospital with her and to have her bag packed ready; the least you can do is to know where it is so that she doesn't have to go hunting for it in the middle of the contraction while you're getting the car started.

Even the best-laid plans of mice and men can go astray, as I well know myself. When Helen was born, I thought I had everything sorted out. The bag was packed and waiting in the hall, my mother was primed and ready to look after Emma while Sally was giving birth, the car was fuelled and on the starting line . . . but what happened was very nearly a disaster straight out of the *Keystone Cops*. One day after the estimated date of delivery I was woken in the middle of the night by a wife who was obviously on the verge of giving birth. She strode up and down the hall while I got Emma up, sat her on the pot and tried to get her ready. Within five minutes I was dressed and revving the car in the darkened street, with a pyjama-clad Emma in the back seat. I was just about to drive off when Emma said, 'Where's mummy?' Sally had, in fact, gone back into our flat to collect the bag, which I had completely ignored, while I prepared to drive off to the hospital without her. I didn't . . . but we only just made it.

## The first signs

The best advice is, don't panic. You'll probably have plenty of time when the big day comes and your partner goes into labour, especially if it's her first baby. Some women having their first do deliver very quickly, but they are the exception. Helen was our second child, and second labours are often much shorter than first ones. It seems that wombs get more efficient with practice.

We still don't fully understand how labour starts, but it is thought that it's your baby who sets the whole process in motion. Current research suggest that late in pregnancy, your baby releases a hormone called *cortisone* into his bloodstream which eventually finds its way into your partner's system through the placenta. This stimulates a change in the hormone levels in your partner's body, which in turn is thought to start the womb contracting. This may all happen at the time of lightening, and it's probable that the whole process is quite

## WHAT HAPPENS IN LABOUR?

complicated – as well as simply being related to the fact that your baby reaches a stage where he can't grow any more within the constraints of the womb.

One very clear sign that your baby is on his way could be that your partner's waters 'break'. These waters are in fact the *amniotic fluid* which has been surrounding and cushioning your baby in the womb. This fluid can gush out of the womb quite spectacularly when the membranes holding it break, something which is usually caused by the contractions which puts them under stress. In some women the fluid only seeps away gradually, while others hardly seem to have any fluid at all. The membranes can sometimes break later in labour, and a few babies are even born inside the intact membranes. Your doctor would advise you to start making your way to hospital once your partner's waters have broken, or even if you suspect that they might be leaking. This is because your baby is far more vulnerable to infection from the outside world.

Another common sign is *the show*. All through the pregnancy, your partner's cervix is sealed with a thick plug of mucus, and this usually comes loose just before labour starts. Women sometimes notice the show as a bloodstained piece of mucus on their underwear, perhaps when going to the lavatory. It's easily missed, of course, and you shouldn't think that labour has definitely *not* started simply because your partner hasn't had a show. In any case, it can appear a couple of days before the birth, or immediately before. But again, if your partner does have this sign, it's time to start thinking about getting into hospital.

Of course, the most significant sign that labour is on the way is the fact that your partner's womb starts to contract in what can only be described as a business-like way. Even though her womb may have been contracting throughout pregnancy, when labour begins she'll probably realise fairly soon that the contractions are different. For a start they'll begin to come more frequently, last longer and involve a little more discomfort. Braxton-Hicks contractions don't have the regularity of true contractions in labour, which begin by coming every 20 or 30 minutes or so.

They often start off mildly, so mildly, in fact, that your partner may not notice them for a while. It's worth timing them as soon as she does begin to notice them, and noting down the interval between each one. Each one will begin quite slowly and mount to a peak after which it will die away again. The sensation has been described as being like a cramp in the muscles of the stomach, or even like having a belt tightened across your middle. At this stage it's very unusual for the contractions to be distressingly painful. They don't last very long – about 30 to 40 seconds – and many women experience a sense of relief once they feel them begin. 'I was just glad that the long wait was over and that soon I'd be meeting my baby,' was the way one woman described her feelings to me.

You'll have to make the decision at some time to get in touch with the hospital and ask their advice about coming in. Bear in mind that as with most events in life, it's wise not to arrive too early and certainly even wiser not to arrive too late. The latter needs no explanation, but if you do arrive early you may just have an awful lot more waiting to do in an environment which isn't as pleasant as the one you've just left. If the contractions are still a long way apart – more than 20 minutes or so – you may as well stay at home, put your feet up (and that means both of you), have a cup of tea, relax and watch the television. You're both going to need all the strength you can muster, both emotional and physical, for what's coming, so make the most of the time beforehand. If you're at all worried at any stage, ring the hospital and ask their advice. Once the contractions are getting down towards every 10 minutes or so, it's probably time to make a move; leave earlier if you've got a long journey. It's also a good idea to ring the hospital and let them know you're on the way.

Obviously this isn't something you should leave too late. You don't want to have to try and beat the world land speed record to get to the hospital; that won't do your nerves any good at all. But don't be surprised if you get to the hospital with your partner apparently on the verge of delivering the baby only to find that the contractions stop. It happens quite often. Sometimes the doctor will send you home again, but usually they'll keep you there, especially if they examine your partner and find that she is well advanced into labour.

Your doctor might also recommend *induction* in this situation. Induction of labour simply means bringing labour on by artificial means. It's something doctors have done for many years, and the method used these days is fairly standard. Your doctor may break your partner's waters manually, either directly with his finger during an internal examination or with a specially designed probe. In hospital this is often combined with giving your partner hormones to stimulate her womb to contract. These are usually administered by a drip direct into the vein and sometimes combined with glucose to give her energy for the birth. Your partner may also have a *pessary* placed in her vagina, and this will contain *prostaglandins*, hormones which stimulate the womb to start contracting.

Induction has been the subject of heated controversy in recent years. Supporters of natural or active birth have spoken out against induction, claiming that it has become far too common in our maternity hospitals, and the evidence does seem to support their claim. A survey conducted in *Parents* in 1981 revealed that *one in three* mothers had their labours induced, and that the rate was higher among first time mothers. Other surveys have indicated that even higher percentages of mothers are induced in certain areas of the country or in some individual hospitals.

Opposition to induction has focused on several key issues. Campaigners say, for example, that in the majority of pregnancies, a baby is only ready to be born when the time is right, and that induction represents an unnecessary and overly disruptive interference in a natural process. Natural is the key word here; for a healthy woman, birth should be a normal, natural event which needs little interference of this type. Opponents of induction point to the fact that many induced labours seem to involve more discomfort and take longer than natural labours. Induced labours usually involve a lot of 'technology'; a drip is needed so a woman is likely to be confined to bed, and she's also likely to be attached to a machine called a *fetal monitor*. The electrodes of this machine will be in a belt strapped round her middle; their purpose is to keep a running check on the baby's heartbeat throughout labour.

Induction is only one aspect of 'technological' birth which has been attacked in recent years. Those same campaigners have criticised some of the other things hospitals do. That same *Parents* survey also discovered, for example, that 87 per cent of mothers had their pubic hair shaved off before the birth, and 75 per cent were given an enema. This was called 'preparing' the mother for labour, the reasoning being that it made it easier for medical staff to see the mother's genitals and *perineum*, the area between the vagina and the anus, and ensured that the pressure of birth didn't result in an involuntary bowel movement. But many people have said that not only is this sort of medical interference unnecessary, it was demeaning, undignified, and put women at a psychological disadvantage by making them feel as if they were no longer in control of what was happening to them or their bodies at a crucial time.

Doctors say, quite rightly, that there are cases in which induction is necessary, because either the baby or the mother or both are at risk and the pregnancy needs to be brought to a safe conclusion as quickly as possible. In some cases where a baby is overdue, for example, the placenta may begin to work less efficiently than it should. Such an 'old' placenta may not supply the baby with sufficient oxygen or nutrients, so it's definitely time to get her out. Yet many doctors now admit that a procedure designed for coping with emergencies may have become too widespread, and that the results can be harmful in terms of how positively a woman experiences the birth of her child. So although a follow-up survey in *Parents* in 1983 found that the rate of induction was still the same — at one in three mothers — there was some real evidence that attitudes were changing. It was found that fewer mothers were shaved or had enemas, although the two figures were still high, at 60 and 50 per cent respectively, showing that there is still need for improvement. Other surveys, however, have shown that the rate of induction may also be falling now, albeit slowly and then only in certain areas.

Again, it's important that both you and your partner should at least be aware of the issues. Some couples handle the induction question by discussing it with medical staff during pregnancy; it's for this reason (among others) that it's a good idea to develop the positive sort of relationship with your doctor and midwife I talked about in the last chapter if you possibly can. It's up to you to make your wishes known to them and you'll probably find that if you do it in a reasonable, well argued way, you'll get what you want — always remembering that you should listen to their advice first, especially where the health and safety of your partner and your baby is concerned.

Many couples manage to avoid an induction by using the do-it-yourself method of bringing on labour provided by nature — sexual intercourse. Among other things, semen contains a good dose of prostaglandins. So if you get tired of waiting for your baby to arrive, the best thing you can do is to make love. And I can't think of a nicer way of bringing a pregnancy to an end than in the way you began it – with love.

## The three stages of birth

Like Caesar's Gaul, birth is divided (at least by doctors) into three stages, the first, second and third. The first stage is the one we've already been looking at in talking about the first signs of labour. In this *first stage*, your partner's body is working towards opening the cervix or *dilating* it, as the textbooks say; that's what the contractions are doing – the long muscle fibres of the womb contract rhythmically so that over a period of hours the cervix is gradually pulled open.

This gradual dilation of the cervix is described in terms of *centimetres* or *fingers*. The midwife or doctor may say, for example, that your partner is 2, 4 or 6 centimetres dilated (which corresponds to 1, 2 or 3 fingers). The cervix is said to be fully open when it's reached *10 centimetres* dilation. At that stage, the cervix will become part of the womb, and womb, cervix and vagina will then form one single unit which is called, quite simply, *the birth canal*. This is your baby's route into the outside world. It usually takes much longer for the cervix to reach the halfway point in its dilation than it does to go from halfway to being fully open. It almost seems as if the womb needs to get up some steam at the beginning of labour, especially in a first pregnancy.

Once the birth canal is ready, your partner will begin to move into the *second stage* of labour, in which the baby is actually pushed out of the womb. During this stage your partner will probably find that she has an irresistible urge to 'bear down', to push the baby out. This may be the hardest part of the whole experience for her, the one that involves most pain and effort, although as we'll see, it needn't be as dramatically painful and long drawn out as you might think. The key part of this stage is the moment of *crowning*, when the largest part of your baby's head – his crown – passes through the last part of the birth canal and emerges through the vagina into the outside world. That's the point of no return, and the rest of your baby's body follows soon after.

The *third stage* of labour is one few people take much notice of after the excitement of the birth. It involves the delivery of the placenta, which is also called – for obvious reasons – the *afterbirth*.

You won't be surprised to hear that all this is not the work of a moment. In an average first labour, the first stage can take up to 12 hours or even longer, while the second stage – the actual delivery – can take 30 minutes or more. However, there is a very wide variation in the length of time different women take to have their babies, and very, very long and distressing labours are now a thing of the past. If your partner is taking more than 12 hours in first stage, it's likely that the medical staff may offer her a way of speeding up the delivery – of which more a little further on. Some women, on the other hand, have very short labours, and second or subsequent births are likely to take less time in any case – only 6 to 8 hours in most cases or even less. The third stage of labour is usually very short indeed; I didn't even notice it happen in two of the births I attended. Again, if it's taking your partner a long time to deliver the afterbirth, the medical staff may well take action to speed things up.

## The pain of labour

One question is likely to be uppermost in your mind as you watch your partner begin to experience labour: how much will it hurt her? 'I'd been thinking about that all through Lynne's pregnancy,' one man told me. 'I was really worried about it. Once the contractions began I became very concerned indeed. They seemed quite painful to start with, and I knew that she probably had a long way to go yet.'

You'll probably find that your partner's just as concerned about the pain she's going to face, although she might not want to admit it. Most women do worry about it before the birth; that's only normal. But when it comes to talking about the pain after the event, women vary enormously in their assessments of how severe the pain actually was. Some women – even some having their first babies – seem to have very little pain at all during long labours, while others report very high levels of pain and discomfort in short labours. Each birth is, in fact, unique, and the same woman can experience the births of her children in very different ways. Sally, for example, found Helen's birth easier and less painful than Emma's, mostly because it was so quick. But when she gave birth to Thomas, she said that it was much harder than when Helen was born and that she had felt it necessary to exert greater effort to push him out, although he was almost exactly the same size as Helen.

How your partner experiences birth will depend on many factors. First of all, it's important to bear in mind that different people have different pain thresholds. You may be one of those people who passes out if you prick your little finger with a pin, while your partner might be able to stand much more severe pain. Part of that is in your own mind. Pain is usually a signal that something is wrong, an indication that you need to do something, perhaps to prevent damage to your body. That's why we instinctively react when we experience pain; we pull our hands out from underneath the tap when we realise that the water's far too hot and it's hurting. An essential part of that reaction is *fear*, and pain and fear usually go hand in hand.

The point is that fear can make pain worse. You know how it is when you're going to the dentist – your fear of injections, drills and pain often makes even minor discomfort much more unpleasant than it would be if you weren't afraid at all. The same is true of birth, and interestingly enough, this is something that's been shown by research. It's often those women who haven't prepared for labour, who don't know much about what's happening to them who are the most frightened when the time comes. The result is that their experience of the pain involved is much more acute and distressing than it is among women who have prepared both mentally and physically for what's coming. It's during labour and birth that preparation in the form of reading, antenatal classes, learning breathing exercises and relaxation techniques can really pay off. In some ways, all this preparation comes down to one thing: helping your partner become aware that labour and birth isn't necessarily agony, and that it can be coped with. 'Once the first stage got going and my contractions were coming strongly,' said one woman, 'I just kept telling myself that if everyone else could get through it, then I could too.'

Some women find it easy to develop a positive attitude towards the pain of labour. 'I was glad when it all started,' one woman told me. 'When I started to feel the contractions I knew it wouldn't be long before I held my baby in my arms. The long wait was over, almost.' Women also often talk of 'constructive' pain, of pain with a *purpose*. Unlike the pain of an illness or an injury, the discomfort of labour – and these are often the women who are more likely to think of it as 'discomfort' rather than pain – is part of a very positive, creative purpose, the bringing of a new human being into the world. Another point is that labour doesn't involve a constant level of pain. Contractions usually start off mild and get stronger, and each contraction itself builds to a peak, then tails off. So your partner may only have to face the worst of the contractions for a comparatively short time just before the delivery. But bear in mind that your partner is likely to have plenty of time to get used to what's happening to her – it's unlikely to be a very sudden event, especially for a first baby.

## Pain relief

There are various methods of pain relief which your partner may be offered during labour, and this is certainly a matter which you need to talk about with your doctor and midwife before the event. Certain types of pain relief have to be set up before proper labour gets underway. This is true of *epidural anaesthesia*, for example. The nerves from the cervix, the perineum and the vagina all meet at the base of the spine, from where impulses are sent on to the brain, which is why women often experience what's called 'gynaecological backache' in the lower back during birth or a miscarriage. By inserting a needle into the spine at this point and passing anaesthetic into the *epidural space* between the vertebrae and the spinal cord, the impulses can be 'headed off'. The anaesthetic has to be kept topped up during labour, and to do this, soft tubing is threaded through the needle and taped to the woman's back. If the epidural is given by a skilled anaesthetist, it will mean an almost complete absence of pain. The trick is to remove all the pain and leave the woman enough sensation so that she still knows when to push during the second stage of labour.

The commonest form of pain relief offered to women is probably *gas and oxygen* (you may sometimes hear it referred to as *gas and air*). This is a combination of nitrous oxide (otherwise known as laughing gas) and oxygen. It comes ready mixed in a cylinder, complete with a rubber mask attached. The midwife or doctor may recommend its use towards the end of the first stage when contractions are likely to be at their most painful. Breathing the mixture in deeply at the beginning of a contraction should take the edge off the pain. Another common method of pain relief is the drug *pethidine*, which is supposed to eliminate the pain of contractions without putting a woman out completely. It's given by injection and takes about 15 to 20 minutes to start working.

We've already looked at another form of pain relief in labour, although it's one which involves a conscious decision to try and do without drugs of any sort. I'm talking about the relaxation and breathing exercises you learn at antenatal classes, a technique of preparing for labour which has been given the imposing name of *psychoprophylaxis*. Interest in this has, it seems, grown by leaps and bounds in recent years, mostly as a side effect of the swing towards active birth. Supporters of active birth say that it's better for both mother and baby to do without drugs as far as possible, and that women who are properly prepared for labour, and who get the right help and support during delivery shouldn't need them anyway.

There can be problems with all these methods of pain relief. Pethidine, for example, affects different women in different ways. Some mothers find it useful in taking the pain away, while others don't seem to get any benefit from it – and that can be a real disappointment. Alternatively it can have a very powerful effect on some mothers, almost knocking them out completely, or making them feel very woozy. Another problem is that pethidine can travel across to the placenta and affect the baby if it's given a long time before the final delivery. That can mean that both mother and baby are very sleepy after the birth, which will make it difficult for them to establish feeding and to get to know each other, a process called *bonding*, which is very important indeed. Gas and air can also make a woman feel very peculiar, while many mothers simply don't like the smell or feel of the rubber mask. It can also fail to take away the pain.

Epidurals have also come in for some criticism, principally because they guarantee to make birth a highly technological affair. For a start, an epidural removes almost all sensation from the lower part of the body, so that means the woman is bound to be confined to bed. She'll also have very little room for movement within the bed because she'll have the 'topping up' tube taped to her back. She'll probably also find herself attached to a drip containing an artificial hormone called *oxytocin* to speed up her contractions. She may well be attached to a fetal monitor, too, and have a catheter to help her pass water – without any sensation below the waist she's likely to be incontinent. In fact, a woman with an epidural may end up looking like a laboratory animal in an experiment rather than a woman giving birth. Another problem can be that if the epidural takes away all sensation, as it sometimes does, then the woman won't know when to push. Her baby may then have to be delivered by *forceps*, special instruments designed to grip the baby's head and ease him out of the birth canal, or by a *vacuum extractor*, an instrument in which a cup is attached to the baby's scalp by suction so that he can then be eased out. Either way, the woman is almost certain to have an *episiotomy*, which is a surgical cut made in her perineum to give the baby's head more room through which to emerge.

Episiotomy has, in fact, become a major part of the debate about birth. Those same surveys in *Parents* revealed that in 1981, 69 per cent of women were given an episiotomy, and that the figure was still the same in 1983. The rate of episiotomy was also higher among first time mothers and those who gave birth lying on their backs. In defence of 'the unkindest cut of all' as it's been described, doctors say that it's necessary to help the baby out more quickly when labour has gone on too long and there's a chance that he might now be suffering. They also say that it's done to prevent a woman tearing, on the grounds that a surgical cut is easier to repair by stitching than a ragged tear.

Opponents of episiotomy have much the same to say about it as about induction – that it is an emergency procedure which has become too widespread. On the basis of the figures in *Parents*, it seems almost to have become a matter of routine. They say that women who have them often tear as well, and that a significant number of women have problems with the stitches afterwards. If an episiotomy cut is stitched poorly or if it becomes infected – as sometimes happens – it can make the early weeks of motherhood very painful and unpleasant. Even if there are no problems of this sort, an episiotomy can be very sore for several weeks.

## Natural childbirth

Campaigners for active birth say that there's a link between the episiotomy rate and the position in which a woman gives birth, and it's a link which seems to be borne out by the statistics. It's been said that the worst possible position in which to give birth is lying on your back in bed, what's called the 'stranded beetle' position. Quite simply, in this position a woman has to work much harder to push the baby out; because she's lying down, the area of her birth canal is actually less, and she has to push in a straight, horizontal line. If she stands up her birth canal may be as much as 30 per cent bigger, and she has one major advantage – she has gravity to help her.

Active birth really means allowing a woman to move around as much as she likes during labour and letting her adopt the position she finds most comfortable and useful for giving birth. When women are encouraged to do this, they take up all sorts of positions. Many women squat or get on to all fours, while some stand or move around a lot. Others like to have the support of their partners holding them from behind, while still others even like to lie in a bed propped up on pillows. The point is that labour is a dynamic, changing experience and that the only person who ultimately knows what is best for her as far as dealing with the positive, purposeful pains of labour is your partner. Active birth allows her to be in control of what's happening, which is something that doesn't apply to a technological birth. In many hospital births, everything is in the hands of the medical staff – and often that's what women find most disappointing about them. 'I just felt like a piece of meat in the end,' one mother told me. 'I felt that I didn't have any say at all in what was happening to me.'

The evidence seems to show that active birth can be a more enjoyable and less distressing experience for a woman. Fewer women need episiotomies, forceps or painkilling drugs in active birth, and in general, active labours tend to be shorter – even in first time births. Women's subjective accounts of active birth usually stress the positive, pleasant side of bringing a new baby into the world, whereas women who have had painkilling drugs and a high level of medical 'interference' in the process of birth seem to talk more about the pain and suffering. Another advantage to a drug-free, active birth is that mother and baby will probably be in a better condition, more alert and better able to respond to each other, at the crucial moment when they come into contact for the first time. The evidence seems to show that women who have this positive experience of birth tend to suffer from fewer problems in the early months of parenthood, and are also less likely to suffer from severe postnatal depression. It's a theme which runs through the whole process of becoming a parent: those people who are most positive about the experience from beginning to end and take steps to remain in control of what's happening to them tend to fare better than those who don't prepare or who are negative about it.

We mustn't forget the most important person of all in this context — your baby. Birth is a very traumatic experience for him too; some would say that it's the most traumatic experience anyone ever undergoes. In a very short space of time your child is pushed out of the only environment he has ever known, an environment in which everything is controlled. It's warm and peaceful in there (most of the time, at least), and all his needs are taken care of. Then the walls of his world start to contract and push him down towards a narrow opening in which he's constricted, twisted, squeezed and finally ejected into a world of light and noise and total stimulation of his senses, all of which are in working order and which relay sights, sounds, smells and sensations to a brain which as yet can make very little sense of them. Is it any wonder that your baby's first instinct is probably to cry?

It was looking at birth from the baby's point of view which lead Frédéric Leboyer to develop his ideas about peaceful, natural childbirth. He said that birth should take place in an atmosphere of calm, preferably in a darkened room, and that once the baby was born, voices should be hushed and the baby handled gently and with consideration. Michel Odent is another Frenchman who has developed Leboyer's ideas in his maternity clinic in Pithiviers, just outside Paris. He encourages women to have active births, and there is very little medical interference at all in his clinic, although it's fully equipped 'technologically'. He also sometimes lets women give birth in warm water, an idea which others have developed, both for the sake of mother and baby; it's said that it's more relaxing, and that as the baby is coming from a liquid-filled environment, emerging into water reduces the shock of birth. The emphasis in these births is on making the surroundings and reception for a baby as calm and welcoming as possible.

These days, 97 or 98 per cent of all births take place in hospital, and for some campaigners that's the problem. Hospitals by their very nature can be frightening, impersonal places; we tend to associate them with illness and pain and death rather than warmth and love and life. Births often take place in coldly sterile surroundings, and to ordinary, non-medical people like you and I, a delivery room with all its equipment probably looks more like an operating theatre than anything else. With all this in mind, some people are saying that we should allow more women to give birth at home, where the surroundings are familiar and more human. Most births are completely normal and problem free and could take place at home, they say; it's only the fact that the medical profession is so opposed to the idea that means more women don't have their babies at home. Campaigners say that with the right back-up, home births could be as medically safe as hospital births – and much more enjoyable.

Doctors, on the other hand, tend to say that the reason birth is so safe for both mother and baby today is that it takes place in hospital where there are all the facilities to handle any emergencies, should they arise. It's true that most births are normal and go smoothly, but problems can happen, and they need to be sorted out quickly. There was a time when many births took place at home, but with the growing dominance of hospital births, facilities for home births have been run down. Local area health authorities and hospitals simply aren't used to the idea of home births, so they don't usually have 'flying squads' of staff with the right equipment ready to go out and handle emergencies in home births. There are also very few midwives who deliver babies at home.

So if you and your partner want to have your baby at home, you might find it very difficult to arrange. Your doctor might be opposed to it, and you'll need his support in arranging for antenatal and postnatal care, whether he gives it to your partner himself or helps you to find another doctor who will. You don't necessarily need a doctor to be present at the birth; in this country the only legal requirement is that you have a midwife. Your doctor will almost certainly be opposed to your partner having a home birth for a first baby, or if she's at risk in any way because of medical factors (if she has diabetes, for example). But it is possible to have a home birth if you try hard enough, and there are some organisations and books which will help you to get what you want. Remember that you do have the right to have a home birth so long as you can get a midwife to attend your partner. Thomas James Bradman was born at home, and I must say that of all three births, his was the one Sally and I enjoyed the most – and we also found it quite easy to arrange.

Perhaps that's a sign that times are changing; I think they are, and I hope that the 'humanisation' of birth will continue. There does seem to be evidence that doctors and hospitals are taking criticism of their impersonality and 'coldness' to heart. One solution which is being adopted in some areas is simply to make hospitals more friendly places, with labour wards and delivery rooms which look more like home, it's hoped. These 'birthing rooms' often include carpets, soft music and subdued lighting, and they're a long way from the cold, antiseptically white wards we normally associate with medical institutions. I've noticed in talking to people that there even seems to have been a change in attitude on the part of medical staff. One woman I talked to said that when she had first given birth, five or six years before, the doctor and midwives had adopted a 'we know best attitude' from the start and told her what to do as if she'd been a child. Her partner had been excluded and also made to feel a nuisance. 'But it's all different now,' she told me, four months after having her second child. 'They couldn't have been nicer and more friendly.'

The important point is that these are all issues of which you should be aware before the time comes when you can no longer do anything about them. You need to have the sort of relationship with the medical staff who will be looking after you that means you and your partner can discuss with them things like episiotomy and pain relief. They need to know what you want, and you need to know what they're prepared to go along with. Obviously, if you want an active birth or Leboyer-style birth, or a water birth, then you're going to have to make special arrangements well in advance, and the same is true if you and your partner want to have your baby at home.

We started this section by talking about the pain of childbirth, and I feel very strongly that as a man you shouldn't allow yourself to be carried away by interest in alternative styles of birth. I am a supporter of active birth, and having experienced both hospital and home births I would go for a home birth every time. I think it's probably better for a woman to do without drugs, and I would like every couple to experience birth as a joyful and completely natural event. However, as a man, I don't have to suffer the pains of childbirth. I've seen them in action, and I wouldn't hesitate in saying that no woman should be forced or even pressurised into trying to do without the assistance of modern medical technology or pain relief. The choice is your partner's. Something else that can be a problem is that because it's in vogue at the moment, many women set out determined to do without drugs and have an active, natural birth, and feel terribly disappointed if they don't manage to stick to their high ideals. One doctor I've talked to even put 'Failed natural childbirth' very high on his list of factors causing postnatal depression. I don't think any woman should be made to feel a failure if she's gone through the pains of birth, however many painkilling drugs she has and whether or not that's what she intended to do; they all deserve a medal at the very least, *and* the gratitude and devotion of fathers. Remember, the important thing is that your baby should be born safely, and that you should all be happy; in the end, little else matters.

# 9 The father's role

Traditionally, a father's role in labour ended when he drove up to the hospital and handed his partner over to the midwives inside. He was then free to do the things that expectant fathers still do in films and novels, like going down to the pub to get drunk or pacing up and down in the hospital waiting room smoking cigarette after cigarette and looking extremely worried. Older films are sometimes kinder to fathers, allowing them to boil kettles of water and rip up sheets into swaddling for the baby. But whichever way you look at it, you're not really expected to be of very much use on the day your child enters the world. One book about pregnancy and birth which I've read actually goes so far as to say that you should take a good book with you when your partner goes into labour so that you don't get 'bored'.

During your partner's labour you'll probably feel a wide range of emotions. You'll feel terrified, ecstatic, exhausted; but you won't be bored, even if you decide that you don't want to be present. I'm assuming that you will decide to be there, mostly because the figures show that the majority of fathers are these days (it seems to average out at around nine in ten fathers being present throughout the birth), but also because you *can* have a very definite – and very important – role to play. In fact, your presence at the birth can make all the difference between it being a positive experience for your partner and it being a disappointment, or something worse.

The decision to be there or not is obviously a very personal one, and one which should be made between the two of you. Some women say they don't want their partners to see them giving birth because 'it might put them off', the idea being, I suppose, that a woman should 'look her best' for her partner at all times. If that's what a woman feels, then of course she's perfectly entitled to her opinions, although I feel that it's a great shame for any couple to live their lives together under such constraints. The classic reason for a man not being present at the birth of his child is, of course, squeamishness; we've all heard stories of men passing out at the sight of blood in the delivery room. From talking to doctors and midwives it seems that it's very rare indeed for a man to faint during a birth; in fact, I've not yet met a doctor or midwife who has had personal experience of such an event. Nevertheless, some couples decide that they simply don't want the father to be there. If you and your partner look at all the options and understand what happens during birth and what it means, and you make the decision together, then that is up to you and it should be respected. Don't think that just because you aren't at the birth itself you're going to be a bad father. There are plenty of fathers around who didn't see their children born, and who couldn't be faulted in any aspect of their approach to fatherhood and their attachment to their families. This is an important point to remember for fathers who find that they're excluded from the birth for reasons beyond their control – like an emergency Ceasarean, for example. If you wanted to be there and then suddenly you can't be, it can be very disappointing – although it needn't be the end of the world.

It's also important not to be too blasé about what you're going into. Birth is a total, sometimes overwhelming experience which can catch you completely unawares. 'When Diane went into labour and I got to the hospital,' one father said, 'I thought I was prepared for what was going to happen. I'd been to classes, I'd read about birth, I thought I was confident. But it wasn't too long before I was reduced to a quivering wreck. I couldn't believe what I was feeling, what was happening. It was such a powerful experience.'

One thing you're almost bound to feel at times during the labour is a sense of being an outsider. It's not so bad at the beginning, especially if you and your partner are able to stay at home and be calm and relaxed about what's going on. But once you get her to the hospital, you may find that you are literally left out in the cold at times. 'When we arrived at the hospital the midwives took Jane off to examine her. They just left me standing in the corridor waiting for something to happen.' Even if the staff are more helpful and understanding than they were in this father's experience, you should remember that their attention is going to be focused on your *partner* and not you – which is the way it should be, after all.

That's why it's important to make your presence felt. The fact is that if you hang back, you're not just going to feel left out, you probably will *be* left out. Again, there's no need to go into the hospital in a spirit of confrontation; that will only be counter-productive. But there's every reason to make sure the midwives and doctor are aware right from the beginning that you want to share the experience with your partner. If it isn't in her notes, let them know as politely, but as firmly, as you can, that you want to be with her at all times wherever possible, and that you won't get in their way. These days you'll probably find that the staff will be glad to have you there. However, you may well be asked to leave the room when your partner is examined, especially when the midwife or doctor want to find out by an internal examination how dilated her cervix is. This practice of asking the father to leave isn't as widespread as it was when my first child was born. But if it happens to you, make sure that the staff let you know when it's all right to go back in again.

You may find that you and your partner spend a fair amount of time alone together, at least in early labour. Once your partner's been seen by a midwife and it's established that labour has actually begun, she'll probably be put into a side ward or room on her own where her womb can get on with the business of contracting. If you aren't with her, that time may well be spent alone. I remember that when Emma was born, Sally spent the first three or four hours of labour pretty much alone, except for the occasional visit of a midwife to 'see how she was getting on'. Of course, at this stage, there may be little that anyone can do except wait. Your role is quite simple: you can be with your partner, hold her hand, talk to her – and generally be a good companion.

Although at this stage the contractions may still be fairly well spaced out, many fathers find this period of waiting the most difficult time of all. I remember very intensely during Sally's first labour sitting next to the bed in which she was lying. I held her hand and tried to help her through the contractions, but early on there was still plenty of time for us to talk. I was, quite simply, terrified, and I could see a certain amount of fear in Sally's eyes, too. As the contractions became stronger and started coming closer together, I became quite anxious. I grew even more anxious, even alarmed, when she started making the most appalling faces during each contraction. I was convinced that she was going through unspeakable agonies; the grimaces on her face, the terrifying expressions could mean nothing else, and I felt very guilty that I wasn't suffering them too. I asked Sally about it after the birth and discovered that she hadn't felt as much pain as I had thought. 'You looked so worried,' she explained, 'that I wanted to smile during the contractions to show that they weren't too bad.' The result of a smile on top of the expression imposed on her by the contraction had been the grimaces which had horrified me.

## Feeling anxious

Guilt and anxiety are very common feelings for men in this situation. 'I just felt really worried about the pain,' said one father. 'I could see that it hurt and I wanted to share it with her. If I could have done, I would have gone through all the pain for her. I couldn't, and that made me feel useless.' We do worry about our partners at such a time, and we do feel useless; but we're not. Just being there and holding her hand is reassuring for her. Your very concern shows that you feel for her, that you appreciate what she's going through for you. 'It was wonderful to have him there right from the beginning,' one woman told me. 'I don't think I could have done it without him, really.'

Time may seem to drag very slowly in the early stages of labour, but it won't be long before things start to happen. As we've seen, the medical staff may want to speed the whole process up by putting your partner on a hormone drip, and they're more than likely to want to use fetal monitors. It's at this point that one of the most important parts of your role during labour can begin, and that part is to be a mediator, even a translator, between your partner and the medical staff around you both. A problem that sometimes occurs is that in their concern for the baby, the staff may forget to keep a mother completely informed of what's going on. A new machine or drip may suddenly appear which isn't explained to her, and she then becomes worried that something might be wrong. At the same time, a perfectly reasonable request for information might be ignored by a midwife or doctor not because she doesn't want to answer, but because she's too busy or concentrating too hard on something complicated, like setting up a fetal monitor.

That's where you come in. You're likely to be sitting or standing closer to your partner than the medical staff; you're also likely to know how she's feeling and what is worrying her at any one time. You can ask her questions *for* her – again, politely but firmly – and explain *to* her what's going on. At the same time you can remind the medical staff of her wishes as far as painkilling drugs, speeding up the contractions and episiotomy are concerned. You can be a central source of information for both sides in the team which is delivering your child, and just by doing that you'll be a great reassurance to your partner. 'John was amazing,' said one mother. 'He kept me calm, and stayed cool throughout. He let me know what the midwife wanted and told me what they were doing all the time.'

## Active support

Of course, if your partner has learnt relaxation and breathing exercises, and you have learnt them with her, you have a great role to play in helping her to use them. Some women find that under the pressure of their emotions during labour and in the excitement it all goes to pieces. This can be a great disappointment, for if a woman has taken the trouble to learn the exercises and has put great faith in their ability to help her through labour, losing that help at a crucial moment can be almost worse than never having had it. You can help her to keep going by keeping her calm, by being reassuring, by reminding her of what she should be doing, and when and how. At the same time, don't forget to use the magic power of touch. Hold her hand, of course, but respond to her request for other forms of touch. Many women find massage of the lower back a marvellous relief during labour. The National Childbirth Trust also recommends that you should take a natural sponge along with you into the labour ward. Soaking it in water and then using it to mop your partner's brow and face may also be very comforting for her. And if your partner is having an active birth, then your role may be very physical indeed; you might spend a lot of time walking around with her, supporting her during a contraction and generally giving her the strength and resources of your body to help her through the labour. That can be a marvellous experience, and one which brings you very close together.

Remember in all this to take your cue from your partner. She is the one who knows what she wants and how she feels; she is the one who's really under pressure. If you let her, she will tell you what she wants and when she wants it. One problem for some couples these days seems to be that fathers are sometimes so keen to make a contribution that they almost become *too* involved. 'Steven was a great help most of the time, but at one stage he really began to shout at me about my breathing exercises,' one mother told me. 'It was almost as if he was coaching a football team or something; it seemed as if he was taking over, and quite simply I resented it. So I ended up shouting at him "Who's having this baby anyway, you or me?"' It's also easy sometimes to become too interested in the equipment around you, or to get too chatty with the midwives and doctors. Always keep in mind that the star of the drama unfolding before you is your partner, and that she should be the centre of your attention.

Also remember that women can behave very oddly during labour and birth. Some curse and swear and tell their partners that they'll never go to bed with them ever again. Others simply get very irritable at different times during labour. The period of *transition* between the first and second stages is notorious for this; at this stage, your partner may feel very odd indeed, quite understandably, as this is the time when her body is building up to pushing the baby out. The woman I quoted above delivered her baby less than half an hour after she shouted at her husband. The point is that your partner is under a lot of pressure; it's hardly surprising that she should have little patience and that she might lose her temper. You'll notice that midwives and doctors won't even bat an eyelid if your partner swears like a trooper; they've heard it all before. So don't worry, and don't think that your partner means what she says. Laugh it off – and try to make her laugh about it, too (that's not always possible!). Remember that by the time she's getting close to the moment of birth, your partner's whole being is likely to be concentrated on what's going on in her womb and birth canal; she won't have much time for anything else.

# 10 The delivery and after

Labour speeds up once the cervix reaches and goes beyond the halfway point as far as dilation is concerned. The contractions begin to get stronger and stronger and come ever more closely together. Once they start coming less than two minutes apart, they'll almost seem to merge into each other, and your partner will probably go into transition. It then won't be long before she's feeling that irresistible urge to bear down, to push the baby out into the world. The staff should keep a close eye on her throughout, checking her cervix to see how dilated it is, and if they have, she will probably have been moved to a delivery room by this stage. If they haven't, and you are on your own with your partner when she begins to want to bear down, let the staff know immediately.

You also have another choice to make at this time: do you want to watch the actual birth itself or not? If you don't like the idea of seeing your baby emerge from your partner's body, you can stand at the head of the delivery couch and concentrate your attentions on your partner. No one will force you to watch anything you don't want to. But if you're like me, you'll be fascinated. I watched every second of the deliveries, and each was an unforgettable experience.

It's at this time, too, that your partner will need as much of your support and reassurance as she can get. It's the climax of her pregnancy, the climax of the efforts and energy she's expended in the labour so far. If it's been a long labour, she may well be getting tired and even feel that she can't go on; in that case, she really does need the sort of positive encouragement which will tell her that not only can she do it, but that she's doing it really well. The important thing at this stage is to make sure that she doesn't waste her energy. The midwife will certainly tell her when to push, and how to use her pushing so that her efforts work with the contractions to push the baby further and further down the birth canal. You can play a crucial role here in 'echoing' and passing on the midwife's advice and instructions. It's vital that you don't just stand there shouting 'push' at the wrong time. This is really the moment when you all need to be working together.

It's a very exciting, climatic time. 'It seemed as if the whole world centred on what was happening in that room,' one father said. 'Nothing else mattered except the struggle for life that was going on in front of my eyes. It was heart-stopping, terrifying, awe-inspiring, amazing, and it all seemed to be happening in slow motion.' Fairly soon you may even be able to see your baby's head coming down the birth canal. The tissues of the vulva and the perineum begin slowly to bulge outwards (at least they do in a calm, well-managed birth). The lips of your partner's vagina will actually begin to part, and unless your partner is giving birth in a position which makes it impossible (like standing), you'll probably see a patch of flattened, damp, dark hair. When Emma was born I saw her head coming down towards me (it also seemed to be covered in jelly) with what looked like inexorable, irresistible force. It receded twice as Sally stopped pushing after a contraction faded. With Helen, I saw the head coming, and then it popped out, as it did with Thomas.

## The crowning moment

For that's the next stage, the *crowning*. It's also probably at this moment that the midwife or doctor will perform an episiotomy if one is deemed necessary. As I've said, the reasons for doing this are to speed up delivery if the baby's as risk or if the mother is getting too tired. Sally had an episiotomy when Emma was born (and she shot out of her mother after it was done like a cork from a champagne bottle), and we both felt that it was done too soon. If Sally had been allowed to push a couple more times, we were sure that she would have made it without the episiotomy. Again, this is where you can act as a mediator with the staff; if you hear that they want to perform an episiotomy, you could try asking them to let your partner have another go before they do so. Obviously, you don't want to get into a big argument at such a moment, and if the staff have medical reasons for wanting to perform an episiotomy, you shouldn't argue at all.

The moment when the head crowns has its own magic, whatever has led up to it. 'I looked down, and there was my baby's head,' said one father, 'a tiny, purple and black blob with its features all scrunched up. It didn't look any bigger than my fist.' Sometimes the cord is hooked round the neck, and if it is, the midwife may either gently prise it over the baby's head, or clamp and cut it there and then. It's a moment of tremendous relief for your partner, and she's likely to want to sit up and touch the baby's head just to prove to herself that she really is on the last lap. She'll be advised to change her breathing patterns – perhaps to light panting – and to ease the rest of the baby out on the next couple of contractions. Sometimes it all happens much more quickly, and this is especially so when there has been an episiotomy. Whatever the case, the baby's head will twist round, one shoulder will emerge before the other, and the midwife or doctor will lift your baby clear of his mother's body and into the world.

You may already have heard your baby cry by now, too. Some babies start crying as soon as they emerge – some even before they're fully born – which means they've already taken their vital first breaths. Others need a little help, and that's why attention will turn to your baby once she's been delivered. To start with, the midwife will clamp the cord in two places, perhaps after it's stopped pulsing, to make sure that the baby gets as much blood as possible. She will probably then cut the cord (some midwives and doctors ask fathers if they want to do this), and your baby will then be completely separate from her mother. If the baby hasn't started crying yet, the midwife may have to do a little work on her. She'll probably use a small tube to suck out mucus and debris from her throat and nasal passages to make it easier for her to breathe, but it's highly unlikely that she'll slap your baby as they do in Hollywood films. If everything is in order, and in most cases it is, the baby will be wrapped up, and given to her mother, who probably can't wait to hold her newborn baby in her arms.

Something which you may not be aware of at the time is that the midwife will actually give your baby a score out of ten. This is called an *Apgar score* (the name is derived from the name of the doctor who came up with the idea), and your baby's score is made up of five different elements. She'll be marked out of two for each of the following: pulse, breathing, muscle tone, response to stimulus and her overall appearance and skin colour (whether she's pale or not). It's a way of determining whether a baby needs any extra help. A baby with an Apgar score of under six or seven may not be doing too well, in which case the midwife and doctor may bring into operation some of the resuscitation equipment in the delivery room, such as giving the baby some oxygen, for example. Most babies score over six or seven, anyway, and scores of nine or ten are by no means unusual. Some midwives do an Apgar score straight after birth and then again five or ten minutes later, especially if a baby has room for improvement.

Your partner still has a little work to do, though; she has to go through the third stage of labour and deliver the placenta, the afterbirth. Many women are given an injection of a substance called *syntometrine* which speeds up the contractions to expel the afterbirth. This practice has been criticised by campaigners, and there is some evidence that syntometrine can pass into breast milk and make a baby unsettled in the early days after birth. If you and your partner don't want the syntometrine, then it's up to you to say so; it's not necessary in most cases. Some women do have a problem in delivering the placenta, and in a very small number of cases it's even necessary for the doctor to remove it manually (usually with the woman under a general anaesthetic). But many women don't mind the syntometrine; they're too busy getting to know their babies to worry about other things.

These first few moments after the birth are very important. They're the time when three new people meet – a newborn baby and a new mother and father. It is, of course, a time of very real emotion. 'I felt overwhelmed, speechless,' said one father. 'I didn't know what to say, so I burst into tears instead.' That sort of reaction is very common; few of us ever experience feelings of such intensity in our lives, and they can be especially difficult for men. It's the very fact that we are sometimes unable to deal with strong emotion because of our conditioning that can make birth such an overwhelming experience. Nevertheless, most of us end up swimming with the emotional tide at such a time, and it's very common to feel a very deep love and admiration for our partners. Your partner will herself be going through some pretty strong emotions, one of the main ones being relief that it's all over. Another kind of relief will come too as you and your partner look at your beautiful new baby (and all new babies, however ugly, are beautiful) and see that she's perfect. Those fears of handicap which have haunted you throughout the pregnancy will make you count her fingers and toes and explore every inch of her body; and the relief will be enormous. Don't feel guilty or worried about it; we all do it.

## The first feed

If your partner intends to breastfeed, now is the time for her to put the baby to the breast. She may need some help and advice from the midwife in getting the baby 'latched on' to the nipple properly (this is looked at in more detail in chapter 11). But even if this first attempt at breastfeeding isn't a complete success, it's vital that she should try. Many mothers (and many fathers, too) are in fact amazed at how well it goes. Your baby is born with an instinctive ability — and desire — to suck, an ability that she may well have practised by sucking her thumb or fingers while she was in the womb. She will also display what is known as the *rooting reflex*; that is, when her cheek is stroked with a finger or a nipple, she'll instinctively turn towards that side with her mouth open, ready for a feed. 'Within minutes of being born there she was sucking away for all she was worth,' said one father. 'I think that was an even more awe-inspiring sight than the birth itself.'

This first feed is important for two reasons. Obviously, it's vital to get breastfeeding established straightaway; it will be your baby's sole source of nourishment for months to come, and it's been shown that the sooner a woman gets into the swing of it, the more likely she is to manage to breastfeed successfully. But it also plays a part in that important process I've already mentioned, the process of *bonding*. In simple terms, this word describes the way in which a mother and her baby get to know — and to love — each other. It's dependent on early physical contact, and the better it goes, the less likely a mother is to have problems in her relationship with the baby afterwards.

It's important to remember that no woman should expect to fall in love with her baby immediately. Interestingly enough, a survey in *Parents* revealed that most women expect themselves to do exactly that — and most women don't. I'm not saying that women hate their babies when they're born; but few actually feel a deep, maternal love for them immediately, either. It's hardly surprising, after all. The baby might look very ugly, for a start. She may start off looking pale or even blue. She may be covered in a greasy, cheesy substance called *vernix*; she may also have a fine down of hair (called *lanugo*). Her head may be misshapen from the pressure it's been subjected to in the birth canal. It's not a solid box, but made of overlapping plates with softer cartilage between them (the junctions are called *fontanelles*, or *soft spots*, of which the one on the top of the head towards the front is the most obvious – they harden during the first year of life), specifically so that it can change shape without fracturing during the birth. She may be red-faced and wailing, she may be covered in blood, and she'll have an ugly looking cord stump on her middle. She may have skinny legs and arms too, and she'll definitely look very unlike the standard image of a baby. In short, your baby might be quite a surprise.

But love comes, and usually very soon. If the birth has gone well and both mother and baby are lively and wakeful, these first few moments can lead to the creation of a very strong bond. Even if the birth has been very difficult, the same can happen. But mothers should remember that they need time to get to know their babies and to get used to being parents; love comes in its own good time. Fathers need to bear the same thing in mind. Don't forget that you need to hold your newborn baby and get some of that physical bonding, too. 'I was really scared I'd drop him when the midwife handed him to me,' one father told me, 'but the fear evaporated when I looked into those eyes. He was staring at me with the biggest, clearest, most beautiful blue eyes I'd ever seen. I spent ten minutes talking to him, saying all sorts of things, introducing myself to him, I suppose. I didn't want to give him back to the midwife to be weighed and messed around with.'

These days, midwives and doctors will probably be tactful enough to leave you and your partner and your new baby alone together for a while. Use this time as well as you can; don't worry about the things you say to each other or to the baby. Say what you feel, do what you feel, and you'll probably discover that what you say and do is just right. Ride with your emotions, and enjoy these moments; there is nothing quite like them.

After a while the world will reassert its presence. The baby will have to be weighed, bathed and probably examined by a doctor. You may be asked to leave while the doctor examines your partner, and perhaps stitches her episiotomy cut or any tears she might have suffered. Those feelings of exclusion, of being an outsider can come back at this time, especially if you're ushered out into a silent hospital in the dead of night. But in these early hours after the birth you're likely to feel so high, so exhilarated (if it's all gone well) that very little will be able to dampen your mood.

I remember that I was walking down the corridor of the hospital after Emma was born when a midwife asked me if I was

Tony Bradman; if I was, my father-in-law was on the phone and wanted to speak to me. He asked me if everything was OK, and whether Sally and the baby were all right, and several other questions. To my surprise I found that I literally couldn't speak; I just howled into the phone, and the midwife had to reassure him that everything was all right – and that I was still sane. After Helen was born I emerged from the same hospital into a dark, cold October morning. It was raining, and I stood at the hospital threshold and laughed and danced in the rain, much to the amusement of another midwife. And I will never forget the moment when I brought my two beautiful daughters home from my sister's house, where they had been looked after during Thomas's birth. I watched their faces light up with wonder as they met their new brother; and although I cried partly because my father wasn't alive to know he had another grandchild, it was also because I knew that such moments don't happen too often in your life and should be felt to the full.

## Possible problems

Most births are straightforward, but some women do experience certain problems. For example, the baby might be in a position which makes a normal birth through the vagina difficult or even impossible. The commonest and safest position for your baby to be born in is with the back of his head towards his mother's front, and his face towards her back. It's the safest because it means his head will form a wedge shape as it emerges, which makes it easier to get the biggest part out.

Sometimes babies face the other way, with their faces towards the mother's front. This means that a larger area of head is coming first, and it can make labour longer and more difficult. If the baby is coming *brow first*, then it's almost impossible for him to be born through the vagina. Babies in this position usually need to be delivered by a Caesarean. Babies who are in the *breech* position at birth – that is, with their heads up and their feet presenting first – may also have to be delivered by Caesarean, although this isn't always the case. Some doctors and midwives are very skilled at helping a woman deliver breech babies normally. Other reasons for women having Caesareans are a baby lying in what's called the *transverse position* – that is, across the womb – or the sort of problems with the placenta we

## THE DELIVERY AND AFTER

looked at in chapter 7, such as the placenta coming away from the wall of the womb. Some women have to have Caesarean deliveries because it's discovered during pregnancy that their pelvises are simply too narrow for the baby to get through, although this applies to only a few women.

A Caesarean might also be necessary if a baby is thought to be suffering from *fetal distress* during labour. The medical staff will try to keep a constant check on the baby's heart rate throughout labour, either with a fetal monitor, or with the old-fashioned method of using an ear trumpet pressed into the abdomen. If it appears that the baby is distressed at all – perhaps the heart rate speeds up or becomes erratic – it may be necessary to get him out as soon as possible. It could be a sign that he's not getting enough oxygen; a long labour is very tiring for the baby, too. Sometimes the cord becomes squashed (something doctors call a *prolapsed cord*) or caught up in some way in the womb.

A Caesarean is very safe these days, although it's still considered to be major surgery. If you and your partner know it's going to happen, then you can prepare yourselves for it. Some hospitals even perform them under an epidural anaesthetic so that the mother is awake when the baby is actually delivered; it's felt that it's better for her to meet her baby straightaway rather than to wait until she wakes up a little later. It's completely painless, and a screen across her middle prevents the mother from seeing anything unpleasant. It's also possible in some cases for fathers to be present at these epidural Caesareans, and that can obviously make them feel less left out than they would have done otherwise in a normal Caesarean performed under a general anaesthetic. Again, they won't see anything unpleasant, and they'll have the added bonus of seeing their baby straight after the delivery – although they still have to be prepared to leave at the request of the medical staff should this be necessary.

The important point to remember about any Caesarean is that it is major surgery, and your partner may need more of your support – both practical and emotional – if she's going to be able to cope properly. It takes longer to recover from a Caesarean birth than a normal birth simply because there's the problem of abdominal stitching. But unless your partner has got a small pelvis, having a Caesarean once doesn't necessarily mean that she'll have to have all her babies in that way. Many women go on to have completely normal births for second and subsequent children.

Support is the key word in any case wherever there has been a problem. If your partner has had a distressing time at the birth – if it's gone on for a long time, or if she's had a difficult forceps delivery, for example – she's going to need plenty of help and tender loving care from you. Some women react to a difficult birth by becoming very depressed, and in some cases of severe depression (a subject we'll be looking at in more detail further on) they may even reject their babies temporarily. Most mothers overcome their depression, but they do it sooner and more lastingly if they can feel that their partners are right behind them.

It's sometimes more difficult for both of you if there's a problem with the baby. *Very, very few babies are born handicapped*, but when they are, it can of course be extremely distressing for the parents. Handicaps come in all shapes and sizes and degrees of severity, and to a large extent, the effect on parents depends on what the handicap is and whether anything can be done about it or not. Parents of babies born with a hare lip and cleft palate, for example (in which the roof of the mouth doesn't close during pregnancy and which sometimes involves the upper lip and the nose) are bound to be distressed, but they can gain real consolation from the fact that modern techniques of plastic surgery almost guarantee that their child's face can be made normal. That's a consolation not available to the parents of children with *spina bifida*, children who will be paralysed for life and who will face enormous difficulties; neither is it available to the parents of children who have been brain damaged during birth, or those who have Down's syndrome (Mongol children).

This isn't really a subject I can go into here. All I can say is that parents of children such as these will be offered help and counselling, but however sympathetic the people who deal with them, however much help they get, their experience of parenthood is going to be much tougher and more demanding than it is for parents of normal children. They deserve all the help and support they can get, and they need to help each other. It goes without saying that not only are fathers deeply affected by this sort of tragedy, they have a real, positive role to play in helping their partners to deal with what can be a devastating blow. A list of useful books and addresses for further information are on pages 265-70.

Fathers also have a role to play when a baby needs special care after birth. Some babies are born too soon – these days they're

## THE DELIVERY AND AFTER

called *pre-term* rather than *premature* – and are too small or too immature physically to survive without expert help. Some babies born at full term (that is, after a full, nine month pregnancy) are also too small or need extra help. These are often referred to as *small-for-dates* babies, and various factors will have played a part in causing their problems; a less than efficient placenta is a common cause. At any rate, these babies may well end up in an intensive care unit with tubes and pipes and electrodes all over them, and essential equipment helping them to breathe and to get the nourishment they need. Doctors these days can perform near miracles in saving the lives of tiny babies, but obviously, the smaller and less mature they are, the less chance they have. They may have to spend days, weeks or even months in incubators, their tiny lives hanging by a thread.

Obviously this can be very distressing for parents. They may have to sit and watch a tiny baby struggle for life, feeling absolutely useless. They'll be unable to take the baby home, and although many hospitals now encourage mothers to express their breast milk so that it can be fed to the baby, it's much more difficult to do anything directly for the child you've been waiting for throughout pregnancy. You'll need to help and support each other if this happens to you, and for fathers that may mean getting time off from work to share the burden of long hospital visits and vigils. Happily, many parents who face these worries are rewarded with a healthy baby after a while.

But sadly, babies sometimes die. If a baby is born dead it's called a *stillbirth*, and this can be very distressing indeed. It seems doubly tragic for a woman to have to go through all the months of pregnancy and the pains of labour only to give birth to a dead baby. In the past, doctors and midwives sometimes tried to make sure that the mother and father didn't see the baby, which was hurried away for anonymous disposal. It's now known that this can make the natural depression after such an event more of a problem. A stillbirth is the loss of a child, just as a miscarriage is, and that's something that needs to be worked through. Parents need to be able to mourn for their child and to express their grief, and it's sometimes much harder to do that if you don't even know what the baby looked like. That's why, these days, midwives and doctors will ask parents if they want to see their dead baby and spend some time alone together with their child. It's important too for some parents to have their baby buried properly in a place where they can visit the grave;

and this is a feeling we should all respect. Again, I hardly need to add that fathers feel the grief of a stillbirth just as much as their partners and need to be helped and supported through the difficult time. They also need to allow themselves to feel the grief and work it through.

## Coping with an emergency birth

Many fathers I've talked to have been secretly worried about what to do if their partners go into labour and there's no chance of getting any help, or of getting to a hospital. I'm very grateful to *Parents* magazine for allowing me to adapt and reproduce a set of guidelines for dealing with an emergency birth written by an obstetrician and published in a *Parents* special issue on pregnancy.

It's a fact that some women – although they're rare cases – do have very short labours, even for a first baby. It might also be a combination of adverse circumstances that means a woman can't get to a hospital on time.

There are two points to keep in mind about these fast labours. They're often *easier* than births where the mother is surrounded by helpers. That's because the faster a birth is, the less distressing it's likely to be for both mother and baby. But the other point to remember is that no matter how advanced labour might be, you should try to get help right up until the last moment. It's also important for both mother and baby to be seen by medical staff as quickly as possible after the birth.

So if your partner goes into labour, and it feels as if the baby's coming very fast, *don't panic*. Ring the hospital or your doctor for help, and if you know that it may take them time to get to you try getting more immediate help, even if it means shouting out of the window to someone in the street. But if it really looks as if the baby is going to be born before any help arrives, follow our guidelines for dealing with an emergency birth. Try to make sure your partner sees them too!

*What to do*
- Make sure that your partner is as comfortable as possible. If the room is cold, heat it. If you can, place a pile of newspapers or plastic sheet under the mother. Wash your hands thoroughly, and get some towels or something warm

## THE DELIVERY AND AFTER

to wrap the baby in, and also clean cloth pads or handkerchiefs.

- Try and get your partner to relax, and to let nature takes its course as smoothly as possible. Boil some water in a kettle and several saucepans, then pour into bowls to cool.
- At some time the bag of waters surrounding the baby will break and release some fluid. This is normal. As the baby gets nearer to being born, your partner will be feeling quite strong contractions at fairly short intervals – every two to five minutes. Let her get into the position where she feels most comfortable – she may need support behind her back.
- When the baby's head appears it will make the vulva bulge, then eventually emerge through it. Just as it seems about to emerge, stop it from doing so too quickly by gently cupping your hand over it to control the speed. Ask your partner to take quick, panting breaths at the same time to stop her pushing too hard.
- If the umbilical cord is wrapped round the baby's head when it's out, feel carefully round it with your finger. If you can, gently try to loop it over the head or shoulder so it's free. Wait now for the next contractions, which will get the baby's shoulders out. Then firmly hold the baby under his armpits and gently lift him out. Hold him with his head low to let any fluid in the mouth and nose drain out.
- Don't move him in any way which will pull on the cord, which will also partly have emerged. Lie him on the mother's abdomen. Wrap towels around him and cover the back of his head.
- The next contractions should deliver the afterbirth. Once this is out, cover it with a towel. If it doesn't come out after 20 minutes, get your partner to kneel and press on her lower abdomen. It should slip out then.
- Slowly and gently – but firmly – rub her abdomen over where you feel the upper end of the bulk of the womb. This should be at about the level of the navel. Use the cooled, boiled water to wash between her legs. Put a clean cloth or pad over the vulva.
- If the baby doesn't breathe within two minutes of birth, give artificial respiration very gently with small puffs. When he's ready to suck, help your partner to put him to the breast and see that the nipple is well back in his mouth. Now's the time to get back to the phone and see where that help is!

- If you're unable to get hold of a doctor or midwife, boil up some shoe laces or soft string for tying the cord, and scissors for cutting it. Wait until the cord has stopped pulsating and then tie it about 4 inches (10 cm) from the baby and again about 6 inches (15 cm) from the placenta. Cut with sterilised scissors or a sterilised, new razor blade between the ties. Check that there's no bleeding from the baby's cord stump. If there is, do another tie nearer the baby.

PART FOUR

# BECOMING A FATHER

Oh . . . the grand old Duke of York,
He had ten thousand men,
He marched them up to the top of the hill,
And he marched them down again.
And when they were up, they were up,
And when they were down, they were down;
And when they were only halfway up,
They were neither up, nor down.

*Traditional nursery rhyme*

# 11 Early days

The first few days of your baby's life – the first few days of fatherhood, in fact – may be a very strange and confusing time for you. If it's your first baby, your partner will probably spend at least a week in hospital to recover from the birth and to get to know the baby. Some hospitals insist that first time mothers should stay in for up to ten days, which means that you will be relegated to the status of a visitor.

It can be a very odd, and even upsetting experience to be separated from your partner and child, especially after the 'peak experience' of birth. 'I felt very strange going home alone after I left the hospital on the day Ben was born,' one father told me. 'The house just seemed so empty and cold. I couldn't sleep, I couldn't eat, I couldn't do anything. All I wanted was to get back to that hospital and see Linda and Ben again.' Some men instinctively avoid this problem by going to stay with parents and friends, and this can be a great help; I stayed with my mother when both Emma and Helen were born. Apart from the practical support this affords, it will also give you someone to talk to – and you'll find that you probably want to talk about the birth over and over again.

However, your life will centre on the hospital while your partner is still there, and you may discover that visiting hours can sometimes be a problem. When Emma was born, for instance, I was only allowed to visit for something like an hour a day. It seems that things are a little more relaxed in some hospitals these days, although you're still unlikely to be allowed unrestricted time for visiting. You'll probably find too, as I did, that there's a restriction on the number of people allowed round each bed at visiting time. Obviously, friends and close family will want to visit your partner and to see the new baby; a newborn child seems to exert an irresistible attraction over everyone you know, and they'll all want to come and peep, gurgle and say 'Coochie-coo'. So you may well find yourself spending half of what little time there is for visiting marooned outside in the corridor waiting for great aunt Doris to stop finding resemblances between your child and relatives you've never even heard of.

Many fathers do feel very left out and on the edge of things at this time, a feeling which grows out of everyone's attention being firmly focused on your partner and the baby. Most of us realise that this is as it should be and are happy to accept the fact; after all, your partner is the one who's done all the hard work, and if she never is at any other time of her life, she should be in the spotlight in these early days after the birth. But you do still need to feel part of what's happening; you've become a parent too, even if you didn't give birth, and the less involved you are at the beginning, the harder it's going to be to catch up later on.

This is a problem which can be made worse by hospital staff and routines. In the hospital where Emma was born, there was a rule to the effect that fathers were not allowed to pick up their babies and hold them. At the time, this was a rule we conspired to infringe with the greatest circumspection. I remember picking up my baby from her cot and being terrified in case a nurse should catch me. I also sneaked into the nursery on the ward, a room which was strictly off-limits to all dads at all times, just so that I could see Sally change Emma's nappy. This was on the fourth or fifth day after the birth, and it was the first time since she'd been born that I saw any more of my baby than her face and the top of her head. I felt like a naughty schoolboy in the school stock cupboard as I watched Sally's apparently deft and practised fingers deal with nappy, cream and safety pin. I felt even more naughty when the door flew open and a tyrannical nurse came in to order me out.

Times have changed since then, but not all that much, and you may still come up against that sort of rule or attitude. If you do, then I can only advise you to do what I did when Helen was born: take no notice. If your partner stays for a week or more in hospital, she'll spend much of that time learning how to change nappies, establishing feeding and so on. In other words, she'll be getting a head start on you in learning how to be a parent; you'll have a lot of catching up to do. To a certain extent, there's no way of avoiding this, but it's vital that you should try to minimise its effects. Visit as often as you can, stay as long as you can, and don't let anyone stop you from picking up or getting to know *your* baby. That's an important point to remember; it's your baby, not the hospital's. You're the one who's going to have to do the fathering in the future, so try to give yourself a good start now.

Of course, you may start coming into an area of conflict with your employers at this stage. (I'll be looking at the subject of paternity leave in more detail further on.) It is very important indeed for you to take as much time off as you possibly can to be with your partner and baby, though it is best to take it when you're all at home together. This means that you'll probably still be at work while your partner's in the hospital, and if your company isn't particularly sympathetic or considerate, then you may find it difficult to get the time you need. If that's the case, try and have patience; you can make up for it when you're together at home. And if you're lucky enough to have more human employers, take every advantage of their generosity – you don't become a father every day of your life.

## Coming home

The day eventually dawns when it's time for your partner and your new baby to come home. For them, that last day in hospital will probably be marked by a final physical examination. A doctor will examine your partner to make sure she's fit enough to go home and that she's well on the way to complete physical recovery from the birth. The same doctor may examine your baby, or it might be a specialist paediatrician who looks him over. Either way, it will be quite a thorough inspection to make sure that there are no problems. Once they've both been checked over and given the all clear, you'll probably be summoned to take them home.

Coming home with your new family can be an exciting, even nerve-wracking experience. 'A nurse carried the baby down to the car for us,' one father told me. 'I made Janet sit in the back seat and then the nurse handed the baby over. After that I drove home so slowly and carefully that Janet thought there was something wrong with the car. There wasn't; it was just that I couldn't stop thinking about that tiny, defenceless baby in the back in my wife's arms. I had to protect him, to make sure that he was safe. I felt so worried about his fragility.'

Rule number one for all fathers on this day of days is to make sure that your partner is coming into a clean and tidy house. There really is no excuse for you not to make sure that everything is under control. To my eternal shame, it's a rule which I completely ignored when Sally came home with Emma. I hadn't been in our flat for most of the time she'd been in hospital, and the sink was still piled with dirty dishes from the day before the birth, there was a thick layer of dust on everything, and I had dumped presents, bunches of flowers and other assorted acquisitions all over the place. Sally was decent enough not to say anything, although she would have been perfectly justified in letting me have it right between the eyes. Even so, I do remember feeling very guilty, although guilt is never much help; it always comes *after* the fact. That's why it's important to get into the habit of housework and sharing the chores *before* a time like this. That way you won't simply forget that such things have to be taken care of, as I had done.

Life is going to be very difficult indeed for your partner in these early days if you haven't got *any* experience in handling the domestic chores and cooking. However easy the birth was for your partner, and however quickly she seems to be recovering, she'll still need plenty of rest for a couple of weeks. And of course, if she had a difficult birth, or a Caesarean, she's going to need as much help as she can get. These days few of us can afford to pay someone to come in and help. Your parents – the baby's new grandparents – probably won't be able to take time off from their jobs and commitments to help you out on a major scale, either. That means the role of chief supporter, head cook and bottle washer falls squarely on to the shoulders of the new father. You will be worth your weight in gold to your partner if you can simply get on with what needs to be done, whether it's the cooking, the cleaning, the washing or the ironing or the shopping, without having to ask what needs to be done. It helps if you can be there, and the evidence is that even though few companies grant paternity leave to fathers, either paid or unpaid, most fathers take up to one or two weeks off work to be with their families. In one survey in *Parents*, it was found that only 11 per cent of fathers took no time off at all.

Mind you, by the end of my first day as a fully fledged father with wife and baby at home I was almost ready to go back to work. That was because I had discovered the unique nature of those early days of parenthood, that combination of terror, joy, awe and total exhaustion which no one who has experienced it ever forgets. The first two things which seem to strike everyone at this time are the responsibility of caring for a new human being who is totally dependent on you, and just how demanding that new person is. 'It wasn't long before we realised that babies are hard work,' said one father. 'Every time we changed her nappy, she filled it. Every time we put her in her crib she cried. Every time we closed our eyes or sat down to a meal it seemed that Lucy woke up and had us on the go again. Inside a week both of us looked – and felt – like the living dead.'

These early days of parenthood are very much an up and down time, which is why I put that old nursery rhyme *The Grand Old Duke of York* at the head of this chapter. Apart from the fact that it's our baby's favourite rhyme at the moment, and the one we use to calm him down when he begins to let rip, it's also a perfect description of what it feels like to be a new parent. Sometimes you're up, like when you look at your beautiful new baby sleeping in his crib, or when you look at your partner breastfeeding him or when you hold him in your arms yourself. And sometimes you're down, like when that same beautiful baby wakes up for the fourth time in one night and is still crying after the feed which you were both sure would send him off to the land of nod for at least two or three hours. It's at this time that you'll really begin to understand what sort of an impact becoming a parent can have on your life, and if you had any illusions about parenthood, now is the time when they'll be blasted into smithereens. Being 'neither up nor down' is something which will come later, once you've settled down and got used to all the changes. But the early days are when they're just happening, and the sudden transition from pregnancy to having a baby around the house can be disconcerting, to say the least, because your new baby's got to get used to the world – and you, too!

In fact, no matter how well prepared you think you might be for parenthood, the reality often comes as something of a shock. By saying that you might think I'm going back on what I said in earlier chapters about the need to prepare – I'm not. What I'm saying is that even the most prepared parents find these early days a struggle, and the less prepared you are, the more difficult they're going to be. The important point to bear in mind is that these early days in a new situation may well set the tone for the months and years to come. If you get used to doing things in a certain way, you might find it very difficult to get out of those habits later on, even if they're bad ones.

That's why it's important not to overdo the housework and cooking and 'background behaviour'. Of course it's vital for you to make sure that the house isn't continually in a terrible state;

of course you must make sure that you both get meals and that those vital cups of tea and coffee arrive when necessary. *But you also need to get to know your baby*, especially if your partner has that 'hospital head start' on you. This brings us back to the problem of conditioning I discussed earlier on, the conditioning which makes women believe they should be instinctive mothers, and men that they're incapable of looking after a baby. Don't forget that your partner will probably have been unconsciously conditioned into thinking of herself as a 'natural' mother, and to a large extent she will have many qualities which will help her. But in these early days of motherhood she'll be finding out that she has an awful lot to learn as well.

Take bathing and changing your baby, for example. It's not as easy as it looks, and to most first time parents – although few mothers will admit it – it doesn't look very easy at all. You and your partner may have experimented with a doll at your antenatal classes, but you soon discover that a real live baby is a very different kettle of fish (or barrel of monkeys if you'll allow me to mix my metaphors more accurately). If you could be present in the hospital the first time your partner handles your baby in the bath, the first time she changes his nappy, the first time she dresses him, you'd see that in many ways there's no such thing as an instinctive mother (although there is much about parenthood which is instinctive, as we'll see in later chapters); she has to learn how to do these things, just as she has to learn how to breastfeed properly, just as you'll both have to learn to get on with this new person who will be making such an impact on your life.

Why then do so many new mothers look so relaxed and competent to their partners, us, the new dads? It's the result of a combination of factors, the main one being the almost complete inexperience of most men in this field, a lack of knowledge which means that a hospital head start coupled with your partner's assumption that she *should* know how to do these things is translated in your eyes into dazzling competence. But it's also caused by attitudes. You partner's conditioning may make her feel that she should be competent, and so she gives that impression; your conditioning may make you believe that you're incompetent in these tasks, and turn you into a cack-handed father every time you attempt them.

It's amazing to see the pressure of prejudice and stereotyping in action at such a time. The new mother takes a pride in showing her partner how well she can cope, to the extent that when he tries to change a nappy or dress his child she loses patience with his inefficiency and good naturedly says, 'Here, let me do it.' He, of course, having been brought up to defer to women in all such matters, immediately retreats, however much he'd really like to be involved. Gradually it becomes easier and easier for both mother and father to relax into traditional roles; it may even feel more 'comfortable' for your partner to look after everything to do with the baby while you handle everything else. The problem is that the more your partner does, the more skilled she'll become at every aspect of childcare, while the less you do, the less skilled you'll get. The pressure to conform to stereotyped roles is enormous, and often comes very much from within. Even couples who want to share childcare more evenly may find the pressure hard to cope with. If you allow yourselves to be pushed in this direction, it's going to be very hard to change your habits later on, especially if your partner stays at home full time to look after the baby, while you go back to work after this short period of time off.

## Making an effort

I've called this part of the book becoming a father because that's what you're going to have to do. Of course, in one sense you're already a father, *but fatherhood isn't a state of being, it's something you do – it's an activity*, and it starts as soon as you make it start. If you take a back seat and let your partner handle all the practical tasks you'll only increase the sense of exclusion and being left out that you'll probably be feeling somewhere deep inside anyway. At the same time you won't be establishing a relationship with your child. You need to make the effort, and change nappies; you need to hold your baby; you need to take every opportunity to get used to the idea of doing things for and with your baby. The more you do, the more your partner will appreciate you, and the better you'll get at being a practical parent. It will mean that when you do go back to work, you'll find it easier to take up the reins of parenthood when you're at home, you won't have so much 're-learning' to do every time you want to help out. At the same time it will mean your child gets used to the idea of having *two* parents who can do almost everything, which should make him feel very welcome indeed.

Think of parenthood as something to share with your partner, something you can both learn together; you'll all benefit.

Obviously, you can't breastfeed your child. What you can do, however, is to be encouraging and give your partner all the support she needs in this vital area. It's been shown in various surveys that women whose partners are understanding about breastfeeding tend to have far fewer problems than those whose partners aren't very helpful or even hostile to the idea — which isn't very surprising. Breastfeeding is a very important subject which few men know anything about. Every woman is equipped with breasts, and there are very, very few women who are physically incapable of feeding a baby with their own milk. Breastfeeding is, in fact, a marvellous system. The baby's sucking at his mother's breasts stimulates the milk producing glands to make milk. The more he sucks, the more milk they produce, and vice versa. The milk is perfectly suited to the baby's needs, and contains all the right nutrients in exactly the right proportions. It also helps to confer immunity to many infections on the baby by passing on antibodies from the mother. At any one breastfeed, your baby is therefore receiving food specifically designed for *him*, possible immunity to infections, *and* he's getting plenty of comfort, too. That's a very important part of the activity for him; the physical action of sucking and the satisfaction of his needs is comforting in itself, but the skin-to-skin contact it affords is also very important.

Despite the fact that mother's milk is just right for your baby, by far the majority of women bottle fed their babies with substitute, artificial, formula milks until recently. These come in packets in powdered form, and have to be made up with hot water. You have to be careful to keep the bottles and mixing equipment sterilised, and all in all, bottle feeding is quite a complicated business. Formula milks are also usually based on cow's milk, and there is a growing body of evidence to show that exposing a baby to cow's milk at such an early stage may be implicated in causing allergies of the type which lead to eczema and other problems, for example.

There has therefore been a swing away from formula milks in recent years; breastfeeding is all the rage. This has a lot to do with the move away from 'medicalised' birth and the 'scientific'. It seems that in many areas we're moving back to more natural, less 'technological' ways of doing things. Bottle feeding's heyday coincided with the years of the 'technological revolution' in the

1950s and 1960s, and it was often promoted as the more 'scientific' way of feeding your baby. Breastfeeding is also growing more popular for the simple reason that it's much easier – there's no mixing of feeds to be done in the middle of the night when your baby's breastfed. All you need is a baby and a breast to make the system work.

Although that's not to say breastfeeding is completely instinctive and works without any problems. That's not so; women often experience difficulties and these range from the minor to the major; they can also make a woman give up breastfeeding if they're not sorted out soon enough. In basic terms, to succeed with breastfeeding, your partner will need to relax and to operate a 'feeding on demand' system. Women used to be told to feed their babies to a rigid schedule, such as every four hours, and to ignore their cries otherwise. It's now known that babies need to be fed when they're hungry, and will cry until they get what they want. At the beginning, your baby may want to feed every half hour or so, although most babies settle down into some sort of feeding pattern eventually. The important thing is to be flexible, and to make sure that the baby sucks enough to stimulate the milk supply. If your partner starts to panic, then her milk won't flow properly. She has what's called a *let-down reflex*, a reflex which starts her milk flowing once she picks the baby up – it works in some women even when they hear their babies cry. It certainly won't work if she's worked up and anxious. It's a common problem for first time mothers, or a mother at any stage who's worried that feeding isn't going well. Her anxiety hinders her milk supply, her baby cries because he isn't getting enough, which increases the mother's anxiety and so on. Soon you've got a vicious circle going, which ends with the mother reaching for the feeding bottle.

You can play a crucial role in making breastfeeding work. Help your partner to relax; encourage her by telling her how well you think she's doing. Find out everything you can about breastfeeding, and understand things such as why it's important to make sure the baby's *latched on* properly (that is, with the whole of the nipple and areola in his mouth the right way). If you make this sort of positive effort, you'll be a great help to her. If she has any problems, like a blocked duct, a sore nipple or *mastitis* (an infected breast), make sure she seeks help and also that she gets it. You can talk to your midwife, your health visitor, the doctor, or seek help from a specialist organisation like the National Childbirth Trust or the La Leche League (see page 266).

Many women still do choose to bottle feed, and it's important for your partner not to feel guilty if she does so. With all the emphasis on breastfeeding at the moment it's easy for bottle feeding mums to feel like failures, especially if they wanted to breastfeed and found that they couldn't, for whatever reason. It's important to remember that although breastfeeding is the best and easiest way of feeding your baby, there are millions of children and adults around today who have been bottle fed and are none the worse for it. If your child does have problems, such as the allergy problem I mentioned, there are formula milks based on other foods, such as soya, which will help. Obviously, fathers can and should play a greater role in feeding a baby who gets his milk through a bottle. You can help your partner to mix feeds, too (always remembering to be scrupulously careful about hygiene and ensure that all equipment is sterilised), and fathers who give their babies a bottle often feel very involved in parenthood indeed. Mind you, fathers of breastfed children can have that experience – it's possible to express breast milk and give it in a bottle, and that's something some couples do from time to time to give the mother a rest.

Talking of rest brings us to the vexing question of who gets up in the night. The fact is, as you'll soon discover, that babies are no respecter of your golden slumbers. When your two week old baby is hungry, he's hungry, and he'll want feeding immediately, whether it's two in the afternoon or two in the morning. If your partner is breastfeeding, you might think that there's no point in you getting up in the middle of the night; there's nothing you can do, after all. I didn't feel good about making that excuse when Emma was born, though; I could see that Sally was very tired, so I decided that I would try to get up and help out. I could change Emma's nappy, for example, and make Sally a drink if possible. I soon found that once I went to sleep, nothing would wake me. So I went through a period of trying to force myself to stay awake until two or three in the morning to make sure that I would be around to help out for at least the first feed of the night.

Various surveys have found that few fathers do actually get up in the night, even when their babies are bottle fed. It's something which can become a very contentious question between you, and obviously has a lot to do with the roles you carve out for yourselves. In the early days, one advantage of taking time off work is that there aren't so many demands on your energies, so if you can get up in the night to help out in whatever way you can, it's worth making the effort. Even if your partner says she doesn't mind you sleeping through it all, she'll appreciate the fact that you're trying.

These early days don't have to be all gloom and doom. Many fathers experience them as a joyful time, a time when they begin to understand the good things about becoming a father. 'There were the times when both of us just stood and looked into the cot at our beautiful baby,' said one father, 'and the times when I looked at my wife and saw that she was really enjoying being a mother, despite the broken sleep and the worry about whether we were doing it right or not. It was wonderful.' It's a time you should try to enjoy. That same father described it as like a 'honeymoon period, after the birth, but before the real world of work and daily concerns came back into our lives.' Don't fuss about being too tidy or too much cooking; have some takeaway meals and spend the time getting to know your baby and yourselves in a new role.

If you do have any problems or are particularly worried about anything, don't just sit there, seek help. You'll be visited by a midwife for the first week or ten days, and she'll help you and your partner to do things like bath the baby. She'll also weigh him, and make sure your partner is well on the way to full recovery. Your health visitor will come to see you at least once or twice as well. She's not 'checking up' on you so much as finding out if you can manage or whether you need some help. You don't really have to go out for advice, therefore – it will come to you. So use the opportunity if you need to.

# 12  Back to work

'I don't thnk I'll ever forget the day when I had to go back to work,' one father told me. 'All my friends, everyone at work, they all said things like "I bet you're glad to be out of it now" – but I wasn't. I couldn't bear it. I would much rather have been at home with Anne and the baby.' I know exactly how that father felt, and if the truth were known, many fathers feel much the same. Contrary to popular belief, and in opposition to much of our conditioning, after we've had a taste of it, many of us do miss being at home with our partners and children. In that first day or two back in the office or at your workbench, you may experience a real sense of being excluded, of being left out. I remember feeling very strongly that I was missing out, and that's a common reaction among those fathers who have made the effort to be as involved as possible during their time at home after the birth. It seemed that when I'd kissed Sally goodbye and shut the front door behind me, I was walking into a world of exile – the world of work.

Your partner may well be feeling less than happy about you going back to work, too. Now she's really on her own, and it's worth trying to put yourself in her shoes. Remember that although in the UK only 5 per cent of *all* households conform to the traditional pattern of a housewife and mother at home full time with her partner out at work, when we're talking about households with babies or small children, that figure is much, much higher. In one survey we reported on in *Parents*, less than 10 per cent of mothers with a baby under a year old were back at work, and a high proportion of that 10 per cent were doing part time jobs. Your partner is very likely to have given up work for a period of months at the least – and probably years.

Your partner may begin to discover when you go back to work that the transition to motherhood can involve considerable loss. She has gained a baby, but she has also lost the status of being fully independent with her own money that working involves. From now on she will be financially dependent on you, and however much she may have wanted to become a mother, that dependence is likely to rankle. The only income most mothers can really call their own – unless they're fortunate enough to have private means – is their child benefit, which in the UK at the time of writing stands at a paltry £6.85 per child, per week. Obviously enough, that doesn't go very far at all, and when it's gone, your partner probably has only one source for any more – and that's you. Different couples have different ways of handling their financial arrangements. In some households, the man gives his partner a set amount of 'housekeeping' every week or every month to pay for specifics like food or certain bills. Other couples have a joint bank account into which they both dip freely according to need. But whatever method you use, your partner is still likely to feel the loss of her independence. 'We never argued about money,' one mother told me, 'and Chris is always very good about it. He hates me to feel that I have to ask him for money; he says that what he earns belongs to both of us. But I can't feel that way. It still feels as if I'm taking *his* money all the time. I'd love to be more independent.'

At the same time, your partner will begin to realise that being a mother isn't all sweetness and light. Social conditioning combined with the sort of idealised view of parenthood portrayed in television commercials gives many of us a set of rosy illusions about having children which are shattered by reality. Your partner will discover that babies make a lot of work, but at the same time the work isn't particularly demanding of her brain. In fact much of the routine of looking after your baby is very tedious. Yes, your baby is lovely and wonderful and a delight to be with – sometimes. But when your partner is rushing around trying to get the shopping done, the washing and the ironing under control and all the other domestic chores finished, *and* get a meal ready for you to eat when you come home, playing with baby in the way television commercial mums play with their babies is likely to come very low down on her list of priorities.

You may have noticed that we're peering into that great divide again, the great divide between men and women. For in what I've just written, I've implied that being a mother at home with a baby is a job which includes *all* the domestic chores. The simple fact is that *that's the way it is* for most couples. What it means for your partner is that she may have given up a demanding, full time job which gave her plenty of stimulus and interest to become an unpaid skivvy, a domestic cleaner who also has to look after a demanding baby all the time. Even those women who were glad to give up boring, underpaid and tiring jobs soon find that they miss one key component of being a working woman – adult company. Babies are lovely, but when you're at home alone with one for most of the day, you don't get much adult conversation or variety. 'The only other adults I saw were people in the supermarket, old people in the park, and other mothers with their babies and small children', one mother told me. 'Inside a few months I was desperate to talk about something else other than the weather or disposable nappies. I felt that I was becoming a vegetable.'

Society, and men in particular, can make this sort of thing much worse for women. The title 'housewife' often seems to be synonymous with 'moron' in the mouths of many. This is something which was brought home to me with some force quite recently. A friend of ours told us the story of how she had rung an office in connection with a bill she'd received. The man on the other end of the phone asked her what she did for a living. When she said she was a housewife, he said that he 'would write to her husband about the matter'. It's the sort of callous, unthinking chauvinism which causes great distress and inequality, and is also still very powerful indeed in our society.

## The Great Divide again

And what about you? How will you be coping with the other side of the great divide, the world of work? In a sense, the moment when you shut that door on your wife and child and go back to work is the point at which your life begins to diverge from hers. You'll soon find that the world of work takes very little notice of the fact that you're a father now. In fact, you'll find that nothing has changed around you; it's all still the same. 'That was the weirdest thing,' one father said to me about this time. 'I was completely different, at least that's what I felt. I was a father, and there was a whole new side to my life. But no one at work was really very interested. It just seemed that children and being a father wasn't a subject you brought up in the office very much, if at all.'

In a broader sense you'll begin to discover that there are no concessions for most fathers. You might want to sneak off early to go home to your wife and baby, but your company will expect you to do the same number of hours you did before you had a baby. Indeed, as I've already explained, the pressure might be on you to work longer hours. You may need the extra money that overtime brings in simply to help balance the family budget now that your partner's given up paid work, however temporarily. At the same time, the years when you have young children are usually exactly the same as the years when you need to put a lot into your job – and to be seen to be doing so, often – in order to get on in your chosen career.

It's a trap that many of us fall into, a trap it's very hard to avoid. The result is very simple. For me it meant leaving home early and coming home late; it meant barely seeing my baby daughter, except at weekends. What that meant was that I did less and less in terms of practical care for my child, mostly because I simply wasn't around very much, but also partly because I lost whatever skills I'd developed during my 'paternity leave'. Sally and I found that our lives were going in completely different directions – and that we had less and less in common.

Interestingly enough, various research studies have shown the effect of this great divide between work and home on something as precise as the amount of help fathers give their partners in practical terms. One survey showed that the amount of housework fathers did was generally at a peak in the first few weeks after the birth, and then fell off rapidly once they went back to work. In many cases it was found that men actually ended up doing *less* around the house after they became fathers than they had done before. Some men seem to feel (often unconsciously) that now their partners are at home full time looking after the baby, they should have plenty of time to do all the housework, too. I've even heard it said, 'I don't see why I should do a full day's work *and* do the housework too now that she's at home all the time.' The problem is that we're brought up to look down on housework as something which isn't really 'work' at all, and many people – especially men – tend to have the attitude that most mothers at home have a fairly easy time of it. Remember that few men know much about this side of life at all, or about what it means to care for a baby, either.

Involvement with the baby on the part of fathers also falls off fairly rapidly once they go back to work. A survey conducted for *Parents* discovered, for example, that 30 per cent of fathers *never* gave their babies a bath, 23 per cent *never* dressed their children, 43 per cent *never* got up in the night to the baby, 24 per cent *never* changed a nappy and 22 per cent *never* took the baby for a walk. If you added in the percentages of fathers who only occasionally or rarely did these things, you ended up with a figure closer to 50 per cent or higher of fathers who very rarely did anything practical for their children. Admittedly, there was a 'hard core' of around 50 per cent of fathers who did these things either every day or at least once a week. Another interesting statistic was that well over half the mothers felt that their partners did 'as much as they were able', something which accords with my own experience and that of the people I've talked to. Most mothers realise that their partners are under a lot of pressure, just as they are. Add this to the fact that many women feel uncomfortable with the idea of their partners helping out around the house because of their conditioning, and you have a simple reason why a lot of women don't expect or even ask for more help from their men.

However strong your relationship, however well you communicate, there are still bound to be times when the pressures of early parenthood cause a certain amount of friction between you. The problem is that those pressures are relentless, and there's no escape. You can be pushed into your separate, diverging, traditional roles before you're even aware of it – and end up very disappointed with your own performance as a parent, as well as your partner's.

You may well feel under enormous pressure in your job, a pressure compounded of several factors: the desire to get on and succeed, for example, or your new feelings of responsibility for your family, or the simple fear of unemployment. All these are linked with each other, obviously enough; in any case, many of the jobs fathers do are exhausting, stressful and tough even without the added burden of overtime or the extra responsibility parenthood brings. Traditionally, a man's home has been seen as his 'refuge'; home is where you retreat at night from the hurly-burly of the competitive working world outside, where you shut the door behind you and wait for your partner to serve your dinner, find your slippers and calm you with a cool hand on your fevered brow. There's still a lot of power in that image, even today. Many fathers find themselves hoping – or even expecting – that their partners will be sympathetic and understanding about the pressures they have to face in being the family's breadwinner.

But your partner may well have had a pretty tough day herself. Don't forget that she'll probably by trying to cope with the feelings of isolation and loneliness I've been talking about. She may have had no adult company to talk to all day, and even though she very probably loves your baby, even the brightest, perkiest, happiest baby has his off days – and he certainly isn't going to be any great conversationalist. Your partner's day may well also have been very monotonous and tiring. Babies need feeding and changing and playing with, but your partner will soon discover that she spends most of her time doing the housework or the shopping. No one can convince me that doing the washing or cleaning the house are deeply fulfilling tasks: they're just plain boring.

## Outsiders at home

There's another aspect to all this which I felt myself in our early days of parenthood, although it was something I couldn't articulate. A friend did it for me when he talked about feeling like 'a lodger in his own house'. Mary Ingham found this to be a common feeling among fathers when she interviewed them for her book *Men*. We might do the work which brings in the money to pay for the mortgage, and so in that sense we *own* the house. But Mary Ingham's distinction between ownership and possession is a revealing one. Women *possess* the home in the sense that they are actually in it, usually, far more than their partners; they also know it intimately, having cleaned it from top to bottom more often than they'd care to remember. At the same time, although it's usually men who do most of the decorating, it's their partners who choose the colour schemes, the curtains, the colour of the carpets, even the furniture. I know that many of the men I've spoken to feel that they're intruders in their own homes, sometimes, that they're only 'messing things up' and getting in the way. Sally and I have often had arguments about tidying up which touch on this sore point; if she dusts my desk and even slightly rearranges what's on it, I can feel almost irrationally upset. But then to a certain extent, my desk is the one place in our house which I know is truly mine. In most of the other rooms, I often feel like an *outsider* once again.

The problem for your partner is that she probably unconsciously expects too much from herself. The traditional pattern has been for mothers at home to combine housework with motherhood, and the implication in your partner's conditioning is that she should not only be good at what she is now doing, she should also be satisfied with her lot. All that playing with dolls, all the emphasis in society around her on how 'natural' is the bond between mother and babies, conspires to make her think that it should all come naturally, instinctively. At the same time – and this is especially so in women who have really wanted to become mothers – your partner may feel that she shouldn't complain. There's a real sense in which a woman's status is wrapped up with how good a mother and housewife she is. Even if it's unconscious, your partner may feel that people will think badly of her if the baby's not always tidy and clean and happy, and if her house isn't spotless. That's why she'll probably try very hard to live up to your unconscious expectations that she should have your slippers ready when you come home, and a meal on the table.

Life, however, isn't like that. Some things about parenthood *are* instinctive, as we'll see further on. Much of it isn't, mostly because practical parenthood is to do with things like establishing a weekly or daily routine for tasks which have to be done. You'll find out that babies generate a lot of washing which has to be fitted into your schedules. Shopping with a baby in tow is a much more complicated affair than a solo dash to the supermarket. Babies, you'll discover, have their own time-table which often differs from – and usually clashes with – yours. In fact all of our children were the same in having an awkward period in the late afternoon and early evening which perfectly coincided with the time Sally needed to prepare our evening meal. What that meant was that she often had to stir the stew with one hand, and hold a screaming baby with the other.

It will take time for your partner to sort out routines and schedules; it will take time for her to learn how to arrange life in a way which suits her and the baby. At the same time, you should both bear in mind that babies and their needs change constantly. It's no good trying to be rigid with a baby; you have to be flexible. More importantly, you have to be flexible in your attitude. 'Our first really big row after the baby was born happened one night when I came home from work,' one father told me. 'When Gail opened the door, the baby was screaming her head off. Gail practically threw her at me and stormed off upstairs. I didn't know what on earth to do, and it was all that much worse because I'd had a pretty lousy day myself. So I just lost my temper, and bingo – we had a steaming row.' That couple settled their differences and began to understand that their problems were the result of the sort of pressures they were under. 'We began to realise that it was no good looking at parenthood as something we did separately. We had to start looking at our lives as something we had to arrange together, as a team.'

# 13 Sex – and other problems

There's one character in this story about whom we've talked very little so far, and that's your baby. That's partly because I've devoted a whole section (the next one) to talking about fathers and their children, but also because you'll probably find that your attention as a 'beginner' father will be focused less on your child than on the circumstances of parenthood. In simple terms, you really won't be around very much, and that can be a real problem. 'I felt very left out, very jealous of Jane's involvement with the baby,' one father said. Feeling like that can make it very difficult to work together with your partner as a team in sorting out your problems, and in the early months of parenthood it can seem that there is nothing but problems. It's a very stressful time of life; what's happening is that you're trying to adjust yourselves to a massive change in your lives and circumstances, a change which comes suddenly and totally. That stress will sap your energies; even if you don't realise it, you'll both be feeling pretty anxious about everything, and that can be very draining, not forgetting that you'll simply be tired because of the broken nights, the extra work, the extra responsibility.

'It was a great disappointment to me,' the same father went on. 'We had felt so close when the baby was born and in the couple of weeks afterwards. Now we just seemed to be growing apart.' Many couples report a deterioration in the quality of their relationship after the birth of a baby. It's important to remember that some experts have described the first year or 18 months with a new baby (especially a first baby) as an 'emergency situation'. Everything is thrown up in the air to settle who knows where, and the pressure is immense. You wouldn't be human if you didn't sometimes resent your partner, and we all do. Men resent women because most of us still have the feeling that life at home with children is still somehow easier and more pleasant than life in the working world, however much lip service we might pay to the idea that it isn't. Women often soon

## SEX – AND OTHER PROBLEMS

resent the fact that their partners seem to have a wider world to operate in, that they have adult conversation and can go to the pub at lunchtime with colleagues, that they simply seem to have much more freedom.

Freedom is a key word in arguments between the sexes over parenthood. It's an argument Sally and I have had several times. In a fit of pique, I've said that she has more freedom than me because she can arrange her life without the constraints of doing what bosses tell her to do. Some women do appreciate that, but as Sally so rightly says, it's often an illusory freedom because children, housework and all the other demands on her time usually take up more hours than she has available, so she's constantly under pressure. She says I have more freedom because it's a man's world, and I can go out without being tied to the children. It's true that few fathers automatically think of what needs to be done for the children before they go out, even if it's to do some sort of leisure activity. With most couples it's the woman who gives up her outside interests after she has a baby, and not the man. But my argument has always been that that freedom is also sometimes illusory; it's part of our conditioning, and often really means a freedom not to play a part in our children's lives.

The quality of your sex life is often a good indication of how healthy your relationship is. In basic, physical terms, your partner will probably be ready to resume intercourse within a few weeks of the birth. Some women who have had no tearing or didn't need an episiotomy are ready to resume sex within a couple of weeks, while others may still feel uncomfortable up to four, five or even six weeks after the event. Your partner should have a full postnatal examination at six weeks after the birth, and any problems can be sorted out there. It's an unfortunate fact that occasionally some women are stitched up inefficiently and may need a certain amount of treatment. Obviously you need to be careful about your first attempt at intercourse after birth; some women like to use the woman on top position to make sure that they can control the depth of penetration. But if you and your partner find that she's still in pain after her postnatal examination, or that the pain is severe, then she should see the doctor as soon as possible. The sooner the problem is sorted out the better; there's no need to suffer in silence, and there will probably be a simple solution.

Nevertheless, you'll soon discover that sex as a parent is

different, to say the least. The mechanics might be the same, but the ambiance certainly won't be. For a start, if your partner's breastfeeding, you may find that intercourse is an even damper affair than it used to be. Pressure on breasts full of milk can result in substantial leakages. Many is the time when I've woken up in the night to find that my wife's affectionate cuddling of my back has soaked us both! Some women also find that orgasm can stimulate their let-down reflex and make the milk start to flow.

Also bear in mind that our society is riddled with the idea that the primary purpose of women's bodies is to give pleasure to men, and that only those women who are young, slim, beautiful, well dressed, immaculately coiffed and made up can be considered as truly sexy women at all. This idea forms an essential part of your partner's conditioning, and it can make life very difficult for her in early parenthood. First, just as with pregnancy, society's attitudes make it difficult these days to associate being sexy with being a mother; 'playmates' don't have children, or if they do, they don't pose with them for centrefolds. Second, motherhood makes it difficult to keep up in terms of fashionable clothes and buying make up; you're probably short of money and one thing that's been discovered through research is that mothers are often reluctant to spend money on themselves. They feel guilty if they buy make up, for example, a point which is intimately linked to the idea of now being dependent on *your* money. Third, with all this in mind, your partner may well feel very depressed if it takes her longer than a few months to get her figure back. She'll feel fat and ugly and dull, and her head might be full of the dire warnings of older generations about what happens to marriages in which the wife 'lets herself go' after she has a baby.

The great divide also plays a part here. If you work in an office, for example, you might have to look quite smart; you might wear a suit and tie and take great care over your appearance. Even if you don't, there are probably a number of women in the office: young secretaries, married or unmarried, mostly without children, though. Put yourself in your partner's shoes; she may feel that in the outside world, the world of work, you have plenty of opportunity to meet young, attractive women while she deteriorates into dowdy housewifery and motherhood. Confidence is a key word in this context. However much you might reassure your partner, she's still likely to feel that her self-confidence has been battered by the transition to parenthood. Much of this has to do with the low status of parenthood in our society. Having children is not a glamorous occupation; the emphasis these days is on being young, slim, single, rich, and unencumbered. Few people think that being a mother (or a father, for that matter) is exciting at all. So bear in mind that your partner has to try and cope with all this; she has to come to terms with not only a different status in society, but one which is deemed by many as being a *lower* one.

It's not surprising therefore that sex problems are a common feature of early parenthood. Sex is a bridge between a man and a woman, and early parenthood can be a time when the gap between you widens – which makes sex a much more tenuous, more difficult business. Your partner may feel reluctant to give herself wholly to you if she feels you don't understand what she's going through. Don't forget that she'll also have the demands of the baby to cope with, and that those demands can seem total and all consuming at this early stage, especially if your partner is breastfeeding. It's a very close, intense physical experience for many women, and to a certain extent the physical needs which she satisfied in sex before the birth may be partially satisfied in this contact with the baby. Add the fatigue which you'll both feel at this stage and you've got a very good reason for your partner not being all that interested in sex. In fact some women see their partner's interest in sex as 'just another demand' on them which they can resent intensely. Even women who have no inhibitions and may be very interested in keeping their sex lives going may find the sheer exhaustion of early parenthood is sometimes too much for their libidos.

Touching is an essential part of a relationship, yet often men are reluctant to associate touch with anything other than full sexual intercourse. Many women resent the fact that – after the honeymoon period, at least – their partners never seem to kiss them or offer any other physical affection unless they want intercourse. 'He never kisses me, he never told me he loved me, he barely even touched me,' said one women, 'except when he wanted to make love. Then he was all over me. But that wasn't good enough for me. I don't like it that way.' It's something which can make a woman feel used, exploited as a sex object.

So even if your partner may not be as keen on the idea of sexual intercourse as you are, she's still likely to want some physical contact with you: a cuddle, and some physical reassurance and support.

Not all women react this way, of course. Some find that the

experience of pregnancy, birth and breastfeeding only serves to enhance their sexual needs and pleasure. It's as if becoming a mother makes them feel more complete, more whole as a woman, and it certainly can help to lessen the internal force of any inhibitions in some mothers.

As far as new fathers are concerned, you still sometimes hear it said that men shouldn't be present at the birth of their children because it 'puts them off' sex; the idea being that you'll find it hard to place your penis in your partner's vagina after you've seen a baby emerge from it. To be honest, I've never met anyone who's even been remotely concerned by anything like that. Indeed, being present at the birth seems sometimes to enhance a man's sexuality in the sense that he may be more considerate towards his partner afterwards; it may actually help him to broaden his ideas and appreciate his partner more.

A more likely reason for a man to go off sex after birth is his sense of being left out, of being excluded. It might seem to you that your partner is concentrating on the baby to the exclusion of you. To a large extent, there's no other way it can be after you go back to work. Your partner and your child are literally thrown together all day, every day and so your partner *has* to establish a relationship with the baby simply in order for both of them to get on with what they've got to do. But it can be very disconcerting to come home every night to find yourself almost an observer outside the charmed circle of mother and baby. Even those fathers who are very much involved, and who have prepared themselves for these problems, can feel left out. So the less involved you are, the more difficult it's going to be for you to feel included. Some men deal with these negative feelings by denying them and retreating into 'traditional' fatherhood, refusing to help out, refusing to do any housework, even sometimes refusing to have much to do with the baby at all. I've heard men say that 'babies are uninteresting' and that they'll take notice of them when then they're older and 'can hold a conversation' – by which time it might be too late to build a real relationship.

Still other men are simply jealous of the link between mother and baby, a jealousy which sometimes focuses on breastfeeding. I've known men who haven't liked seeing their babies breastfed because they felt that their partner's breasts belonged to them; it was as if the baby was some sort of sexual challenge, or sexual competition. Some men react to this by making sex – its frequency, duration and quality – an issue; others withdraw their favours, something which can be bewildering for a woman. Problems come when a couple can't and don't talk about their feelings, because suppressed or unexpressed feelings fester, expecially when there's a sexual element in them.

## Postnatal depression

The first point to make is that there are several different types of postnatal depression. Your partner may well have felt very weepy and depressed three or four days after the birth. She might have burst into tears at the slightest upset, or even taken some perfectly harmless remarks in completely the wrong way and been very distressed. Doctors have long blamed this on the dramatically falling levels of pregnancy hormones in a woman's system after the birth, although it's also probable that a certain feeling of anticlimax plays a part, as well as a feeling of panic that now there's a real baby to be looked after. Most women get over these 'baby blues' fairly quickly, usually within a day or two. It's thought that at least one in three mothers have this sort of depression.

But about one in 500 mothers are thought to suffer from a far more serious and long-lasting form of postnatal depression. Doctors give it the grandiose name of *puerperal psychosis*, and it can involve serious depression, a rejection of the baby, even attempts by the mother to harm herself or the child, or commit suicide. Women with this illness often behave in a very odd way indeed; they may have bizarre hallucinations, for example, and imagine all sorts of morbid happenings. In cases where women have actually killed their babies and committed suicide, they've sometimes left notes saying they believed that the world was coming to an end, or that they couldn't look after the baby properly and it was best for all concerned.

Even in cases – and they're by far the majority – where a depressive illness of this sort doesn't end in the tragedy of a suicide, it can still have a devastating effect on a marriage. Obviously, the burden of dealing with his partner and looking after the baby (or making arrangements for the baby to be looked after so that he can hang on to his job) falls squarely on the shoulders of the father. Thankfully, these days he's likely to get plenty of help and support; the symptoms of serious postnatal depression are well known to doctors and midwives, and they'll take steps to help a woman in whom they're spotted, although they're occasionally missed for several months as a woman struggles on and tries to act normally. If your partner seems to be suffering badly from depression of this sort, don't hesitate to seek help as soon as you can – any delay could be dangerous. She'll probably be put on a course of anti-depressant drugs and, hopefully, be offered some counselling. In the most serious cases, women are given psychotherapy as well as drugs, and some are treated with electro-convulsive therapy, although ECT is a controversial technique. Most women with this problem get over it, and end up living normal lives. A woman who's had postnatal depression once, however has a higher than normal risk of suffering from it again after a subsequent birth.

Between these two extremes there lies a vast spectrum of postnatal depression. Indeed, it's been said that almost all women suffer from 'early parenthood depression' at some time in the first year or two of motherhood. Any major change in your life lays you open to the risk of being depressed afterwards; and as you can see from what we've been talking about so far, the social context in which we become parents today lays us more open to the risk of depression than ever before. Our expectations tend to be higher; your partner will expect more of herself, more of the baby, more of motherhood, more of you. You'll probably have high expectations of her, of fatherhood, of the baby; depression is almost inevitable. I'd like to stress, too, that fathers can – and do – suffer from postnatal depression, although it's rarely called that and people rarely take notice of the fact that fathers can feel very down in the early months of parenthood.

Even the most saintly couple can soon find themselves arguing with each other out of sheer exhausted irritability. The problem is, of course, that babies are sensitive creatures. The more tense you are, the more tense you're going to make your baby. Tense babies cry and don't settle; crying and not settling makes *you* more tense – the perfect vicious circle.

Parents who are violent towards their children are often those who are so totally unprepared for the experience of parenthood that the shock of what it's really like is too much for them. There are very few parents who, in their heart of hearts, haven't felt like strangling their beloved children sometimes. It's hard for most of us to admit, but when you do feel as if you're at the end of your tether, you're tired, and the whole world seems to have forgotten you and your problems, it can be very easy to take out your resentment on the cause of all your troubles – your baby. Don't think that all 'baby batterers' are young, poor and illiterate, either; there's many a progressive, educated couple who have had to face and overcome the violence in their lives. The important thing to remember is that if you really do feel as if you can't go on, or that you might be violent towards your child, then it's time to seek help. You mustn't be afraid to ask for it, either; many people are not only trained specifically to be of assistance to families with this problem, they're more than willing to use their skills to make sure you get the chance to enjoy parenthood.

## Positive solutions

Knowing what sort of problems you're likely to face and understanding something about their causes is the best preparation for having children there can be, though even if you do know what you're letting yourself in for, the reality is something of a shock. The secret is to try and relax and to take things as they come; you can't be rigid with babies, and that's a principle you need to extend to parenthood as a whole. Ride with the punches, don't try and fight back all the time – remember the old cliché about what happens to trees who don't bend in the wind (to mix my metaphors once again): they break. In simple terms, so long as you're aware of the need to work together with your partner in coping with the impact of parenthood on your lives, then you shouldn't go far wrong. In effect, what you'll find yourself doing in these early months of parenthood is re-drawing the map of your common world; you'll be re-negotiating the lines of demarcation, carving out new areas for yourselves alone and together. This has to happen anyway, under the pressure of accommodating this new person in your lives; but it's far better if you take positive action to make the redrawn map as fair as possible and to try and make it approximate as closely as you can to what you both want. A first step here is to ensure that the lines of communication between you and your partner are still open and in operation. Remember that no problem can be sorted out unless you talk about it. So if you're feeling resentful and left out, then it's up to you to tell your partner. It's also up to your partner to let you know how she feels – if you know, then you'll be able to do something for each other.

What you can do for your partner is very simple. She needs support, reassurance, encouragement. You need to make her feel that she's doing a great job, that she's a terrific mother and that you're full of admiration for her. At the same time she needs to know that you still find her attractive; don't come home and tell her that she looks dreadful, even if she does. If you can't say anything positive, don't say anything at all until you can. At the same time, be interested in what she's been doing, which to a large extent means being interested in your child. You probably will be anyway, but social conditioning may make it difficult sometimes for you to be able to show your interest. The baby might seem to be driving you apart at times, but he can often be a means of bringing you closer together, just as he may have been on the day he was born.

Try and be open and receptive when your partner talks about the problems she's had during her day. Remember that she may not have anyone other than you to 'sound off' to about her problems, and that a sympathetic ear is a major benefit to anyone. At the same time, your solutions might be just what she needs; it's sometimes easier to be objective about day-to-day problems when you're not as heavily involved in them. It's important to remember too that much of what you learn about your child will have to come through your partner. As your child grows, she'll also be able to remind him continually of your importance in his life when you're not around.

*Staying involved* is vital at this stage, and most men really need to make an effort to combat the pressures which take them away from their families or keep them excluded while they're at home. The plain fact is that the more you do around the house, the more your partner will appreciate you; and the more you do with and for your baby, the better your relationship with your child is likely to be. You'll feel less excluded, more valued, more of a *parent*. I can't say often enough that being a father is an *activity*; well, so is being part of a family. It's the things you *do* that count.

There are also some other, even more practical things you can do to help out. If your partner is feeling lonely and isolated, encourage her to find some friends. There are various groups designed to bring mothers together, such as mother and toddler groups, of which there are bound to be several in your local area. Many women find these a great help in making friends in the early months of motherhood. I know that Sally did, although she needed my help in finding out about them because she was unsure and had lost her confidence (I got the address through a contact I made via the National Childbirth Trust) and my encouragement to get her actually to go along. It's important to keep an eye on your partner to make sure that she isn't just 'struggling on' under the misguided notion that she shouldn't ask for help. You're the best person to see if there are any problems, and you can play a vital role in making sure that your partner doesn't suffer from postnatal depression badly enough to spoil her enjoyment of parenthood. You can also help by making sure that you both go out alone together once in a while. It's easy to get into the habit of staying in, especially when you haven't got much money, but getting a babysitter and going out for a couple of hours, even if it's just for a cheap meal, can make an enormous difference. You may be parents, but you're still people with needs of your own.

Something else you can do for your partner is to try and give her some time completely alone once in a while. At the beginning, when the baby may be dependent on your partner for breast milk, the best you can do is probably to go for a walk with the baby for half an hour or so. But even that half hour of freedom and independence can make your partner feel a lot better. As the baby gets older, you'll be able to extend these periods; they don't have to last for hours, and you don't have to do it every other day. Once a week is usually enough. Some women use the time to have their hair done, or simply to have a long bath or just to read quietly for a while. However your partner uses the time, she'll appreciate the freedom to recharge her batteries.

Another benefit of doing this is that it gives you a chance to get to know your child better. 'It was on the afternoons at the weekend when I took Paul for a walk in his pram that I really got to know him,' one father told me. 'We were on our own, so I could talk to him how I liked, get him out of the pram, do what I wanted. It made me feel more like a father.' Obviously, being alone with your child can be very daunting if you haven't got the experience of coping with a baby; that's why it's important to take a share in the practical side of babycare right from the beginning. But time spent alone with your child is very valuable indeed, especially if you use it properly.

As far as any difficulties with your sex life are concerned, the answer is to relax and to try to be patient. Accept the fact that it will take a while for things to settle down, and don't make sex an issue between you. Bear in mind too the importance of touch in your relationship, touch in its broadest sense. Make sure that you offer your partner the cuddles and physical affection she'll appreciate, and don't put pressure on her to turn every physical encounter between you into a sexual episode. If there's a wider context of touch and sensuality in your relationship, sex should blossom naturally from time to time as an expression of your mutual affection. That is so at any time of life, and good sex has a lot to do with good communication. Remember too that you need to have positive physical contact with your child as often as possible as well, which means you should be giving him plenty of kisses and cuddles too!

There's also a point here for women to note. Your partner needs just as much encouragement and reassurance as you do. He needs to feel that he's doing a good job, that you appreciate what he's doing, and that you understand some of the pressures and problems he's going through. He needs to have someone to whom he can 'sound off' as well, and although you might think that he has colleagues at work to whom he can talk, don't forget that often they're just the people he doesn't want to talk to about his real feelings. You should also remember that men have no tradition of airing their feelings or talking things out, and although it's something we need to do, we often find it difficult. You have a vital role to play in helping your partner open up; all he might need is a little nudging from time to time, a little help in exploring his feelings. Again, if you can be open and receptive to this, you'll be helping him, and therefore helping yourself. Something else it's vital to do is not to put him off when it comes to sharing babycare or the housework. We've seen that women can sometimes be jealous of their traditional role and reluctant to hand over anything to their partners. It's the old 'Here, let me do it, you'll only make a mess of it' syndrome. If your partner is willing to help, swallow your pride and let him do it. Let him change nappies, let him clean the house, let him cook the dinner if he wants to, even if he makes the kitchen look like a bomb's hit it. He'll learn with practice; what he needs is encouragement.

At the same time, it's important to draw your partner into the charmed circle of mother and baby. Many fathers feel acutely embarrassed about even much minor things as watching their partner breastfeed the baby. You need to overcome these feelings by making your partner feel welcome. Keep him informed of what you're doing, of what progress the baby's making. If the baby suddenly starts smiling or crawling, ring your partner at the office and tell him, even if he's not supposed to have personal calls. Some things are more important than rules and regulations, and it's the sort of thing that might help to make your partner feel a lot more part of what's going on. He needs to feel that he's not being left out.

## Surviving parenthood

'It was funny,' one man told me, 'but one day we woke up and it was as if everything had suddenly settled down. We'd got used to the baby, and the baby had got used to us. We'd worked out a lot of our problems and we seemed to be getting on OK. Parenthood didn't seem all that bad, after all.'

It might seem strange to say it after all the gloom and doom of what's gone before in this chapter, but like that couple, most of us do survive the early days of parenthood and even get to quite like it. Things do settle down, you do establish routines, you do find your feet as parents. So even if you think you're never going to make it, remember that you very probably will; the bad times don't last. What few of us realise before we actually become parents is that there are any bad times at all; but I guarantee that there will be times when you'll wish that you'd never become a father (or mother).

There is an important point to be made here, though. If you feel that your problems aren't getting any better, whether they're problems in your relationship, problems with money or problems with your baby, don't hesitate to seek help. There is a strong element in our conditioning which makes it difficult for us to admit that we're anything less than perfect when it comes to parenthood, and that in itself can be a pressure on us. The fact is that we all make mistakes as parents; none of us is perfect, and anyone who tries to make you believe that early parenthood in particular has gone like a dream is either lying through their teeth or certifiably insane.

But remember too that these same couples who report a 'deterioration' in their relationship during the first year or 18 months of parenthood also usually report that they feel their relationship is 'stronger' after that period than it was before. It seems sometimes that we discover new qualities in our partners; men see that their wives can be efficient, capable, and can work extremely hard for little reward. Women see whole new areas opening up in the men they thought they new. As one woman put it to me: 'When John became a father it seemed to change him. I never knew he could be so tender, so considerate, so *parental*.' Under the pressure of parenthood, many people discover they have a depth of feeling which they've never tapped before, and this can be especially rewarding for men. The important point is to make sure that our conditioning doesn't block that flowering of new and different qualities in us.

Most couples, however, seem to feel that after the struggle to accommodate themselves to this massive change in their lives they're 'bloody but unbowed'. Another interesting point is that it becomes very hard to think of the possibility of life without a baby. 'I just couldn't imagine not having him around,' was the way one father expressed this feeling. 'It was as if he had made our lives much fuller, and that was a good thing despite all the chaos and the fatigue and the worry. I couldn't imagine how anyone without a baby could get any real fulfillment in their lives at all. I know that's arrogant. But it was the way I felt about my son, my baby. At that moment, I felt I'd truly become a father.'

PART FIVE

# FATHERS, MOTHERS AND CHILDREN

Throughout our formative years he was what may be called a 'weekend father', if as frequent as that... Such a father might well be an awe-inspiring figure to small children, and that was the aspect he sometimes assumed... It is fair to say that he came to us generally in the guise of Father Christmas, loaded with presents; but if we or the dogs were in disgrace he came as a figure of retribution, and it may be that, for this reason, he did not perfectly earn his way into my childish heart.

from *My Father and Myself* by J. R. Ackerley

# 14 Your child's development

However involved you want to be as a father, the simple fact is that you will probably spend less time with your child than your partner does. One survey by Ross Parke showed that mothers spend on average around nine hours a day with their babies when they were awake; the figure for fathers was just over three hours. Another survey, this time by Julius Segal and Herbert Yahraes, went into far more depth. It was conducted among middle-class men in the United States and showed that fathers spent an average of only 20 minutes a day with their one-year-old children; and out of that 20 minutes, only 38 seconds was judged to be contact of a 'meaningful' nature.

It's difficult to understand figures like that. Surely, you might think, surely I spend more than 38 seconds a day doing something meaningful with my child? But think about it for a moment; think about what your average day is like. Like me, perhaps you crawl out of bed, hurriedly wash and dress, rush through breakfast and fly out of the door (after a brief peck on the cheek for your partner and a pat on the head for your child) so that you won't be late for work. Then you'll work hard all day, and maybe fit in some overtime. You might stay late to finish a particular piece of work or go to that important meeting. Either way, by the time you get home your child is likely to be asleep or about to be put to bed. If you were actually to put a stopwatch on the amount of time you spend with your child you might be very surprised indeed.

Even if you decide that you want to spend as much time at home with your child and partner as you can, it's still going to be very difficult to combine involved fatherhood and working for a living. It's that old great divide again, the divide which means that most of us end up doing our fathering at weekends – we're 'weekend fathers', in J. R. Ackerley's phrase. This is, after all, our traditional role, part of which is also being the family's seat of authority and discipline; 'Wait till your father gets home' is a phrase which is supposed to have quelled generations of children, as it did J. R. Ackerley and his dogs.

In this sense, the traditional father had two faces. The weekend father was — and still is — a playful dad. Those figures I quoted earlier from the *Parents* survey which showed that few fathers did much practical childcare on a daily or even weekly basis also revealed that 90 per cent of fathers or more played with their children every day (or at least claimed to). To a certain extent this doesn't gell with what I've already said about the woefully small amount of time you're likely to be able to spend with your child. But in another way, it does. Even if all you do is gently tweak your baby's nose and tickle his chin as you're saying goodbye in the morning, the 38 seconds you spend together is far more likely to involve play than it is changing his nappy or feeding him. It couldn't really involve anything else — there wouldn't be enough time!

Traditionally, too, this pattern has been interpreted as meaning that fathers don't actually make that much of a contribution to any area of their children's development. In fact, fathers are conspicuous by their absence from the research that's been done into child psychology. Up until quite recently, the only research that was done very rarely featured the good, and much more often concentrated on the bad and the ugly (and the absent). There were a number of studies of families in which fathers were alcoholics, violent, criminals, mentally ill, or of families with no fathers at all. What's been missing — and the gap is only slowly being filled — is any research into what normal fathers can give normal children in the context of ordinary family life. Men are still under the shadow of the enormous emphasis that's been laid on the link between mother and child. Let's call it *the Madonna complex*: what is means is that because of the way society is organised (that is, because of the 'great divide'), and because our conditioning tells us not only that motherhood is instinctive in women but that only women can be effective parents, men feel inferior as fathers.

Yet from the research that has been done (meagre as it is), it's quite clear that fathers can be an important and very positive influence on their children. What's more, in some areas, it really can be said that we're essential, that without our positive, uniquely masculine contribution, our children are likely to be worse off in terms of their development. Up to now, because we've felt inferior as parents, it's been easier for many dads to stay in the background and to allow their partners to take a greater share in shaping our children, even where we've had time to do more. What I hope to show you in this chapter is why you should get as involved in parenthood as much as you can for the sake of your children – and how you can make the most of the time you spend with your family. To understand how you can make a positive contribution, you've first got to understand a little about how children develop in the early years of life.

## Your talented baby

It used to be thought by the experts that newborn babies weren't capable of very much, that they were a blank slate on which their parents and the world would write in a character and experiences. After all, they seem only to want to feed, sleep, fill their nappies and cry for the next feed. But we now know that your newborn baby is capable of a lot more than those simple facts of existence; indeed, we know that your baby is actually a very talented little human being.

As I explained, babies in the womb can see and hear, so it's no surprise that your baby is born with all her senses in full working order, although as yet, she won't be very skilled at using them. She can see very well, and will tend to focus on objects 8 to 15 inches from her face. She can hear, too, and she can certainly taste and smell. And of course she can feel; we've already seen just how important it is to have skin-to-skin physical contact between baby and parents after birth for bonding.

Much more important is the fact that your baby is born ready – and even eager – to respond to your partner and you, and to find out about the outside world. She focuses on 8 to 15 inches from her face because she's born with an instinctive desire to look at human faces, and that's how far away her mother's is likely to be during feeding. In fact it's been discovered that a newborn baby will look at a face in preference to almost anything else. That's something you'll probably have found out for yourself; you might find that you spend an awful lot of time looking into your baby's big, beautiful eyes and be amazed that she'll stare back at you with such intensity.

Your baby's talents and skills don't end there. Babies have a highly developed sense of taste and prefer breast milk to any other drink. She can also suck when she's born, a vital skill which she's probably spent a lot of time practising in the womb – babies have actually been observed in the act of sucking their thumbs during pregnancy. Newborns also show what's called *the rooting reflex*; if you stroke the baby's cheek gently, she'll turn towards the stimulus and open her mouth, ready to start sucking. Another reflex which newborn babies have is called *the grasp reflex*. If you put your finger in your baby's palm, she'll grasp it very firmly. Some babies can even hold on tightly enough with both hands to be lifted into the air.

The point of these various skills, reflexes and instincts is a simple one: they are there to help your baby survive. At birth, she's totally dependent on you for all her needs. She needs to create a link with you and your partner in order to get the food she needs to grow and the protection she needs for survival. Your response to your baby is part of this, too; your child evokes in you a response, a protectiveness and affection, which will make sure you do what's necessary to keep her alive.

All this is the base from which your child will develop over the coming years. At birth she can't walk or talk, and she certainly can't fend for herself. But by the time she's five years old – and in Britain, that's the age at which she's likely to start full-time school – she'll be able (among many other things) to run, jump and climb trees, and she'll probably talk so much that you'll sometimes feel like giving anything for some peace and quiet. It's a process which always seems miraculous to me whenever I think about it; from that tiny, fertilised egg created by the fusion of your sperm and your partner's egg, a unique new human being grows.

There are several things which you need to bear in mind about your child's development, though. The first is that although it's a subject which is often talked about under separate headings – how your baby learns to walk, or learns to talk, for example – it's a process which happens as a whole. Your baby is learning to talk *at the same time* as she's learning to walk. Development in every area of your child's life happens as one dynamic, continuous process. In fact, an advance in one area such as learning to crawl – will give your child greater opportunities to develop her skills in other areas, such as using her hands on new and interesting objects she hasn't been able to reach before.

It's also important to remember that there are no set ages at which any of these developments *have* to happen. Some children, for example, learn to walk at eight months (as our daughter

Helen did) while others don't take their first unaided steps until they're 13 or 14 months (as Emma did), while still others might be 18 or 21 months old before they graduate to the status of 'toddlers'. The important point is that the age at which your child learns a particular skill or reaches a particular stage of development is probably perfectly normal for him or her. Doctors talk about 'average' ages at which children achieve certain things, and the range of what is to be 'normal' can be very wide indeed; in the case of learning to walk, for instance, the range of normal is perhaps nine months or more.

Your doctor and health visitor will encourage you to take your child for regular check-ups at your local *well baby clinic*. These clinics have been set up with one simple aim in view: to make sure that babies are healthy and developing normally. Your doctor will probably want to see your child at regular intervals – at six weeks of age, six to eight months, one year, 18 months, two or three and at the age of five, just before full-time school begins. At each stage, your child will be weighed and measured and checked; she'll also be given special tests to see how her development is progressing and whether she's within the range of normal for her age. You'll also be offered the chance to have your child immunised against specific illnesses like polio, tetanus and whooping cough. It's also intended that these clinics should give you and your partner the opportunity to ask about anything which might be worrying you. Of course, one purpose of the clinics is to detect any problems as early as possible so that treatment can begin at an early age, which will mean that the child will have a better chance of overcoming any problem she may have.

The doctor will be looking at how your child is progressing in four main areas. These are: *gross motor development* (learning to crawl, walk and generally become mobile); *fine motor development* (learning how to use the hands in co-ordination with the eyes and other senses, and so on); *language* (which involves learning to understand as well as use words); and *personal/social development* (which basically means learning social skills and getting on with other people).

## Walking and talking

It's fascinating to watch a baby developing increasing mobility, to see how development progresses *downwards* in your child's body. Control of her body depends on the maturity of her brain and central nervous system, and so the first parts of herself that she'll learn to control will be her eyes and her head. Then she'll learn to control her hands, which will be followed by control over her legs and feet. Consequently, in her early months, she'll spend a lot of time working on the second of our two categories, fine motor development, and especially the co-ordination between her hands and eyes.

In the early weeks of life, your baby's ability to focus will get better, slowly but surely. Soon she'll learn to follow objects which move across her field of vision — a skill called *tracking*. By the time your baby is six weeks old, she'll begin to explore one hand with the other, and within a couple of weeks after that she'll start to look at her hands for the first time. From then on your baby will increasingly want to grasp the things which interest her. Once grasped, they'll be conveyed immediately to the organ which she probably considers her most important at this stage — her mouth. It isn't just that she gets her food through her mouth which makes it important (although that's obviously part of the reason); sucking also gives your baby comfort, which is why many babies like to suck their thumbs or other comfort objects. At any rate, your child will explore everything with her mouth, which means you'll have to keep a watchful eye to ensure that she doesn't put anything dangerous into it.

At about three to five months of age your baby will be able to look directly at something she's interested in and reach out to touch it. By then she'll probably be able to lift her head and control its movements quite well. At six, seven or perhaps eight months old, she'll be able to sit up, although she may still need some propping up to stop her falling over. Of course, in terms of hand-eye co-ordination, this is a very important moment as it means her arms are now completely free. The result is that most babies at this age seem to spend a lot of time just sitting with some interesting toy or object held firmly in both hands and stuck squarely in their mouths. Part of the stimulus for becoming more mobile is that objects sometimes get dropped and roll away; and sometimes there are even more interesting things that your baby will be able to see in the distance . . .

By the age of eight months or so many babies have become mobile. Most start rolling over before that age; at the time of writing, six-month-old Thomas spends much of his day rolling over and over and over. He's also now beginning to raise his bottom and push with his knees, although he hasn't worked out yet that it's a good idea to lift your face up if you want unimpeded, painless forward motion. That will come when he has developed the necessary strength and co-ordination in the muscles of his neck, back and arms. Many babies do learn to crawl at about this age, and it can be a fantastic, hilarious sight to see a tiny baby suddenly discover the joys of scampering around on her hands and knees. Some miss out the crawling stage and go straight to standing up and walking, while others simply shuffle along on their bottoms.

Most babies start pulling themselves upright by the time they're around ten months old, and those first few unaided steps usually happen between the ages of about 12 and 15 months. Your child will be very unsteady at first, but she'll soon become more assured, although she'll have plenty of falls. Once your child starts to walk, she isn't really a baby any more but a *toddler*. Those steps represent more than a simple physical achievement, too; they're symbolic of the central meaning of your child's development, which is no less than the process by which she grows to independence. It might be hard to imagine, but just as Neil Armstrong's first steps on the moon represented a 'giant leap for mankind', so your child's first unaided steps represent a major milestone for her on the road to becoming an adult.

Growing mobility means more opportunities for improving hand and eye skills. These will be very good by the time your child reaches toddlerhood, although clearly there will still be a long way to go. Your child's development doesn't stop; it continues right through childhood, although it will cover more ground more quickly in the early months and years than at any other time. It is fascinating to watch a child learn new skills. I've seen my two daughters learn how to feed themselves, first by using a spoon (quite clumsily), and then progress to using a fork. Using a knife is quite difficult; even at the age of five or six many children still find it beyond them. I've also seen my daughters progress from fumbling with buttons and zips when they were toddlers to being able to dress and undress themselves completely. Three-year-old Helen may still have the odd problem with complicated clothes (like dungarees), but she manages most of the time. Emma seems to have no problems at all now, unless you count the fact that she's beginning to argue with us over what clothes she wants to wear.

That brings us to the twin subjects of personal/social development and language. Those arguments Sally and I have with six-year-old Emma are a reflection of the complex relationship we now have with her. The relationship grew in the early months and years as her physical development unfolded, and a large part of that process was the communication we built up with her. That communication started off in what seemed a one-sided way, with *us* talking *to* Emma; but it wasn't completely one-sided. It's been shown that even at a very early stage, babies actually take part in 'conversations' with their parents. These 'conversations' take place through gesture and expression as much as through words, and they're an essential ingredient in the way your child learns to speak. It is therefore impossible in reality to separate language from your relationship with your child.

It's now thought that, to a certain extent, human babies are born with an innate ability to learn how to speak. If they are – and the evidence seems to support the idea fairly strongly – it goes some way to explaining the miracle of how a baby learns such a complicated thing as human speech from scratch without any formal teaching whatsoever. You won't sit down and try and teach your child how to speak; you'll simply find yourself talking to her all the time. We talk to our babies as we rock them, we chatter to them as we feed them, we sing them nursery rhymes. In fact we submerge our children in language almost from the moment they're born. The evidence also shows that babies seem to have an inbuilt interest in the human voice to match the interest in faces with which they're born.

And if you listen to the way in which you talk to your baby, you'll find that you talk to her in a very special manner. It's been discovered that we instinctively talk to our babies in a high-pitched, musical way. We repeat what we say and exaggerate our expressions and gestures as we say it. We gaze deep into our babies' eyes, and find them gazing back. Babies, indeed, tend to lead in conversation and we follow; if your baby raises her eyebrows, you'll raise yours; if she coos, you'll do the same. You'll both mirror and repeat her action so that unconsciously you'll be helping her to learn that most basic of human activities, the dialogue, the statement and response on which all social communication is ultimately based. And you'll also probably find that lots of laughter and smiles accompany these conversations; indeed, at this stage, fun seems inseperable from talking to your baby.

Over a period of time your baby will begin to gain more and more control over the complicated physical apparatus inside her mouth and throat which actually makes the sounds; remember that she has to learn how to use her lungs, her vocal cords, her tongue, palate, teeth and lips. On top of that she has to learn the meanings of words and the rules of grammar and syntax, a process which some of us never achieve fully. Your baby will do a lot of shouting and babbling in the second half of her first year. Some children utter their first recognisable word very early, perhaps even as young as nine months; most will have said a word or two at least by the time they're a year and a half or so.

The first word, like your child's first step, isn't an end, but a beginning. By the time your child goes to school she'll have a much firmer grasp of language. Of course she'll make plenty of mistakes, but so long as she still gets plenty of exposure to language, your child's linguistic abilities will continue to grow and develop. However, she is almost totally dependent on you for that exposure to language, and it's been shown over and over again in many research studies that those children whose parents talk to them a lot learn to speak more quickly and develop better language skills than those children whose language skills aren't stimulated very much by their parents. It's a simple supply and demand system; children want to find out about the world, they want to be talked to, they want to relate to you and the world. The more you talk to them about everything with which they come into contact, the more they'll learn; and the more your child learns, the more mature will his brain and nervous system become. Stimulation is the key word in this context; the more your child is stimulated, the more quickly will he develop.

## Play and potties

*Play* is also a very important part indeed of your child's development. In fact it's the way he learns about the world. Several different types of play have been identified, and they roughly correspond to the divisions in development we've looked at. There's *physical play*, which includes the kicking and grasping your baby does in the early months and continues into the running, jumping and climbing she'll do as she gets older;

perhaps even into adulthood, for what else is sport or dancing, for example, than play for grown-ups? *Hand play* is what it says, and includes all the fine things your child does with her hands, from shaking her rattle in her cot to drawing and painting when she's older. *Social play* is something which comes later, too, and as its name implies, it involves playing with other children (or adults) in more elaborate games. *Role playing* is another type of play in which your child will pretend she's mummy going to the shops, or daddy going to work; it's an important way for older children to learn about the world around them – and particularly the people in it – by imitating what they see in their lives. I would add to these categories a fifth one which doctors and child development experts rarely include, but which most parents hear in their children day in and day out: *language play*. Children love nursery rhymes and name games, playing with words and singing songs. Children play with language all the time, and it's an essential part of the development of their language skills.

Of course, as with the different areas of development, these separate categories of play all overlap considerably once your child has gone beyond the baby stage. Physical play continues throughout childhood, and is the basis of the healthy adult exercise which we all need. Role playing games seem to reach a peak in the three to five age range, when children are really beginning to find out about the world around them by 'acting it out'. Social play can last right through childhood, although it may take some time to get established, with most children not really wanting to play with another child until they're around three or so, although many toddlers are quite happy to play alongside another child or in a group of children. Social play will teach your child important skills and lessons, like how to get along with others, how to co-operate with them and, hopefully, how to handle disagreements. Language play is something which can last right through childhood too, and into adulthood. Children of all ages love to sing songs, chant rhymes, play with words – and what else are writing and literature, poetry and song, perhaps even humour and jokes than forms of playing with words and language?

The story of your child's development is one of continual growth towards more and more independence in every area of life. It therefore includes much more than the simple facts of learning to walk and talk. It's also important to remember that your child develops within the structure of a family, something

## YOUR CHILD'S DEVELOPMENT

which isn't rigid but which develops as the people within it develop and change. Indeed, you'll find that, to a large extent, family life will be shaped and determined by the needs and demands of your child. At each stage those needs and demands will change and become wider ranging and more complex, and the way you organise your lives will have to change accordingly.

In the early weeks, life revolves around the feeding, changing and sleeping habits of your baby. But life won't really get any easier once that baby becomes mobile; she'll now be under your feet all the time, and she'll probably get into all sorts of places where she shouldn't. You might have to feed and dress your tiny baby half a dozen times or more a day; but a tiny baby doesn't pull everything out of the cupboards or try to poke her fingers in the electric sockets as a crawling baby or toddler might.

However you look at it, much of your life will centre on putting food in one end of your child and cleaning up what comes out of the other end. You'll probably start to wean your baby from the breast or bottle at around the age of four months (at least that's when most doctors recommend you should leave it until) and on to solid foods, although to begin with they're more mushy than solid, because she hasn't got any teeth yet; they'll probably start to appear around the age of six months, although there's a great deal of variation in this. Your child will probably have a complete set of *milk teeth*, as they're called, by the time she's two and a half or three. During that period your child will become an ever more apparent (and sometimes disruptive) presence at mealtimes. At first she'll probably be in a highchair and have to be spoonfed; in most families this ends up being done by the mother more often than not, who will have prepared the food (and who will also probably have to eat hers cold). Later on your child will graduate to sitting at the table and feeding herself, but she's still likely to need help for a fair while to come. Even some five and six year olds still need to have the more difficult parts of their meals cut up for them!

*Toilet training* is something few of us think about when we contemplate starting a family, but it's a subject which soon crops up once you've actually got a child. There has been something of a revolution in the world of nappies in recent years, and it's certainly gone a long way to making life a little easier for parents. When Emma was born, Sally and I – like most other people – used terry towelling nappies which had to be folded and pinned on, and then washed out afterwards. I remember spending a lot of time rinsing them out in the sink, something you had to do before you could put them in the washing machine, and although it may have been good for my soul, it certainly wasn't the most pleasant of experiences. Terry nappies were also quite hard to put on a baby who's more mobile and who spends a lot of time trying to roll over and wriggle away while you try to avoid impaling her with the safety pin.

These days, however, you can use all-in-one disposable nappies, which many parents have switched to and found to be a great boon. They're generally easy to put on your baby; usually all you have to do is to wrap them round and do them up with the sticky tapes which are attached to the nappy. They cut out all the washing you have to do with terry nappies, and although it might seem that they're quite expensive to buy – you might have to use half a dozen or more a day – you're not using so much electricity with all that washing. Also, the convenience outweighs the cost as far as many parents are concerned.

You still have to do a certain amount of cleaning up, though, whatever sort of nappies you use. Urine isn't a problem for most people, and the bowel movements of small babies aren't really all that offensive. But once your child is eating a wider diet of solid foods, her bowel movements are going to look like yours – and I've not met a parent yet who doesn't sometimes wish that babies were born fully toilet trained from the beginning. Changing the dirty nappy of an 18-month-old toddler can be quite an unpleasant experience, although like most things, you do get used to it. Most children achieve daytime dryness before they manage to go through the night without a nappy; it's a question of developing bowel and bladder control, something which simply won't happen until your child's nervous system is ready to do it. Some children are out of daytime nappies in the latter part of their second year, although if you're to avoid disappointment you'd be wise to think more in terms of achieving full toilet training by the time your child is in her fourth year. Control of the bowels often comes before bladder control, simply because it's more likely that your child will know when something as dramatic as a bowel movement is on its way. But remember that although most children are fully toilet trained by the time they're five and starting school, 'accidents', delays and minor setbacks are so common that they're completely normal.

# 15 Family life

Weaning, learning to walk, the first night without a nappy on... these will be important landmarks in family life for you and your partner as well as for your child. They're the outward signs of a new human being in the full flight of growth. As part of this growth you'll soon notice that your child has a real personality; she'll become part of your family, an influence on what you do and think, a real person in her own right.

In fact it's now known that our children inherit more from us than was ever previously thought before. It's probable that they even inherit a certain amount of their character and personalities from us. After all, if the unique combination of genes we give them determines their basic physical make-up, why shouldn't the same genes contribute to their emotional and psychological profiles? A human being is one indivisible whole whose emotions and body are interdependent and influence each other all the time. It's likely, therefore, that your child will have been born with a certain 'character tendency'. I don't want to go into the nature versus nurture debate here, but I would like to stress that I don't believe that just because we're born with certain personality tendencies, that's the way we stay. It's very clear that you and your partner are an enormous influence on your child's character. If you help him to have positive and stimulating experiences, then you'll help him to develop in a positive way towards fulfilling his potential. If, on the other hand, your child's experiences are negative and unstimulating, they may well have the opposite effect on him.

You will undoubtedly discover very early on a lot about the character and personality of your child. Each of my three children has been very different right from the beginning; Emma was restless, reluctant to be cuddled for too long, in need of constant stimulation; Helen was deeper, more cuddly, more of an observer; and Thomas seems to be more like Emma, although even more active and very, very outgoing.

Something which will also become apparent to you very soon is that your child has a will of her own. In short, you'll discover that just like every other human being there has ever been or there ever will be, your child will sometimes want the things she can't have. For example, when she's a baby, she'll want to grab that enticing object which she isn't supposed to (like an electric cable or a cup of hot coffee), and may scream in frustration when the object is removed from her and placed securely out of harm's way. Later on, your child may be one of the many who throws tantrums when she is denied what she wants; and a tantrum is certainly something to be seen. Some children fling themselves down (wherever they might be, such as in the street or in a shop), most tantrum throwers scream and howl, and some even hold their breath until they're almost blue. The peak age for tantrums seems to come in the third year, a period affectionately known by many parents as 'the terrible twos'.

What we're talking about here, of course, is the contentious subject of *bad behaviour*. All children misbehave at some time. Some are born to misbehave; some achieve misbehaviour; while others have misbehaviour thrust upon them. It's true that some children do actually seem to be born with a tendency to disruptive behaviour of all sorts. Interestingly enough, it's been discovered that in some cases children can have allergies to seemingly innocuous substances (such as dairy products or certain food additives). Part of the reaction to these substances is often extremely bad behaviour and a tendency to sleep very little, among other things. Children like this are said to be *hyperactive*, and it's important to realise that they're not really at fault. If you make sure they're not exposed to the substances which cause the problem, their disruptive behaviour ceases. Medical tests are needed to find out if a child is hyperactive, though.

At the other extreme, it's important to bear in mind that much of what we think of as bad behaviour isn't wilfully bad at all. A toddler may appear to be 'naughty' in knocking over his cup of juice just after you've told him to be careful, but in reality he may well have been reaching out to steady the cup in obedience to your instructions – it was his lack of manipulative skill and natural eagerness which may have caused the problem. It's therefore a good idea to have some knowledge of just what your child is capable of before you start accusing him of being naughty.

Nevertheless, there's a vast grey area between the toddler who knocks over his cup accidentally and the hyperactive child. In that area there are many problems, many rows between parent and child, many battles of will. There is no doubt about it; as your child grows older there will be times when he will want to impose his will on you and your partner, times when he will deliberately knock over that cup just to get at you or be disobedient. In discussing this, we're really looking at something which is close to the heart of family life: the strange love-hate relationship you and your child will develop with each other. Of course you love each other, of course there are plenty of good times. Of course you are vital to your child's development and security; but at the same time, your child will see in you the first people against whom he can assert his own will and independence, and at times there may be real passion in your disagreements with that tiny being.

Problems over bad behaviour with the under fives often centre on major areas of day to day life. *Food faddiness* and a refusal to eat is a common problem, just as a reluctance in some children to go to bed and stay there is for many families. In fact, many parents would say that having a child (or children) is synonymous with giving up all hope for many years to come of getting a full night's sleep. Your child will probably start sleeping through the night at some time during his first year; many children start to sleep better and give up nighttime feeds once they're on solids. However, most babies and toddlers continue to wake occasionally during the night, or – and some parents find this much worse – very early in the morning. You'll find that even a three or four year old will wake up in the night from time to time, perhaps because of an illness (like a cough or a cold) or a nightmare. You will have to calm that child, and that means broken sleep for you. Some unfortunate parents discover that their beloved child may not want to sleep at all. Sally's middle sister is reputed to have been a 'screamer' who hardly slept at all for years, and I've heard other people say much the same about their children.

Taking Emma into our bed worked in our case. In fact, so effective was it in giving us a better night's sleep that we gave in to bedsharing with Helen almost immediately. The result is that she's still getting into our bed at night, although Emma doesn't any more (at least, she only pops in for the occasional cuddle). Having a bedfull of small, warm and cuddly children can be very pleasant; but there have been nights when Helen's fiddling with my ear or Emma's foot in an eye has all proved too much for either Sally or me and we've ended up sleeping elsewhere in the house. Be warned: once you succumb and let your children into your bed, you're going to find it very hard indeed to get them out. Obviously, a lack of sleep is an enormous problem, and one which can seriously affect both your life and your enjoyment of parenthood. The problem, again, is that it's very easy to get into a vicious circle. One couple I know found that their toddler wasn't sleeping at night, and tried to handle it calmly. 'But after a while it got to be such a big thing for us, with James coming into our bedroom every night, that we began to lose our tempers,' said the father. 'It got so that we'd spend half the night shouting at him and taking him back to his bed. It didn't work of course – it only made him upset and spoiled everyone's night.'

That sort of vicious circle can happen over any problem between you and your child. The point is that you play an enormous role in your child's life; any tension in you will be picked up by him, and make him tense and anxious. That's going to make him do exactly the things you don't want him to. And don't forget that because you're important to your child, he'll want your constant attention, and if he can't get the positive attention that he wants, there will be times when he's quite happy to put up with *any* attention, even if it's a telling off.

## A mother's work . . .

Of course, it's likely that the person who bears the brunt of all this is going to be your partner. You're probably going to be at work and out of the house for most of the day; your partner is the one who's going to do most of the nose cleaning, bottom wiping and telling off. She's probably the one who's going to handle your child's toilet training, cook his meals and serve them up to him, and, more often than not, she's probably the one who'll get up to him in the night. Without necessarily meaning to, your partner may well assume the role of primary parent, with you in a secondary role. All the forces of your conditioning and the pressures of society will push you in that direction, and even if you're a father who wants to share these burdens with your partner, you're going to find it very difficult to reconcile that sharing with earning a living.

Your partner may be finding it difficult to reconcile all the things she has to do, too. The fact is that most mothers at home with small children have a very tough job on their hands, and one which is made more difficult by their conditioning and society's attitudes. She may well feel for instance, that she's got to be some sort of Superwife/Supermum; she might expect herself to keep the house spotless, your clothes washed, pressed and ironed, the baby clean and well looked after. An added problem is that the emphasis these days in all the baby books, in magazines and in television documentaries, is on how important it is to *stimulate* your child. Your partner will be told constantly that she should be talking to her child and playing with him, and that if she doesn't, she won't be giving him the start in life he deserves. Let's not forget that part of her conditioning will also be telling her that she ought to be sympathetic and welcoming to you when you get home from a hard day's bringing in the bacon, if not positively seductive, 'to hold on to her man'.

In short, many mothers are faced with a task that no one on earth could do to the standards which seem to be expected – and they *are* still expected. You've only got to listen to a group of mothers (and fathers too) talking to hear some very old-fashioned comments about unironed shirts or untidy houses. But family life with small children can be very difficult, and it's only to be expected that there will be time when your partner won't be able to get the shopping done, or will lose her temper with your child even though he doesn't really deserve it. She'll feel terribly guilty about it too, sometimes, and feel that she's failing. 'It was terrible to realise that I wasn't doing anything properly,' one mother told me. 'I was failing as a mother, as a wife and as a housewife. It all just seemed impossible.' It appears, sometimes, that young mums often have an almost impossible burden to bear; as a society we seem to be saying to them that they've got to hold family life together *and* nurture the next generation.

## Absent fathers

'The worst thing about it is that John can come home and just ignore all the bad side of it,' one woman told me. 'He can come through the door and spend all his time playing with the kids. Sometimes he hardly seems aware that I've spent the whole day dealing with their tantrums and bad behaviour.'

The fact that fathers are likely to come home and have a carefree time just playing with the children can seem pretty unfair to many mothers, especially when they've had a hard day. But that's something which mothers often find hard to admit, too; it seems just as unfair to expect a husband to spend all his time with his children changing nappies and doing practical things. He might seem to have all the fun and none of the responsibility, but in reality he does just as badly out of the deal as his partner.

There is evidence, however, to show that a father's involvement in the lives of his children is very important indeed. As I've said, the research which has been done on the effects of fathers on their children has tended to concentrate on extreme cases. Nevertheless, the results are fascinating. It's been found, for example, that children whose fathers are absent tend in the short term to have more behaviour problems than normal. That is, they behave more badly than normal, they have more tantrums, fears, and other related problems. In the longer term it was found that these children generally had greater problems in adjusting to the people and institutions around them. That tended to mean poor performance in school and antisocial behaviour outside it. In the very long term – that is, in a child's life as a whole – it's been found that the sons of absent fathers tend to have a poorer sense of their own identity and place in society; while daughters of absent fathers tend to have problems in estabishing relationships with men.

The short-term problems of bad behaviour are fairly easy to interpret, especially when they occur in young children. If a father is absent, it's often because there's a problem, such as the break-up of a marriage, in which case there will be plenty of tension around in the family anyway. Even if the absence is the result of something like a job taking a father away for a long period of time, it's still understandable; young children find it hard to cope with people from their close family circle being absent for long periods. Although it might be explained to them as sensitively as possible that daddy hasn't left on purpose, if he doesn't come back soon – or communicate often enough – it can still seem to the child as if he's been deserted. On a much smaller scale, I sometimes find it hard to get it across to my kids that I *have* to go to work every day, that really I'd rather spend my time with them, and that there's nothing I can do about it (for the moment). They would simply prefer me to be with them, and don't really understand why I can't be; which goes some way to explain the odd episode of bad behaviour when I leave the house in the mornings. Helen, in fact, has recently informed me that I'm allowed to go to work only twice more before I dedicate myself entirely to her.

The longer-term problems are slightly harder to explain. They seem to boil down to the fact that having a father in a family teaches the children some essential lessons. For boys, it teaches them what it means to be a man, what men do in society, how they should act with women and so on; it helps them to find out all about their masculinity. At the same time, the way a father relates to a boy's mother – and to his sisters – teaches him about that most important subject, relationships between the sexes. The theory has been put forward that sons of absent fathers swing towards rebelliousness, aggression, anti-social behaviour and so on as a conscious reaction to being brought up in a feminine world. It's as if not having a father around at home makes a boy pick out the most obvious aspects of 'traditional' masculinity and take them to an extreme simply to prove to himself as much as to society that he is truly male. Girls, on the other hand, have a model on which they can base their behaviour as women and their female sexual identity; they still have their mothers. But they have no one to learn about men from. In extreme cases, daughters of absent fathers sometimes go from one sexual partner to another in search of a 'father figure', while many such daughters do have problems in relating to men.

There's a fascinating footnote to this sort of research. It was discovered in various studies that those men who were the sons of absent fathers were more likely to suffer from symptoms of anxiety during their partners' pregnancies. That is, you're more likely to have the couvade syndrome if your father was absent during your childhood. In fact, it seems that the longer the father's absence, the greater the problems the sons are likely to have when they become fathers themselves. You don't really have to be a genius to see why. If you haven't really been the recipient of any fathering while you're a child, you have nothing on which to base your behaviour as a father. It's hard, and therefore very worrying, to try and do something which you haven't seen done at close quarters before.

What seems to happen is that when fathers are absent, there's a real lack of *maleness* in a boy's life. Sons of absent fathers are brought up by their mothers, usually, as I was after my parents separated and divorced. Boys like me therefore tend to get a more female-centred view of life and the world. That explains why sons of absent fathers also tend to have a more female-oriented psychological profile. It's been shown that girls, for example, are usually better at verbal tests, while boys are stronger in science and maths. But boys like me who didn't have a father around for most of their childhood swing more towards the verbal and away from the scientific and mathematical.

I'm not just talking about extreme cases, either. The fact is that absence is an integral part of fatherhood in modern society. Fathers are absent from their children from early in the morning until late at night, and when we're around we're secondary, inferior parents because of our conditioning and our lack of practice. So you could say that most children are already suffering from 'paternal deprivation' to one degree or another. The results of that are all around to see; for families with young children, problems with bad behaviour are very common. At *Parents* our postbag is continually full with letters from young mums who need help and advice in dealing with the sort of problems I've outlined here, and although I wouldn't be so rash as to say that they're caused solely by the absence of fathers from most children's daily lives, it seems obvious to me that it must be a contributory factor. Bringing up young children is a very tough job indeed, and at the moment it's being foisted almost entirely on mothers. At the same time, this book is evidence of a growing dissatisfaction with the old division in parenthood, the growth of a new fatherhood. Obviously the rise of the women's movement has been a major influence. But is it too much to say that the current generation of fathers are the sons of dads who may have dedicated themselves more wholeheartedly to the work ethic and traditional masculinity than previous generations? I don't think it is. I know that my father – and the fathers of many of the men I know now – worked very hard during the 1950s and 1960s, and to a certain extent put his career before his family. At the time, I think that many young men who had fought in the second world war felt that they wanted to strive for something different and better. In many ways, their vision was a materialistic one, and the result was that many fathers strove to get on in their jobs, either simply to make more money, or to climb up the ladder towards 'executive stardom'. I'd need another book to explain all this properly. The fact is that my father's generation was, in a sense, a generation of fathers who were almost completely absent from the daily lives of their children. We are the sons of those men – and we want something very different from life and parenthood.

## Boys will be boys?

There has been a growing interest too in recent years in the study of how we transmit ideas about sex roles and stereotypes to our children. It's been discovered that much of the way this is done is completely unconscious and, what's more, begins almost at birth. It's been found that parents are instinctively gentler with girl babies, and treat boy babies more boisterously. Girl babies are also touched and handled more than boys, as well as kissed and cuddled more often. The differences are compounded as your children get older. Girl toddlers and pre-schoolers still get more physical cuddling and affection than boys, who tend to get plenty of rough stuff and boisterous play – particularly from dad. At the same time, girls are discouraged from getting dirty or being noisy, and often from being assertive or adventurous, which are just the qualities we tend to foster in boys. We also encourage boys to be competitive and 'brave' in not showing their feelings.

There are also some fascinating differences in child development between boys and girls which reveal much about the way we bring up our children. For example, in general, girls learn to talk a little more quickly than boys. This could be the result of the fact that girls are usually *talked to* by their parents rather more than boys, right from babyhood. It's on such differences in treatment that 'the great divide' is built. Girls also tend to get extra kissing and cuddling from their parents, and therefore have a greater chance of developing the communication and verbal skills which will help them in their emotional life and as parents themselves later on.

Boys, however, often begin to outstrip girls of a similar age in terms of physical achievements in later childhood. In simple terms, boys are encouraged to run, jump, climb and throw balls, while any girls who does such things to an appreciable extent is likely to be branded a tomboy. The result is that most boys end up having an edge on most girls in such pursuits. The differences go deeper, though. It seems as if boys are subtly pushed more towards the objective, physical world of things and actions, while girls are pushed more towards their inner selves and the world of feelings. How else can we explain the fact that by the time children reach the level of secondary education, girls' ability in and application to science subjects tends to fall off, while fewer boys than girls are interested in arts subjects?

Of course, this is a huge subject, and one which I can't tackle here with any hope of doing it justice. I'm sure, too, that there are some basic differences between boys and girls on which such different results are, ultimately, based. But there can be no denying that our society puts enormous pressure on our children to go in these directions, and that the pressure is very subtle indeed.

It's interesting to see it in action in another perceived difference between boys and girls. Since we've had a little boy, it's been amazing to see how often people put down some aspect of his behaviour to 'natural male aggression', and even more amazing to realise that they condone it. If, for example, young Thomas crawls over to another child's toys and wrecks them, or tears a magazine to shreds with his two teeth, everyone goes, 'Aaah . . . just like a boy', and leaves it at that. I've seen a similar reaction to bad behaviour many, many times. When a girl misbehaves, she's likely to be told off, and also informed that 'young ladies don't do that sort of thing'. But when a boy shows aggression or is disobedient, destructive, unpleasant or otherwise antisocial, he'll probably get away with it. I've even met parents who admit that they want their sons to be 'tough', to be real 'men' who can stand up for themselves in a tough world. Parents of even quite small children seem to accept that they're going to have to put up with lots of disruption to enable their sons to develop into the sort of men who are happy in the competitive, thrusting world of business, or charging out of the trenches at the enemy. I'll admit that we've found Thomas to be naturally more active than either of his two older sisters, although they were no slowcoaches. But I fail to see why he should get away with bad behaviour just because he's a boy.

One last difference between boys and girls which I think is particularly revealing is in the area of toilet training. Boys in general are said to be slower to achieve full toilet training. I don't think that it's too much to suggest that this is often because mothers – and they're the ones on whom the toilet training burden usually falls – start to train girls sooner than boys. Part of this is to do with the unspoken, perhaps even unconscious assumption that girls should be 'clean' and in control of their bodies more quickly than boys, and that in some ways it's all right for boys not to be too good too soon at this sort of thing. But it's also got a lot to do with the fact that mothers have to train their sons because fathers often aren't around that much, which means that mothers are entering into unknown territory for them. Boys and girls are different in these matters; girls always sit down, but we boys can sit *or* stand. It seems to me that a son's toilet training is something which cries out for the guidance of a father, and that's something many sons don't get, or at least, they don't get enough of. The result is that mothers have to do their best – and sons are slower to be trained. I would even venture to say that for many boys, to be trained in this most delicate of matters exclusively by a mother is one of the ways in which we learn to become outsiders.

The result is that soon even the most progressive parents' children tend to conform to the masculine and feminine stereotypes. That's because the pressures to conform to those patterns are all around us; they're so pervasive we don't even notice them. Don't forget that they're built on a basis of behaviour which is so ingrained that it's hard to catch yourself doing it. Is that such a bad thing? To a certain extent, I believe it is. The great divide starts at the point where girl and boy babies start to be treated differently. It's the fact that we don't kiss our baby sons and cuddle them as much as their sisters that leads eventually to the sort of sexual problems I've been talking about. It's the continual lack of emphasis on warm, positive, physical affection in our sons that helps to turn them into the penis-centred men I've talked about, and therefore helps to cut them off from whole areas of human kindness and physical affection. It's the fact that we tell our sons that 'big boys don't cry' which helps to turn them into men who find it very difficult to express their emotions or talk about the way they feel with the women in their lives, or even with each other. That means most men go through life lacking the sort of emotional support and contact women find in their relationships with other women. As one woman said to me recently, 'After many years I've come to the conclusion that if I want real friendship, real support from another human being, then I can only get it from a woman, and never from a man – not even my husband.' Many women feel much the same, and it's a reflection of just how divided men are from women. And don't forget that the conditioning helps to perpetuate the passivity and dependence we think of as being naturally 'feminine' traits. Subtly, unconsciously, we steer our daughters away from the assertiveness and independence with which they're born and towards their opposites.

I say that girls are born with those qualities because it seems obvious to me that they are, just as boys are born with the need to express their emotions and to receive physical affection. Girls have wills of their own, and boys need to be cuddled. There has been some fascinating research, too, which indicates that there are very few differences between boys and girls when it comes to the 'instinctive' parts of being a parent. For example, parents generally talk to their babies in a way which is slightly different from normal speech; it's rhythmical, repetitive, sing-song. In various experiments it's been shown that this way of talking to a baby is common to both mothers and fathers; that is, fathers instinctively act in a way which has traditionally been thought of as 'maternal'. And yet, in her books, childcare 'expert' Penelope Leach describes this way of talking as 'motherese'! And it seems that fathers don't learn to talk in this way by observing their partners. Young childless men act in the same way when they're given a baby to look after, just as they hold the baby in exactly the same way as young, childless women do when faced with the same task. In short, it seems to me – as I've already said – that apart from the physical facts of pregnancy, birth and breastfeeding, there aren't really many differences between mothers and fathers in terms of their abilities to care for their children.

# 16 The caring, sharing father

So what exactly is it that fathers can give to their children? The evidence, scanty as it is, shows that men have a very positive contribution to make. One part of it is the other side of the coin of father absence; fathers who are around can give their sons a model of masculine behaviour and therefore help them to develop a sense of their identity as males. That in turn should help sons to gain a better sense of adjustment. Fathers can also give their daughters a model of male behaviour which will help them learn how to get along with the opposite sex in later life. And watching their parents in action together and relating to each other will help your children to learn about how the sexes get on – or don't, for that matter.

But it's also been found that the children of fathers who are involved in their families, who are warm and caring and share much of the basic, practical, day-to-day work in bringing up a family, are likely – among other things – to mature more quickly and may even do better at school. Children of fathers like this seem to have a much more positive view of themselves and the outside world; they appear to be better adjusted, both in personal and social terms. The benefits of involved fathering also become apparent at a very early age, and they seem to be related to the simple fact that to a baby, a father is very different to the other main person in his world, his mother.

The bond between a mother and her child is often a very strong one. I know that so far in this book I've tended to play it down, but I've been close enough to three children and their mother to know that the mother-child relationship can be a very intense and rewarding one. That's no surprise; it's difficult to see how else it could be given the facts of pregnancy, birth and breastfeeding. What I've been saying so far is that there's no reason for fathers to be as excluded from that relationship as society and our conditioning tends to make us. But let's look at it another way. Imagine the mother-child relationship as a charmed, magic circle containing two people; it's beautiful, but the world is outside that circle and the child has to get out into it eventually. What your child needs is a welcoming, loving presence inside that circle to lead him out of it – not away from the mother, but with her.

Think of a mother breastfeeding her child: it's an intense experience of infinite fulfilment and love for your child. But your partner can hand him to you after the feed for a cuddle. If he's still awake, the very fact that you're cuddling helps him to learn that there are other people in the world who can be nice to him, and I can't think of a more important lesson. Think about when your child is older: the classic image of learning to walk is of the child leaving his mother's arms to toddle across a short space to his *father*. In a sense, mother is where he starts out, and father is the direction in which he's going.

Of course, much of this is intimately linked to the sort of conditioning that I've been castigating throughout this book. Mothers do the basic childcare, fathers play with their children; mothers therefore do the ordinary things, fathers the more adventurous. I would like to see a society which was arranged so that mothers could play more with their children, while fathers could do more of the basic childcare; if that was so, then fathers would find it easier to be involved with their children on a deeper level, and mothers would enjoy motherhood more. It seems to me that there is sense in the idea that a father can be a sort of stepping stone to the outside world for his child, particularly in the early years when so much of a mother's time and energy are taken up in the physical tasks of parenthood. In many ways, this is a father's unique contribution to his children. And it's been shown that the babies of involved fathers find it easier to deal with new situations and strange faces than children whose fathers aren't so involved. It's on that basis of positive feeling about the world that the children of sharing, caring fathers can build.

It isn't that easy, though. I'll be looking at the main obstacle to spending time with your children – work – in the next chapter. But there's something else that makes relating to your children difficult for most men, and that's the conditioning which I come back to again and again. Children are *total* beings; they demand a total response from the people around them. You can't fob a three year old off with the sort of polite converstaion that keeps other adults out of your emotional backyard. Your child wants to know how you feel, he wants to know everything about you; he wants you to know how he feels, too. And remember that he's a very sensitive creature, too; he'll pick up even the finest nuance of feeling in your household and make it part of his very being.

What all this means for many of us is that we can't respond to our children in the way they would like us to. This emotional block builds a barrier between us, and our children instinctively turn to the person who can give them what they want — their mothers, who, after all, have the conditioning to enable them to deal with the emotional life. 'It came home to me very hard one day,' a father told me, 'when Lucy fell over in the garden. I was standing right next to her, and tried to comfort her — she was very upset. But she just pulled away from me and ran the length of the garden to her mother for the only comfort she wanted. I felt like a complete fool; worse, I felt totally useless.' Such an experience is a common one for many fathers; because we're not around much, because we're often not very good at dealing with the emotional side of life, our children grow up not expecting to find that sort of comfort on our side of the great divide. It can be terribly wounding to get up to your child in the middle of the night when she's upset and crying, only to find that she cries even more loudly until her mother gets up and comforts her. It's tempting to lash out and shout at a child who treats you in such a way, or to escape, to retreat into a don't care attitude which tells your child that if he doesn't want your love and comfort, you're not going to give it to him anyway. Of course, that will only make it worse. Don't forget, too, that the habit of running to mother first always puts an enormous strain on your partner; it means that she is forever your child's first line of comfort, and that can last for years. How many grown-up children go to their fathers to pour their hearts out or get advice? Even if they need a loan they're likely more often than not to go to mum first, and get her to communicate with dad.

## Working at fatherhood

There's a very simple answer to this problem. Fathers who make the effort to respond to their children often find that it becomes progressively easier. I know that in my experience, it's been marvellous to feel that a real relationship has grown between each of my children and me, and those relationships have been built on a base of physical affection and openness about our feelings. I've alway gone out of my way to tell my kids that I love them, that I think they're great, or that I think they're not so great when they misbehave. Equally, I've been pleased to see that they've been able to talk to me about how they feel. When Emma or Helen fall over in the garden, they run to Sally *or* me, depending on who's nearest. I feel involved, I feel valuable, I feel as if I'm a full part of family life and that I'm making a contribution to my children. For a very few partners that feeling comes naturally. But for most of us it has to be worked for. I've known fathers who have felt that their children have actually helped them to come alive in an emotional sense. 'Samantha's response to me was so total that I felt I couldn't hold back from her,' one father told me. 'She helped me to understand that I had to respond to her, that I had to open up, unwind, and not be afraid of being "unmasculine". It was a liberation.'

Having children can therefore be, for a father, a deeply rewarding experience in a very direct way. This is something that many fathers have come to realise. The busy father who takes no notice of his children, and who then changes into a father who sees the magic of childhood is a stock figure in children's literature. We are, of course, talking about Mr Banks and Mary Poppins again. Mr Banks, the father who didn't have time for his children, realised at the end of his story that he was missing out on a vast area of human life which he could have been enjoying. Spending time with your children plugs you into much of the best in human experience; children have a simplicity and directness which can be a revelation. They can be refreshing in their direct response to the people and things around them. Best of all, they can teach you that there is value in even the small, apparently trivial things in life, like fun and games, and finding out about interesting things; simply being together because you like each other's company is something that many fathers experience for the first time with their children. You don't have to compete with them, and there's no sexual element with all its problems as there is with adults of the opposite sex. Your children love you because you are *you* – their father.

But Mr Banks also realised something else; he saw that he could get none of this out of life unless he spent more time with his children. Now I have written many features in *Parents* about the problems of reconciling involved fatherhood with the demands of a full-time job. I've often said in those features that it's not so much the *quantity* of the time that you spend with your child that matters, as the *quality* of the time. In many ways that's true. Your child would far rather spend half an hour with you playing a game or reading books than hours with you mending the car or doing some jobs around the house. But your child needs time with you, time in which you can give him your full attention. Nothing else really satisfies a child, and that can mean a hard choice for you. In essence, your child wants both quantity *and* quality in terms of the time you spend with him – and you're probably going to find that's impossible. You can't pack much quality into 38 seconds, just as it's going to be difficult for many fathers to get away from their jobs long enough to make things easier.

That's why it's easy to end up like J. R. Ackerley's father and be a 'weekend father'. In some ways, one answer is to be a little like Father Christmas; if you really don't have that much time to spend with your children, then one way of making sure that your relationship works is to make it fun all the way, and to concentrate on doing positive things with them. But most fathers in this position find that, in the long run, their relationships with their children aren't as deep as they might have hoped. A relationship with 'Father Christmas' may be superficial, more akin to 'cupboard love' than a relationship based on mutual love and respect. It's also easy to fall into the role of a disciplinarian, like J. R. Ackerley's father, for the simple reason that your partner might use you as an external, absent threat when you're not there simply to enable her to gain the upper hand in handling boisterous young children; and that can lead to your becoming an object of fear in your child's eyes. You'll then find yourself cast in a role which you can't escape, a role for which your conditioning may well have prepared you for, too. But it's my belief that you'll earn a way into your child's heart more easily – and more lastingly – if you do things differently.

Remember that touch is a very important part of your relationship with your children, too. You'll get on much better with your kids if you're prepared to give them plenty of warm, affectionate physical contact. Besides, children are marvellously cuddly creatures, and there's nothing like having a friendly three year old to cuddle at the end of the day for making life more pleasant, and for putting all sorts of external things into perspective. Fathers sometimes find it difficult to express their feelings by touching their children in this way, and often find it particularly hard, for example, to cuddle their sons. Due to our conditioning there's always the ridiculous fear that by being physically affectionate to our sons we're running the risk of turning them into something less than 'masculine'. Yet most of us could do with increasing the amount of physical affection in our lives, especially warm contact of a non-sexual nature, to create a future in which all our sons are unafraid to show their feelings in both physical and non-physical ways – and that future begins in the cuddles you give your baby son now.

But what does it really mean to be an *involved* father? It's a question I've often asked myself in recent years, and I suppose the simplest answer I can give you is that an involved father is one who makes his children a central – if not *the* central – part of his life. I'm talking about remembering that it's your child's sports day without having to be reminded and arranging to take time off (or developing that mysterious cold again) so that you can be there. I'm talking about remembering that your child's packed lunch needs to be prepared for the next day – and doing it. I'm talking about listening to your children from the time they begin to talk to you as toddlers, *really* listening, and establishing good lines of communication with them. To me, this also implies that your partner must form a central part of your life. Being an involved father isn't a cure-all; it won't mean that you never have arguments, or that your children never get on your nerves. It will mean, however, that you won't be an outsider. You'll be an essential part of a team – in fact, you'll be the essential father.

Recently I interviewed John Cleese about his experience of fatherhood. Apart from his 13 year old daughter from a first marriage (to Connie Booth), he now has a young baby (Camilla, aged six months when I met her). John had some very interesting things to say about fathers and children, but one thing struck me above all. He said that he felt it was important to give your whole attention to a child when you were with her. 'Too often,' he said, 'we fathers are pre-occupied when we come home from our jobs, which means we simply can't respond to our children properly. We're thinking about the meeting we're going to be at in the morning, or the bills we've got to pay, rather than on concentrating with a clear mind on what we're doing with our children. They can sense that, and what they want is your total attention and involvement during the time you're with them. And it's very difficult for most men to learn that lesson.'

## Advanced fatherhood

The pressures of family life on both you and your partner are likely to increase, rather than decrease with time. Most couples who have one child go on to have another, and some of the certifiably insane among us go on to have yet another. Having another child may seem a very daunting prospect to you if you've been put off the idea of having one by what I've said so far, but it really isn't that bad.

In fact, most couples find that a second child is actually easier in many ways. To start with, your partner will probably have an easier birth with a second baby; it's almost as if her body – and her womb in particular – is more efficient in pregnancy and labour because it's already had some practice. Your partner may well find that breastfeeding is a lot easier too if she's already done it successfully once. All in all, the experience of having had one baby should stand you in very good stead for your second. You'll also find that having two babies isn't really double the work or double the cost; it means more, of both, of course, but not an enormous amount.

However, if you haven't shared the burden with your partner for the first baby and continue to allow her to do all the work, then things are going to be a lot tougher for her, especially in the early months of broken sleep, nappies and so on.

Fathers have a crucial role to play at such a time. You'll find that life will become a lot more difficult if you don't pull your weight, and as with a first baby – but even more so – your partner will appreciate you very much if you volunteer your services for housework, cooking and whatever else needs to be done. Fathers who have already got into good habits and are sharing family life obviously find it easier to do this.

There's a natural division of labour too when a new baby's on the way. Remember that there are now three of you who need to be prepared for the new baby's arrival, and that while you and your partner have already been through the experience once, it's all new to your first child. She will need a lot of preparation. Up to now she has been your only child, which means that she has had something of a monopoly on your time and attention. She is now facing a period in which she will inevitably feel displaced, however hard you try to include her. Your partner will probably spend some time in hospital (though not as much as she did the first time), and everyone's attention will be focused on the newcomer, for whom presents of all sorts will be bought. Relatives and friends may not take much notice of your older child for a while, and when the new baby comes home with mother, the fun will really begin. Your child will be disrupted just as much as you, with the added problem that your fatigue and irritability may well be directed at her sometimes. That's because children in this position often react by misbehaving; some revert to former stages of development temporarily, which in layman's terms might mean that your clean and dry three year old starts having accidents and wetting the bed, as well as throwing the odd tantrum.

Many, many children ask their parents to 'take the baby back' after a while; many children poke their baby brother or sister in the eye, or give them a loving squeeze which turns into a bone-breaking bear hug. It would be surprising if firstborn children were *not* jealous of their younger brothers and sisters; it is completely normal that they should be. However, you can help to minimise the problem by doing some preparation, by trying to make your child aware that a baby is on the way and that there's going to be a certain amount of disruption. Children can be very reasonable people. If you tell your child what's going to happen, and reassure her that it doesn't mean that you love her any the less, or that you're going to get rid of her (some children have the most peculiar ideas about this sort of thing), then you won't go far wrong. Remember though that it's no good only telling your child once about what's going to happen, right at the beginning of your partner's pregnancy. She'll need to be reminded and reassured regularly – children can have very short memories.

Fathers are uniquely placed to help their older children deal with the arrival of a new baby because, in many ways, they've been in the same situation themselves. Your older child may well feel excluded, left out, rejected and ejected from the charmed, magic circle of the family in which she's been the star up to now. You and your first child may feel like outsiders together, and there's nothing like a common sense of exclusion for bringing people together. Often fathers find they feel closer to their first children during their partner's second pregnancy and in the months after the birth. I know that when Helen was on the way I was very concerned to make sure that Emma didn't feel left out. I spent a lot of time with her before the event, and – although I don't know how I managed it – even more after the birth. In fact I spent so much time making sure that Emma felt involved and not too jealous that I hardly took any notice of Helen at all after the first three or four days. Suddenly I realised, a few months later, that my relationship with my second child was not what it should have been, and I felt that I had to struggle to catch up. This is a common failing in fathers; being so keen to do right by your first child can conceal a fear that you can't cope with the new baby, and end up meaning you don't establish a good relationship with your new child from the beginning.

Just as with many other parts of parenthood, you'll need to perform a difficult balancing act when baby number two comes along. In a way, it's back to the days of the 'You never can win syndrome' which I talked about earlier. You'll need to make sure that you're as involved in this pregnancy as you were (hopefully) in your partner's first, but without making your first child feel as if she's left out of it. The obvious way round it is to make sure that your child is included *with* you, and gets *her* chance to feel the baby in mummy's tummy doing his exercises while you do the same, for example. Indeed, the simple fact that your partner will often probably have to take your older child along to the antenatal clinic with her may help to make her feel more involved anyway.

Obviously you have a very important practical role to play in the early weeks of your new baby's life, which is why it's vital for you to take some time off work. It can be difficult, and some fathers find that it's very hard indeed to persuade employers that they should be at home. If you can be then you'll have plenty to do. 'And it was at that time,' one father told me, 'when I was looking after David, getting to know Clare, the new baby, doing the housework and everything else, that I really began to feel as if I'd passed some sort of test. It was like I was now an "advanced father", capable of tackling anything at all.' This sort of euphoria often doesn't last. I can testify that once you have a second child you can begin to feel sometimes as if you're being pulled in different directions by teams of wild horses. For don't forget that it will probably mean a slightly increased strain on the family budget, which could make you that much more anxious about your job and lead to more overtime; while the demands on your time and energies at home will increase, too. In fact the years in which your children are small and dependent are the toughest years of all, years in which it may seem as if you never have a moment's peace, and during which you'll certainly feel under enormous pressure – and very, very tired.

The writing of this book has coincided with the early months of our third child's life, so I feel well qualified on the subject. It's been a period of intense hard work as we've struggled to accommodate a new child to an already established framework of life. We've tried very hard to give him all the attention he needs and make sure that neither Helen nor Emma feel left out or excluded. It has been very, very hard, and I have to admit that there have been times when both of us have felt low; when we've been unfair to our two daughters in telling them off for things they haven't done or couldn't help; when we've been irritable, or even downright cross with each other; and when Thomas has been left to cry a little longer than he should have been. But I'm unrepentant – we're human, after all.

The point about life with more than one child is that unless you tackle its problems as a *team*, in concert with your partner, neither of you is going to get much out of it. The logic and force of this rule increases with each child you have. It seems to me that a mother-father team is an ideal way of bringing up children, and one which can be very strong. If you and your partner have a good basis of communication, then it should be fairly easy for you to support each other in the day-to-day business of bringing up small children. It's only by being a part of that daily process that you as a father will avoid the problem which one father described to me as 'reporting'. 'Every night when I came home from work Jane went through what the kids had done. It was like listening to school reports about somebody else's children. I know she was trying to involve me, but it just made me feel even more like an outsider.' That father found, in the end, that he wanted to work less and see more of his children, which helped him to feel more a part of family life. If you are involved, if you do have a good relationship with your children, then it's easier to 'pick up the threads' with them when you come home from work or if you have to work extra hard for a period. So staying involved is something which remains important throughout your children's childhood.

Consistency is important, too, and that means working out a joint policy with your partner on the various issues and problems confronting you. Children can be very cunning, and if they see that you disagree with your partner over something they may use that knowledge to try and gain an advantage over you. In

## THE CARING, SHARING FATHER

couples where the father is something of an outsider and uninvolved in the practical side of family life, disagreements between mother and father over things like bedtimes, discipline and so on can be very bitter. Your partner is bound to resent it if you muscle in and start telling her what to do when she's doing all the hard work of bringing up the children. If you want to share the influence over your children, you'll have to share the burdens, too. From our experience it seems that it's usually best to have your disagreements out of sight and sound of the children; they can usually be sorted out when you're both calm, something which is unlikely to be the case when there might be a wailing child between you. Consistency means support, too, so it's vital for parents to present something of a united front to their kids. You don't have to be monolithic, but it certainly helps if your children realise that both of you mean business, and that you can't be played off against each other.

There's a spin-off from this sort of approach to shared parenthood, too, and it's a very simple one. If both of you share the tasks of running a home and a family as much as you can, then you'll probably find that it's easier to share other parts of your lives together. Although, as we've seen, children can put an enormous strain on your relationship with your partner, they can also be a bridge between you. Some couples find that as the years go by they talk less to each other, they touch each other less, they have less in common. I've heard many women say with real bitterness that the only time their partners kiss them is when they climb into bed expecting sexual intercourse. Husbands have told me that their partners don't understand them and never talk to them. This is a product of the great divide, the divide which your children can help you to bridge. If you as a father are interested and concerned enough in family life to want to share it with your partner, and if you both communicate, then out of that common interest a stronger bond may grow between you.

It's something I've felt myself, even in these months of high pressure and hard work. The positive side of children is pure magic. Our children are a constant wonder to me in every respect. I'm amazed by their physical beauty, their grace, their humour, the speed at which they grow and develop. I'm dazzled by the spectacle of real human beings developing their unique personalities before my very eyes, and grateful that I should have the chance to be a participant in such an experience. I'm also constantly impressed by the way in which Sally handles the problems and traumas of life with small children; she's a marvellous parent. In short, having children has given me the chance to take part in some of the most rewarding things in human life, and sometimes I feel it's made me a better person for that. I also find it difficult to believe that I would feel as strongly for Sally as I do now if we hadn't had the children, which makes it all worth while, despite the hard times which accompany the good.

And another spin off of shared parenthood is that it might help to break the mould of stereotypes which perpetuates the great divide from generation to generation. But here we're beginning to enter into areas which really belong in the next section.

PART SIX

# BREAKING THE MOULD

The Scandinavians, in their perennial role of harbingers of the future, are pinning their hopes on marriage. The Norwegians, for example, have experimented in work sharing; the husband and wife alternate in the home and work shifts at the same job. Disrupt the pattern, they are saying, and you change the values: the boredom and exhaustion of both domesticity and salaried work are reduced, the family is strengthened. And when the children see as much of their father as of their mother, the conventional sex roles shift, the stereotypes are broken. No more moonlighting at family life, no more isolation within the nuclear family. In time, the system might even bring life back into the neighbourhoods.

from *Life After Marriage* by A. Alvarez

# 17 Parents and work

I have a friend who is something of a high flyer in his chosen profession. He's achieved a lot in a very short space of time, and is now remarkably successful for his age. In career terms he has everything he wants in a job he loves doing, and to a certain extent, he is also enjoying the material fruits of his success. But inevitably he talks to me about frustration and dissatisfaction, and even of failure.

I say 'inevitably' because my friend is also a father, and one who enjoys the experience of parenthood – that is, what little he gets of it – as intensely as he enjoys his job. The dilemma he faces is that, to a large extent, the competing demands of his career and of his family are seemingly almost irreconcilable. To keep up the pace of his success, he has to put in the sort of hours which mean he is a stranger in his own house for most of the week, every week.

'The worst part about it,' he told me, 'is that I feel I'm missing out on irrecoverable parts of my child's life. When my wife calls me to say that my son has just taken his first steps or said his first word, it sours the whole working day for me. I've missed it, I've missed a moment I'll never be able to recapture.' At the same time, he feels that he wants to put a lot into his job. 'I feel depressed if I don't do a piece of work as well as I can, or as well as I should have done, even if no one criticises. But that's the way it is, sometimes, especially if Peter's been up in the night and I've tried to do my bit as the sharing, involved father. In the end it just feels as if I'm failing everybody – my employers, my wife, my son, *and* myself. At the moment I don't think any of us are happy.'

It's a dilemma I know well myself; it's one of the reasons for writing this book. Men have changed; not so very long ago it would have been thought very strange for a successful young man to have made the sort of comments my friend did to me. But society itself hasn't changed sufficiently to make life easier for fathers (and for families) – and so we have a dilemma. Interestingly enough, there's evidence that this dilemma is often more of a problem for middle-class fathers who have read all the right books. They're often the fathers who might be climbing up the career ladder, but who have also gained a veneer of 'liberation' and want to share parenthood more. As my friend discovered, the two don't mix very well. Working-class fathers, it seems, often face fewer problems in this respect. They and their partners may be happy with traditional roles (or not so unhappy, at any rate), or they may simply find that their jobs aren't stimulating enough to compete for interest with family life. Again, many young working-class fathers find that they end up doing a lot of overtime to keep their families going. But it's often easier for a wife to cope with the absence of a father who's demonstrably doing it to make more money for their *needs*, than for a wife whose husband is simply out of the house so much because he's building the career which is important to *him*.

Of course, it's usually all a lot more complicated than that type of black and white example suggests. The choices we make about the relative importance of jobs, relationships and family life are very often dictated by circumstance, and the solutions we find are sometimes very hard to put into operation. But many people *are* trying to break the mould. Some are trying in small ways, such as not working so much overtime; others are trying more radical approaches. In this section I want to look at the issues raised by these changes, and also suggest ways in which you can make your own decisions about this dilemma.

## Working mothers

So far I've had very little to say about families in which the mother goes back to work after the birth, or takes up some form of paid employment while the children are still young. A woman's right to return to work is now enshrined in the law. So long as your partner has worked for her employers for two years, she's entitled to leave her work 11 weeks before her estimated date of confinement (EDC), and return to the same job 29 weeks after the birth. In terms of cash benefits, your partner is also entitled to the *maternity grant* of £25 which can be claimed at any time after the 26th week of pregnancy and up until three months after the baby is born (the claim form is available from your local DHSS office). There is also a *maternity allowance* which your partner can claim once she's given up work. This is paid from 11 weeks before the EDC and 18 weeks after the birth, and at the time of writing stands at £27.25.

Your partner is also entitled to money from her employer (so long as she fulfills the eligibility qualification of having worked for them for a minimum of two years). She is in fact entitled to six weeks' *maternity pay*. This is calculated as 90 per cent of her normal weekly pay, minus the £27.25 maternity allowance. So if she's being paid £100 a week, she'll get £90, minus £27.25 – which leaves £62.75. Make sure that your partner claims at the right time and gets what she's entitled to. Some companies offer a better deal to their female employees, with a shorter qualifying period and better cash benefits. Your partner should check her contract of employment or company house agreement, or check with her union to find out exactly what benefits she can claim. *You* don't get a penny. It used to be that fathers could claim a tax allowance of £100 per child for each of their children; that was removed, and turned into weekly child benefit payable to mothers a few years ago, which currently stands at £6.85 per child, per week.

If your partner wants to return to her job after the birth, she must inform her employer in writing to that effect at least three weeks before she intends to leave work. She'll also have to write to her employer after she's given birth re-affirming her commitment to return to work; this has to be done at least three weeks before the date on which she intends to return to her job. Again, your partner should check with her employer or her union to find out exactly what she's entitled to at her particular job. If you want to know more about it – and there are various exceptions and problem areas – it's worth getting the appropriate leaflets from your local office of the Department of Health and Social Security.

Making the actual decision to go back to work or not is, however, very difficult for most women. Money is often a crucial consideration in any decision for a young family. Some couples decide that they simply can't manage without the woman's wage, even though they'll probably have to pay the extra costs of childcare to enable her to continue working. But for more and more women it's a question of keeping a career going or of wanting to avoid the sort of isolation and pressure sometimes experienced by mothers at home. 'I just didn't want to vegetate at home,' one working mother told me. 'And I felt that if I did give up work then that was exactly what was going to happen.'

On the benefit side, many women do find real advantages in going back to work after the birth. They have their own money, for a start, which usually means that apart from making a much-needed contribution to the family's finances, they can avoid for the most part that feeling of being completely dependent on their partners for money. The stimulation of adult company is also a definite plus for most women. 'I never thought I'd miss talking to people at work as much as I did when I had the baby,' one woman told me. 'But I did, very much, and within only a few months of not being able to do it any more. I was really glad to get back to work.'

Most working mothers face a range of very difficult problems, however. The first – and most pressing – is the need to find satisfactory childcare, something which can give you real headaches. There are several main types of childcare on offer in this country. If you can afford it and you've got the room, you could hire a *live-in nanny*, who is usually a nurse who has had extra training in handling children, which leads to a special qualification. A nanny can take over completely while you and your partner are out at work. Obviously enough, this can be very expensive. Indeed, it's probably beyond the means of most families, although there are various schemes in which you can 'share' a nanny with another family to spread the cost. There are some agencies which specialise in this, and you can find them in your phone book or advertising in certain magazines such as *The Lady*.

If you can't afford a nanny, you'll probably opt for a *childminder*, and these come in two sorts: the registered and the unregistered. All childminders are supposed to come into the first category, and being registered means that they must comply with certain regulations, such as only having a given number of children to look after and meeting certain health and safety standards. Unregistered childminders are to be found everywhere, however, a reflection of the fact that there's no real state policy towards providing childcare for families in which both partners work, or for single parents. Of course, at one end of the scale, an 'unregistered childminder' might be a grandmother, a sister or a friend who looks after children on an *ad hoc* basis; at the other it could be a childminder in unsafe, unhealthy housing with too many children to look after to ensure a reasonable standard of care. Most childminders, however, fall in the registered category.

Other forms of childcare are state or council-run *nurseries* and *crèches*, of which there are a few, and private versions of the same thing, of which there are a few more. Some companies and other organisations have nurseries and crèches for employees' children too, although again, these are fairly thin on the ground. Childminders, nurseries and crèches all usually have to be paid for, too, so even if your partner does go back to work to the same job and salary after the birth of your child, you're still both going to be slightly worse off than you were before without even taking into account all the baby clothes, equipment and so on.

The problems of satisfactory childcare, however, don't begin and end with money. Mothers who want to breastfeed and return to work sometimes face a difficult decision. Indeed, many working mothers give up the battle to keep breastfeeding after a few weeks of hand-expressing breast milk to be given to the baby by bottle. At the same time, they'll be facing the problems of arranging a much more complicated timetable. If you haven't got a live-in nanny, then not only have you got to get yourself ready to go to work in the mornings, you've got to get your child ready too, and then drop her off at the childminder's before work. Then she'll have to be picked up later on, either by your partner or you, depending on how long the childminder is prepared to have her and when your respective working days end. For most working parents, such arrangements can be very difficult and stressful. Childminders change, move, give up childminding; children grow and develop and have different problems and needs at different stages; mothers and fathers find that their jobs change or other circumstances in their lives become different and affect the entire structure of family life.

More difficult to overcome, perhaps, is the problem of other people's attitudes. At the level of society, the lack of nursery provision and childcare facilities for 'working families' is a reflection of the fact that society as a whole still thinks that a woman's place is in the home, even though more and more mothers are returning to the workforce after having children. This attitude is also reflected in the ways in which women find it impossible to escape their role as 'primary parents' even when they do go back to work. I recently heard a story about a working couple who had two children at school. The father worked locally, near the school, while the mother worked in town, a half hour's train journey away, yet when one of the children fell ill at school, it was the mother who was summoned by telephone, *not* the father, although the school had his telephone number too – an all too-clear reflection of society's attitude that no matter how important a woman's job, no matter how inconvenient it might be for her, no matter how willing or able a father is to take his burden, it is the woman who is expected to sacrifice everything for her family, and in particular, for her children.

It's Catch 22. Society's attitudes are often foisted on to employers and working women along these lines: a woman's place should be in the home; if there is ever a conflict between the needs of her home and family and her job, she is bound to opt for the former, and not the latter; therefore a woman is not a 100 per cent reliable employee; therefore she should not be given promotion to positions of higher responsibility. It's part of the old 'don't-employ-a-woman-because-they-only-get-pregnant-and-leave' syndrome. It's a major reason for women losing out in career terms, and has got a lot to do with the fact that even after equal rights legislation, most women in this country still get paid less than men doing comparable jobs – and often quite a lot less, too.

The problem for working mothers is, however, that balancing the demands of work and family life is a very difficult business. For a start, it's a rare woman who can completely overcome her own conditioning and plough on into her career with the single mindedness that men so often demonstrate. When a woman becomes a mother, her child *is* more than likely to become a central part of her life, even when she does go back to work. Her conditioning will be telling her that she's the one who ought to get up in the night to her crying baby; she's the one who ought to sort out all the childcare arrangements and make sure that everything goes smoothly; she's the one who ought to be there at night to read her child a story and tuck her up in bed. Equally, her conditioning will be telling a working mother that it's her duty to make sure that the housework is done, and because it's impossible for the vast majority of women to be such paragons of wifely and maternal perfection, most working mothers end up feeling very guilty indeed. Oddly enough, most working mothers seem to end up feeling guilty towards *everybody*. As one working mother described her situation: 'I just end up feeling like a failure; I fail everybody, my employers, my child, and my husband.'

## Men's attitudes

Unfortunately, many men only make the situation worse by their own personal attitudes to the question of women working. If you're honest with yourself and your partner, you'll probably admit that you're ambivalent – to say the least – about the idea of your partner going back to work after the birth, or when the children are still very young. There are all sorts of assumptions inherent in our conditioning about the different roles of men and women, assumptions which are contradicted by the image of a working mother. Many of us like the idea of having a wife at home all the time, and it wasn't all that long ago that to be able to keep your wife at home on just your wage was something of a status symbol; it meant that you were earning enough to make sure she didn't *have* to go out to work. Don't forget, either, that our conditioning continues to make us assume at a very deep level that our partners *should* be primarily concerned with the children and leave the breadwinning to us. I don't think it's too extreme to suggest that our partners' growing ability to maintain their financial independence for longer stretches of their lives is seen by some men as a threat. If our role as the family's sole breadwinner is under attack, what is left to us? Not much, apparently, except those traditionally *unmasculine* things – the family, our children, our relationships with our partners . . .

It's hardly surprising then that many men find it difficult to cope both with the idea of their partners working and the reality of it. Some men are openly hostile to the prospect, and try to force their partners into staying at home. If they 'lose' the battle, and their partners do return to work, they can become very sulky and petulant indeed. Other men may go along with the idea but use that familiar tactic in all human relationships (it's one we learn as children when trying to avoid doing something our parents want us to do), *active non-cooperation*. 'He just began to be awkward,' one working mother told me. 'From the day that I said that I intended to go back to work, he started to do less and less around the house. He didn't help with any of the practical details; he simply wasn't interested. In the end I felt as if his indifference was tangible; it was like silent waves of hostility coming out of him.'

Of course, in the face of this sort of attitude, many women give up and postpone their return to work. But even when a man is more positive and supportive, there can be problems. Just because a man says he's in favour of his partner working, it doesn't mean to say that he's actually going to do any more around the house or with the children to help out. In fact I know several working women whose husbands do less than many fathers whose partners are at home full time. Their stories have a familiar ring about them. They leave the house before their husbands and return after; but it's the women who prepare the evening meals and put the children to bed. It's also the women who have mornings off to take the children to the clinic, or to go along to talk to teachers on the school open day. Fathers may say that they support the idea of their wives working; they may even like the higher standard of living that a wife's salary helps to sustain, but all too often the support tends to remain solely verbal, and is not translated into the practical.

Surprisingly, these same working wives and mothers often rush to defend their partners. 'It's not that he doesn't want to help more,' one woman said to me, 'it's that he doesn't know how to.' She has a point. Our conditioning ensures that many of us fathers are helpless in the kitchen and useless at housework. Worse, we tend to forget that these things have to be done, and even if we do remember them, we are led out of habit into endless conniving at getting out of doing them. It's the same with childcare; for all the reasons I explored earlier on, men are often uncomfortable with the role of primary parent, even if we only have to fill it for a short period. The result is that many working mothers are faced with an enormous burden. Not only do they have to do their jobs, they also, in a sense, still have to fulfil the roles of housewife and mother. There's another twist, too; the emphasis on the primary role of the mother, the *Madonna syndrome* I talked about earlier on, often operates unconsciously in working mothers to make them try even harder in their mothering. They feel guilty for working, and so they try to catch up as mothers when they're around – a lot like some fathers, in fact. At the same time there's also pressure on them to be Super-housewife, too, and don't forget either that somewhere at the back of your partner's mind is the feeling that she's still got to make sure she's keeping *you* happy by being the seductive mistress and lover you want. But you won't be surprised to hear that sex is often a casualty in the lives of couples in which both partners work. I for one don't see how they can fit it in!

It may have become obvious to you by now that your role as a husband and father is *vital* in making your partner's return to work a success. Even if your partner isn't among the 10 per cent of mothers who take up their maternity leave option, it's still worth bearing in mind that she is likely to return to paid employment eventually, and these days it's almost bound to be sooner rather than later. The days of women giving up work when they got married or had their first baby in exchange for a lifetime of being a housewife and mother are gone forever. Fewer and fewer of the women in my mother's generation, perhaps one of the last generations who could have grown up with that expectation, actually continue to remain at home once their children are older and off their hands. My mother has been working since I was five years old. The period during which you can expect your partner to be out of the world of work is getting shorter and shorter. If you only have two children, quite close together, it could be as short a time as two or three years at the most before your partner begins to think about what she wants to do, or even starts looking for some sort of employment.

It would therefore seem unwise to adopt a negative attitude to the idea of your partner working. Far better to decide jointly what your priorities are, and for you in particular to accept your partner's financial contribution to the family. Above all, it's important not to see it as a threat to your 'masculine role', as some men do. Being totally responsible for suporting a family financially is a pretty tough burden for anyone to bear, just as being completely responsible for the housework and bringing up the children is. If you can both help each other to spread your respective loads a little, you'll go a long way to making both your individual lives and family life a lot easier in almost every department. It's the same message I've been preaching throughout this book: sharing will help you to avoid or overcome most of the problems. For the partner of a working mother that means volunteering your help in every area of family life and, ideally, more than just help; it means making a real effort to split the burden down the middle. If you're both working, then it seems only fair that you should both share some of the other tasks involved in family life. How you arrange it is up to you, but it seems to me completely unfair for a father not to do any cooking or housework or childcare if his partner is working equal or longer hours.

It really is a question of attitude, and part of the problem is that many men still don't take their partners' jobs or earning abilities seriously. A wife's earnings are often seen as 'pin money', money for luxuries, and her job as dispensable, even where a family is almost dependent on the mother's wage to maintain a certain standard of living. That's an attitude which is sometimes translated into a reluctance to shoulder the yoke of housework, cooking and childcare with equal commitment.

It's particularly important for fathers to take their share of childcare and especially to ask their employers for time off if it's at all necessary. Again, I don't see why this is something that shouldn't be shared between two working partners. At the moment, because of the strength of traditional ideas, employers tend to look askance if a man asks for time off to take his child to the clinic or to visit his child's school. The unspoken assumption – and it's still often spoken – is that it's a wife's job to do that sort of thing. And although some employers might see the logic in a father sharing such duties equally with a working wife, many would still feel uncomfortable in admitting that the logic is correct. That's why it's so important for you to do it. After all, such occasions don't happen every day in most families; we're talking about odd days, odd mornings here and there. But until it's an accepted thing for fathers to do, working mothers are still going to suffer a double bind.

One other important point in this context is that many men are actually a little frightened of housework. It might seem strange to say so, but many of the fathers I've spoken to about it have told me that they'd be willing to do more around the house, but that they were daunted by the prospect. Part of this is the fear that people will laugh at them if they do things like hanging the washing out on the line; part of it is a fear that they won't do it properly and that their partners will laugh or criticise (a feeling which stirs up memories in some men of being told off by mum for making a mess); part of it is, of course, a rationalisation of sheer laziness and unwillingness to be bothered by such things. Housework isn't that bad, though, and the more you do, the easier it gets. Men I know who have made the effort have told me that it's helped them to feel more useful, more of a partner in the household and less of an outsider. 'I never thought I'd see the day when I'd be proud of the way I do the ironing,' one man told me. 'But I am – I'm very proud of it.'

It's also worth thinking about these issues in advance of the time when they become crucial. Part of the problem for many women is that society's attitudes and their conditioning unite into pushing them down the employment ladder into areas with few prospects and little job satisfaction. Part of the reason that many women end up doing poorly paid, part-time, unstimulating jobs is that they're often the only ones which fit in with the demands of home life. If your children don't come home from school for lunch, your partner can avoid the cost and bother of finding childcare by doing a part-time job locally which allows her to be at home before the end of school. And the higher up the career ladder you go, the harder it is to find a job which can be done part time. Jobs which involve responsibility, stimulation, creativity and many of the other things which are reasons for people to enjoy working are usually cast firmly in the mould of the nine-to-five day and five-day week. Indeed, it often seems to me that the higher you go in career terms, the more common it is to work very long hours indeed. I know so many career-minded people who put in 50, 60 or even 70 hour weeks. The few working mothers I know at this level obviously find life very difficult indeed.

# 18 Lone fathers

Single parents form another group of people for whom life can be very hard. It's estimated that in the United Kingdom more than one family in eight is a one-parent family – something like 900,000 families or more, involving over a million, perhaps even as many as one and a half million, children. Of these families, it's thought that in as many as 200,000 the lone parent is a father.

A proportion of one parent families are the result of the death of a mother or father. Such a bereavement will, of course, cause intense suffering for the surviving partner as well as for the children. Losing someone you love is a terrible blow at any time of life; it's as if an entire, integral part of your being has been ripped out of you. A surviving parent has a lot of problems to face. Not only do you have to cope with your own grief, you have to try and help your children to deal with theirs. The younger they are, the more difficult this may be, although a child of any age is going to feel his or her own loss in their own way. It's not a subject I can go in to here at any great length. I will say, however, that it's important both to grieve and to know when you need help in overcoming any problems you might face. Your doctor may well offer you some help, as may your friends and family – take it as and when you need it. Don't struggle on in the misguided belief that you shouldn't be a burden to anyone else.

There are certain practical problems which have to be faced when a partner dies, too, the chief of which is usually what to do about money. You may well have no problems if your partner was covered by insurance, either privately or through a company's pension plan. But if there was no such cover, it's highly unlikely that you'll be able to maintain your stardard of living on any benefits paid by the state, especially if you've got several young children. This is a problem which often becomes acute for bereaved fathers. Many couples make sure that the *man's* life is insured, because he's usually the main breadwinner, and ignore the fact that if he loses his partner he'll have to pay someone to look after the children and the house while he continues to earn the family's income, and that can be very expensive indeed. This can be more than a little awkward, because it can mean that children have to get used to a new full-time caretaker – or several of them in succession – at a time when they need stability, reassurance and support. It's a problem which can be avoided with a little forethought, and a little equality. There are many insurance policies on offer which cover *both* partners' lives equally, so you can ensure that in the event of your partner's death you'll be able to decide whether to continue working or whether to spend more time with your children for a few months or even years, without having to worry too much about money. This sort of policy needn't cost too much, either, and it could give both you and your partner a certain amount of peace of mind.

These days, however, a far higher proportion of single-parent families are created by divorce or marital separation. Indeed, it sometimes seems today as if we're watching the decline and fall of the empire of marriage. Figures vary, but it's been estimated that in Britain, one marriage in four (or more) now ends in divorce; in the USA the divorce epidemic seems to be far worse, with one in three – or even one in two – American marriages not lasting the course. The result is, of course, that large numbers of children grow up in households where there is only one parent for a period of time. People haven't completely given up on marriage, though; second marriages are running at an all-time high, which means that many children also have to get used to having a step-parent of one sex or the other around the house at some time during their childhood. It's been said that there are an increasing number of children who believe that it's normal to have four – or even more – parents!

I grew up in a one-parent family created by divorce long before either was fashionable, and at that time, the idea of awarding custody of the children to a father hardly seems to have entered into anyone's mind in anything except the most unusual circumstances. My mother had custody of my sister and me, and my father had 'access'. To all intents and purposes, this meant once-weekly visits on a Saturday, with telephone calls in between. In fact there was a period after the divorce when we didn't see my father at all. He was working abroad, and the first time he came to see us on his return to this country, I didn't recognise him. But at least both my parents were reasonable people; both of them cared and tried quite hard, within the constraints of society and its attitudes at the time, to make sure that my sister and I kept our relationship with my father going.

That isn't to say that we didn't have our difficulties; we did, and my father, like most dads in his position then *and* now, was forced into being little more than the 'weekend father' J. R. Ackerley described in his book. By virtue of the fact that we saw him only once a week, he played a marginal role in our lives. He wasn't part of the family, he was absent, something he tried to make up for by opting for a 'playful' role. He took us to funfairs and parks, to cafes and museums, to the cinema and events of all sorts. Later on, when my sister outgrew these Saturday outings, it was just my father and me. We did the rounds of London's museums, the Tower, cinemas, bookshops (I've always been a bookbuyer), tourist sights and hamburger bars over and over again. When I'm in a park with my children at the weekend, I often look at other fathers with their kids and wonder just how many of them are going through the same round as my father did with me. I didn't stay overnight at my father's flat until I was in my twenties. It was only in his later years that I ever really established a true relationship with him; the first and last time I told him I loved him was on his deathbed.

I was lucky, though. Many fathers never saw their children again after a divorce, especially if they had been the party 'at fault' and had committed adultery. Because of the lack of importance assigned to a father's influence over his children, it was commonly thought that it didn't matter so much if a father wasn't around. We now know that a father's role is very important to his children's development, and it's been shown over and over again that children who do not see their fathers after a divorce or separation often suffer greatly because of it.

Things have changed to a large extent since my parents' divorce in 1961. The divorce laws in Britain are now less harshly divisive than they were at that time, and we have seen a growth in the number of settlements which involve a much greater share in their children's lives for fathers. Joint custody, with children spending a certain amount of time with each parent, greater flexibility over access, even the granting of sole custody to fathers with access for mothers – all these things have become more common, although it has to be said that in most divorces, the children stay with their mother and the father becomes an outsider; or perhaps I should say *more* of an outsider than he was before. There's no other explanation for those single-parent figures.

## LONE FATHERS

Something the law can't change, however hard we try to make it fair, is the fact that divorce is deeply unsettling emotionally for all concerned. Whatever the reasons might be for a marriage breaking up, it often takes place over a long period of time in an atmosphere of argument, depression, upset and general, all-round anguish. I know, I've been through it, and like anyone else who's seen it from the inside, I know that it's an extremely unpleasant experience. Marital rows, separation, divorce – they're all deeply disturbing to children. It's like watching the two pillars which support your entire universe begin to crack and fall; it seems as if the world is ending. Remember, although it might be relatively easy to divorce your partner, you can never really get a divorce from your children. A very rough rule is that the more acrimonious the split, the greater the upset at the time, the deeper the scars in the children. Those scars hurt for a long time, too – perhaps forever. In fact the effects of divorce are the most convincing reason I know to try and make sure that your marriage survives.

That doesn't mean to say I agree with those who say that you should try and hold a marriage together whatever the cost 'for the sake of the children'. It's probable that life would have been much worse for my sister and me if our parents had stayed together; their decision was the right one. The point is that there are ways of minimising the effect of divorce, and that it's important to try and make the break in as painless a way as you can. Above all, it's important for both parents to reassure the children that just because they don't love each other any more, it doesn't mean that they don't love the children either. In many ways it helps to be honest with your kids; most children can take the truth, and it's far better for a child of any age to know what's going on.

Of course it's difficult to end a marriage in a completely 'civilised' way. I'm not expecting miracles. If our marriage began to break up tomorrow, I'm sure that Sally and I would indulge in plenty of operatic rowing, recrimination and backbiting (real as well as metaphorical); that's what being a (married) human being is sometimes all about. But the less of it you do in front of the children, the better; and the same applies to its duration and extent. It is important to come to some sort of fair and equitable agreement as quickly as possible, and to give your children equal and fair access to both parents as far as you can. How you arrange these matters depends on your circumstances, but if it ever should happen to you, remember two things above all. Firstly, your children will be affected less seriously and less permanently if you are reasonable about the split; and secondly, never under-estimate your marriage's powers of recovery. If you give yourselves a chance, you may well be able to bring your marriage back from the brink. Interestingly enough, there's a peak in the divorce statistics in marriages which have got to about the five to seven year mark. One in five divorces takes place before the fifth wedding anniversary, one in three before the tenth. It seems to me that these are often the mose stressful years, the years of building a home and a family, the years which take a toll on your equanimity and energy. If you can survive the years when your children are young, you'll give your marriage a real chance of staying the course.

But what about those 200,000 lone fathers? In my opinion there are far more than just 200,000; all those fathers I talked about in the park on their 'access' visits with their children are lone fathers, too. The difference is that lone fathers who don't get custody are in the bizarre position of doing something of which society tacitly approves by remaining 'outsiders', while lone fathers looking after their own children are doing something which still to a large extent goes against the grain of society's attitudes.

Single parents face a number of problems in common, whatever their sex. There are the practical difficulties of money and work and childcare, to start with. The children have to be cared for, money has to be earned, the household has to be run. But there is a difference in the way the sexes solve their problems. Many single mothers do try to combine work and parenthood, but in doing so, they face a number of obstacles. I've already said that childcare is not easy to arrange, so obviously that's a major problem for a single mother who may not have any form of back-up in case of illness or other problems. There's also the fact that a single mother is going to find that she's not a very attractive prospect to employers, either, given the context of attitudes about working women. She's a woman, she's a mother, and she doesn't have a man to support her – all of which adds up to an employer looking at her as someone who's probably only worth an unimportant job with a small wage and few prospects for promotion, at best. The result is that single mothers often find themselves pushed more towards being dependent on state benefits and staying at home as full-time mothers than being encouraged to go out and work to support their families by their own efforts.

However, something like five out of six single fathers manage – or make the effort – to combine work and parenthood. This is probably because it's still very hard for many men to see themselves as parents first, and workers and breadwinners second. It's a particularly difficult problem for lone fathers. Our conditioning makes it tough for us to live the emotional life, but that's often what fathers need to do above all in cases where a mother is no longer around, for whatever reason. If a man has suddenly to become a mother and father to his children, life can be very hard indeed for a little while. Children who have lived through a separation or divorce, or whose mother has left them, are often in need of more than their share of emotional reassurance and tenderness – things we find it hard to give our children at the best of times. A lone father will undoubtedly also be struggling with his own feelings about what's happened. So it's no wonder that lone fathers often retreat into traditional masculinity and move hell and high water to keep working, whatever the cost. To this end, they're supported by society's attitudes. In *The Father Figure* edited by Lorna McKee and Margaret O'Brien, a survey is quoted showing that 86 per cent of people questioned in a random street survey felt that single mothers should stay at home to care for their children, and 78 per cent that single fathers should go out to work rather than stay at home as full-time 'househusbands'.

## Swapping roles

Single fathers have a lot in common with another, even smaller group of men – those who have swapped roles with their partners and become full times 'househusbands' and fathers, while their partners become the family's sole breadwinner. I know of no accurate statistics which show exactly how many of these men there are, but there can be very few. For some men, role swapping is the temporary solution to being made redundant or during a long period of unemployment; the idea being, of course, that should a 'proper' job ever turn up, they'll immediately go back to doing what men *should* do – which is being a breadwinner.

Nevertheless, a role swap is something which some couples do freely choose, and role swap fathers do have some unusual and very interesting problems to face. Those that I've met — and you could count them on the fingers of a clumsy butcher's hands — have had some fascinating things to say about what it means to cross the great divide. One father in particular sticks in my mind. He had two children when I met him, a baby son of around nine months, and a daughter of about four. His wife was pursuing a career as a successful model and potential actress, and he freely admitted that he had found full-time parenthood to be a 'great shock to the system'. 'Like most men, I always thought that being a housewife and mother was an easy option,' he told me. 'I'll never, ever think that again. There was a time a few months ago when I thought I'd never be able to cope. I just didn't know what day it was, whether I should change the baby's nappy, feed the cat, do the washing up or play with my daughter. I've never been so tired as this, either. I'm exhausted all the time. It's been really weird to hear myself sounding like a nagging wife when Penny comes home and flops down in an armchair, too.'

Role swap husbands soon find out that there's more to being a housewife than watching afternoon television and yapping with the next door neighbour over the back fence. It is a salutary introduction to a whole new area of life, a world which many men haven't lived in since they were under five themselves. With all the housework and cooking and childcare come those other components of being a housewife and mother, loneliness and isolation. Single fathers face the same problems, and they're compounded by that old great divide.

As that same role swap father said to me, 'It's very hard to go into places like the local clinic, or the local supermarket, without feeling like a square peg in a round hole. At the clinic, for example, when I took the baby for his immunisations, there were all these women who clustered round me as if I was completely unable to cope with him. "Are you sure you can manage?" they kept saying. I felt like General Custer in the middle of Apache territory.'

It's something I've often felt myself. When I first started taking Emma to school in the mornings, few of the mothers who were usually at the school gate even acknowledged my existence. Those who did asked me if Sally was ill or if I was on holiday from work. They couldn't seem to understand or accept the fact that I was taking my daughter to school not because of some emergency or some paternal whim, but because I wanted to be a part of her life and share the burdens of parenthood with my wife. Role swap fathers – and lone fathers – have to face that wall of incomprehension everywhere they go. The simple fact is that we men aren't very good at getting on with groups of women in a non-sexual context because of our conditioning. Equally, women don't know how to cope with a strange creature who looks like a man, but who is to be found behind a pushchair swathed in carrier bags full of the shopping, or changing his baby son's nappy at the local *mother* and toddler group. Another problem is that it's difficult for a man to make friends with other parents he might meet because they're likely to be women – women with husbands, who might take it the wrong way should their partner invite another parent around for coffee during the day if that parent happens to be a man. The sexual edge between men and women is often simply too much for role swap fathers to overcome.

The result is often that role swap and lone fathers give up and retreat from places like mother and toddler groups entirely, which only increases their isolation. Role swap fathers often have some fairly difficult feelings to contend with anyway; the ones I've met have all talked about the problem of other men's attitudes. Former friends and colleagues, however liberated, may look at you as if you're mad to be doing what you're doing, and they may feel driven to tell you so. One man who swapped roles with his partner told me that his father refused to talk to him for several months, and only really began to relate to him properly when he gave up being a househusband and went back to work. It's all part of the same picture; you can't be a proper man unless you've got a job, just as you can't be a proper woman unless you've got children and you stay at home full time to look after them.

A crucial part of the pressure on role swapping fathers to give up the struggle is the feeling that they're simply not good enough as parents and 'housewives'. Remember that our society is still built on the assumption, the engrained prejudice, that men aren't very good at anything to do with childcare and housework; it's women who are the specialists in this area. Men are supposed to be builders and doers, conquerors and heroes – and hopeless at changing nappies or doing the dusting. So it's hardly surprising that role swap men should feel very sensitive and insecure about certain aspects of what they're doing. It's an insecurity I've often felt myself, mostly because there are certain things I'm just not very sure about at all. I've got two daughters, one of whom has long hair which I like to brush; but I'm hopeless when it comes to putting it in a pony tail, and I wouldn't even know where to begin in putting it into plaits. So when I did put it in a pony tail while Sally was lying in after giving birth to Thomas, and a (female) friend laughed to see just what an incompetently managed pony tail it was, I felt a little bruised and unhappy. I can feel equally sensitive when Sally criticises my cooking or comments that I always let the saucepans boil over; it's a sensitivity based on insecurity.

It's far worse for a role swapping father who might be worried that he can't give his children the sort of love and affection that a mother is supposed to. 'I just didn't know if I could be as much of a "mother" to them as they needed me to be,' one man told me. 'I worried that they would be missing out on something very important.' That sort of worry is hardly surprising when you consider that most men are brought up to think of themselves as Action Man, as people who should handle objects and *do* things rather than relate to people. The result for most role swapping fathers, and lone fathers too, is a lot of isolation and loneliness. A man who finds himself on the woman's side of the great divide can feel very lonely indeed, just as it can be very tough and lonely for a career woman who finds herself on the man's side. And yet one role swap father felt very positive about the experience: 'Despite the problems, it's been a marvellous experience for me. And the best part about it has been the fact that I can really get to know my children in ways which I never thought possible.'

# 19 The tyranny of work

Role swapping fathers are very thin on the ground, and for one simple reason; most men would not consider staying at home to look after the children and the house as a serious option at all. In most men's eyes it's still a weird idea, the sort of thing you might expect a few freaks and radical nutcases to indulge in, but out of the question for the vast majority. The fathers I've talked to have mostly said that they wouldn't *want* to do it, either, and even those who said they might consider it instantly retreated into the assertion that it would always be impossible for them because it wasn't viable economically.

Interestingly enough, there seems to be some fairly strong evidence that larger numbers of women who at the moment *have* to work during the years in which their children are small would quite like to spend more time at home, if not to give up work altogether. So it looks as if the sexes agree, and that both sides of the great divide would quite like to stay where they are. Or would they?

I think it's fairly clear that women are not wholly content with the traditional role of full-time housewife and mother any longer; women want more, and they've been struggling to get it for some time now. They've come up against certain obstacles, such as the problem of their conditioning and the way that our stereotyped images of men and women dictate much in our lives, particularly in our working lives. Women have been at the forefront of developing new solutions, many of which are only just beginning to have an effect. We do now have maternity leave; more companies and employers are being more flexible to accommodate the needs of working women; and there is even evidence to show that new ways of working are beginning to creep into the world of employment.

*Jobsharing* is one of the new solutions, but very rarely does it happen in the way in which Al Alvarez writes about it. There can be very few couples who can share the same job, mostly because there can't be many who have the same qualifications and experience in the same area of work. Jobsharing between husband and wife becomes very difficult if one of you is a vet and the other one is a teacher, or if one of you is a policeman and the other a novelist! That's why most people who jobshare are mothers, women with children who share a job – and sometimes childcare – with another woman in the same position. Jobsharing mothers face much the same problems of time and pressure and organisation as any working mothers, but it does seem to work better for them than the more traditional ways of working. One reason for that could be that your jobsharing partner supplies several things which are missing for solitary working mothers – support of various kinds, and the instant availability of someone to fill in as back up in those difficult times such as the school holidays or when an emergency crops up. At any rate, the people I've met who have tried jobsharing have generally been very pleased with it as a means of solving the work versus home conflict, although even jobsharing mothers still feel pangs of guilt about 'not being proper mothers' to their children.

I've come across several jobsharing mothers, but jobsharing fathers are very rare, as are fathers who work part time. Not only are most fathers still locked into the traditional role of breadwinner, the father who goes out to work in the morning and comes back exhausted at night, they often seem to be perfectly happy with it. This is a point I've already looked at from several different angles throughout this book. Your conditioning – and society – will make you feel as if your sole contribution to family life should be that of breadwinner and being the external voice of authority and discipline. On top of that, your conditioning will also contribute to making you uneasy with the day-to-day business of being a parent, the emotional and practical demands of your partner and your children – all of which conspire into making it tempting to escape into your traditional role. And where does your traditional role take you? Outside, to work, away from home and all that messy, problematical emotion. It turns you into an outsider.

The problem is that our traditional, stereotype roles are very, very seductive. It's very comfortable for us to relax as we shut the door behind us in the morning and head off towards the office; it's very easy to turn off and shelter behind our breadwinner role at home. It saves you a lot of effort, helps you to avoid doing anything around the house or with the children (except the things you enjoy, like playing with them), and generally makes life easy to cope with. Women conspire in this too; it's just as easy for your partner to relax into her traditional role and put up with you the way you are, the way all men are supposed to be, than it is to try and encourage you (or nag you) to be different. At the same time, doing anything differently can feel very threatening; it's threatening for a man to feel that his wife doesn't need him any more when she starts to earn her own money; it's threatening for a woman to find that her husband doesn't need her any more because he can do his own washing and cooking. Men and women have established positions of power, fortresses on their own sides of the great divide to protect themselves from the discomforts and rigours of changing into something else. Admittedly, women have had the short end of the stick for a long time; but men are just as oppressed by their own conditioning in many ways. What *we* miss out on is family life.

## Resistance to change

Many men do not seem to feel the sort of conflict between home and work I talked about at the beginning of this chapter. They work, they go on working, and above all, they say that they *want* to work. It's the real desire to work which explains the fact that although the working week is now shorter in most countries than ever before, large numbers of men still work lots of overtime. Of course many families need the extra money that overtime brings, but it has to be said that many fathers work the long hours they do because they simply want to. It might seem bizarre that at a time when there are more unemployed people than ever before, so many of those who do have jobs should be working longer hours than is strictly necessary. But I know men who work 50 and 60 hour weeks, men who take work home in the evenings, men who go into the office at the weekend – even when they don't have to.

These are the sort of men who laugh when I suggest that more men should work part time, or that if they have to work such long hours, then their work is actually concealing a job for another person. 'How could I do what I have to in any less time?' they say. 'I've got so much work I'm running all the time to keep standing still.' To a large extent I must include myself among these men. Writing this book, as I've said before, has meant long hours of 'overtime' for me; it's meant spending a lot of the time left over after I've finished my full-time job during which I could be with my children, at my desk instead, working on what you're reading now. And I've heard myself saying exactly the same things; I never *do* seem to have the time to fit it all in.

But to a large extent, Parkinson's law applies: the available work expands to fill the available time. Those same men who say they can't get home before nine or ten in the evening because they've got so much work to do may spend a lot of time talking to colleagues about golf, the football scores, their wives or just how much work they've got to do during the 'working' day; they may spend two or three hours on 'business lunches'; they may work very slowly at times and even spin things out so that they look to their bosses as if they really are working very hard. Of course some men work very hard all the time; equally, a lot of the work men do, a lot of the time spent at their jobs is unproductive. It's very hard to get a man to admit to that. Just as your partner isn't going to admit to you that she spent an hour or two talking to a friend over coffee that morning because she feels that it was 'selfish' of her to do that rather than something more 'productive'

The resistance to change in our attitudes to work is enormous. Most of the men I've talked to seem to accept the fact that they will have to spend the major part of their lives locked into the tyranny of the nine-to-five day and the five-day week, although increasingly, more and more men are beginning to question that tyranny. For the desire to work, the need to find meaning in life through the job you do, the escape from messy emotions into the outside world of work is now seen for what it is – a solution which brings bigger, and worse problems in its train. Apart from the impact on your health, those problems are the ones I've been talking about throughout this book, the problems of being a parent who isn't a parent, a part of a family and an outsider at the same time, someone who misses out on many of the most rewarding things in life even though they're happening right under your nose. Even if you think now that fulfilling the traditional role of a man is all you want and need, at some time in your life you're going to realise that it probably isn't.

Another major problem at the moment – and one which few of us can do anything about as individuals – is that unemployment adds a dash of fear to everyone's attitude to their job and family income. I've talked to several men who have said that they work as hard as they do because they're frightened of losing their jobs, and most fathers *do* feel a keen sense of their responsibilities towards their families. That sense makes you more aware of the possibilities inherent in being unemployed, and with so many people being out of work now, a generalised feeling of insecurity in even seemingly the most secure jobs has become a real source of fear for many men.

I've talked elsewhere about the importance of deciding where your priorities lie. Fathers like my friend face a very real choice; do they sacrifice their careers for their families, or their families for their careers? For many men there seem to be no real alternatives; it's a question of one or the other. In my experience many of these men fall into the category of 'workaholics', people who work for the sake of working because they're addicted to it. It's very easy for a father to get locked into that sort of pattern, and get stuck in a vicious circle; the harder he works, the less he's at home, and the more useless and excluded he feels; problems in his relationships with his partner and his children ensue, difficulties he can only escape by working even harder for longer hours ... which only makes the problems worse. It's no coincidence that the quote about jobsharing I put at the head of this chapter should come from a book about divorce. Work, and men's attitudes to it, can destroy marriages.

I've already said that for some of us, the answer is to do less overtime, to put less of ourselves into our jobs and more into our families. The problem with making work your life is that work can sometimes disappear; you might get made redundant, and even if you don't, you're still going to have to retire one day. Jobs don't usually go on forever, unless you die in the harness – something most of us devoutly hope doesn't happen. But the disappointments of work can be enormous. My father, in many ways, sacrificed almost everything else in his life – his health, his family life, his personal happiness – to the dream of executive success, a dream he thought he had finally realised in fact when he set up his own company in the late 1970s. I saw the sadness, the bitterness, the great disappointment in his eyes when that company went bust in 1981. It left him a broken man, a man with a truly broken heart. Ironically, once that dream had finally been denied to him forever, he began to warm to his family and soften; he became friendlier, more relaxed, more human. The facade was finally pierced; he had no need to put over a 'masculine', go-getting image anymore. But he had missed so much – and he knew it.

His example is the one I hold in my mind's eye when I tell myself that I won't work so hard in future, and it was similar examples of fathers who had missed out that have led other men I've talked to into the same decision. To begin with it's often a question of saying, 'No, I'll leave that until tomorrow', or 'No, I cant stay for that meeting – I have to be at home'. Gradually, you might find that it becomes easier to make your family a central part of your life and keep work at a healthy distance. 'It wasn't at all easy to start with,' one man admitted to me. 'I began to come home earlier than usual, which meant leaving things undone that I felt should have been done. But gradually I began to organise my day better and in the end I found that I was making sure I didn't waste my time any more. It was because I made the effort to get home to my family that I think I actually became better at my job in the long run – and I felt more a part of home life, too.'

That's a common feeling among fathers who've made the effort to break out of the tyranny of work. You'll probably find that you don't lose your job, or that someone overtakes you in the career stakes. You'll find that getting away from your job might even help you to come back to it with a refreshed mind and a certain amount of objectivity; all work and no play certainly makes you very dull, a factor in itself which can force you into a vicious circle of working less efficiently and more slowly, which will inevitably mean less job satisfaction, and probably longer hours. The benefits of putting work into perspective, a perspective which brings your family more sharply into focus, can spread into every area of your life. In the long run you'll have less invested in your job, which will mean you'll be at less risk of life-shattering disappointments if something should go wrong. That same father who changed his approach to his job found that his change of heart produced a corresponding change of attitude to his employers, too. 'I suppose they began to sense that I wasn't quite so desperate about my job any more; they saw that they didn't have me by the throat. I must have given off an air of being fairly relaxed and confident about it all, and not bothered so much about whether I lost my job. Don't get me wrong, I didn't become irresponsible. It was just that I didn't want them to feel that they could run my life because I was frightened of being out of work – and I found that I got a lot more respect from them for that. They treated me better.'

In some ways, it's a question of deciding on a policy of 'working to live' rather than 'living to work'. But that decision is not always easy; obviously, money must enter into your thoughts, and there's often a very difficult balancing act to perform between the needs of your family budget and your need for time to be with your partner and your children. That balancing act isn't going to be made any easier for most of us until society is changed in certain ways.

# 20 Changing attitudes

The real problem in what we're talking about is, however, of the chicken and egg variety. We won't really be able to change society and its attitudes, and therefore make it easier for families to resolve the sort of conflicts we've looked at, until we can change the ideas in people's heads. But we won't be able to change those ideas until we change the society which does so much to form them.

I've already tried to explain something of the process by which the traditional stereotypes are being passed on in all their glory to our children; it's happening so unconsciously sometimes that it's hard to catch ourselves doing it – but we are. And those unconscious pressures on our children turn into the broader pressures from a society in which the great divide still exists, and in a very powerful way, and so the traditional roles are perpetuated with all their expectations and distortions, their problems and conflicts and inadequacies. Things have changed, but there's still a very long way to go. It takes a long time to change attitudes which are based on conditioning fostered by generation after generation over thousands, perhaps even hundreds of thousands of years. It's not something you can do in a week or so, or even a few years.

What we need now are some practical solutions, some measures designed to make life easier for families. I'm talking about a kind of *positive discrimination* in favour of fathers who want to be involved more in their families. We need to make certain changes, implement certain reforms which will raise both the status of parenthood in general and the status of fatherhood in particular. We need to widen some of the cracks which have already begun to appear in the monolithic facade of the traditional family in society. Life can be very difficult for mothers and fathers of all types (and their children too), and that's because society is forcing us into a mould of parenthood and family life which we have begun to outgrow.

We could make a start in breaking that mould by encouraging fathers to take a far greater role in antenatal care and preparation for parenthood. As Michel Odent says, it's now become a 'rule' for fathers to be at the births of their children; hospital staff often expect it now. But it's grossly unfair of staff to expect a man to play a useful role during labour and birth if the only preparation he's had for it is one antenatal class. At the same time, we've seen how fathers are often excluded from the crucial early days of their children's lives by hospital policy which turns them into 'visitors'. Fathers are still rejected before the birth and ejected after it. What men need is a positive course of antenatal classes specifically for them, or together with their partners on the lines of the NCT course. This course should be made freely available to *all* fathers automatically, free of charge on the national health service, and classes should be held at times when men can get to them. It's no good expecting fathers to be able to get to antenatal classes held in the afternoons – they're at work. They should be in the evenings or at weekends. The course itself should give fathers the practical, common sense information which they need about both the physical and emotional sides of becoming a parent. Such a course would be of immeasurable help to most fathers, and it's something I've heard suggested by many.

Another move forward is an extension of the idea of antenatal classes into the school curriculum. It's already possible for school children to take an examination course in *parentcraft*, as it's called. At the moment these courses are generally taken by girls, although there are several schools in which teenage boys are also being encouraged to take the courses too. I visited one in North London and talked to three boys who were enrolled on the parentcraft course, which involved learning about pregnancy, birth, children and family life. All this was done in a very definite 'non-sexist' spirit, and it was good to see that the three lads concerned were only faintly embarrassed about what they were doing.

Such a course should be compulsory in all schools. There's a lot of talk about how important it is for children to learn in schools the skills they'll need to make a success of life. It seems almost criminally negligent, therefore, not to prepare children for parenthood, as something like 90 per cent of them are bound to end up with children of their own. All children – girls *and* boys – should be taught about parenthood in a practical, common sense way at some time during their secondary school career. What they're taught also needs to be up-to-date and non-sexist; it's that sort of positive discrimination which will really break the mould of stereotypes. Don't forget that tomorrow's managers and MPs also have to go through school, and if we can get to boys young enough we can make sure that they all have a better chance of growing up with a real sense of what it means to be a father. At the same time, if this sort of education is backed up by changes in society which lead to men being more involved as parents, and therefore more visible to their children as fathers who actually do some *fathering*, then the mould will eventually be broken forever.

## Paternity leave

There should also be legislation to introduce a proper system of *paternity leave*. In Britain at the moment fewer than 5 per cent of companies or other employers offer their male employees paternity leave as a matter of course. Those that do are also more likely to be found in the traditionally 'radical' areas such as publishing, or among the left-wing controlled councils. Many companies, of course, say that they're prepared to offer their male staff 'sympathetic consideration for compassionate leave' after their partners have had a baby. As I've said, most fathers do take some time off — it seems to average out at between 70 and 80 per cent — and most of them take it either as part of their annual holiday (which means they miss out on the rest and relaxation holiday is supposed to be for), or as paid sick leave (that is, absenteeism), or as unpaid leave (which means they and their families lose out financially).

A survey we conducted for *Parents*, however, discovered that 72 per cent of Britain's couples felt that fathers should have a legal right to paid time off work after a baby is born. Admittedly, the respondents in the survey were all families with small children, so it's obviously a subject close to their hearts; but in my view what makes their opinion even more important — they're the ones in the front line, as it were. What was most fascinating for me was to talk to organisations like the Confederation of British Industry (the CBI), the employers' organisation, who said that they felt 'paternity leave should not be a matter for legislation, but something to be decided between individuals and their employers'. Predictably enough, this was also the view of the current Tory government as vouchsafed by a spokesman at the Department of Employment. At the time of writing, that is still the government's policy, and attempts by various MPs to get paternity leave into the law by means of private members' bills or by tacking it on to other equal rights legislation have all failed.

Various bodies continue to lobby for paternity leave, however. It's now been adopted as official policy by the TUC, although as a spokesman told me, if it ever came to a straight fight between more money and paternity leave in almost any union-management negotiations, he had a shrewd idea of which carrot most unions would go for and which they would happily lose. Nevertheless, the TUC's policy is also to continue to press the government – any government – to grant the legal right to paternity leave. And as you might expect, it's a fundamental part of the Equal Opportunity Commission's programme. As a spokesman for the EOC said, it would have more than just a practical value, too, although goodness knows, most men would be delighted to know that they didn't have to worry about taking time off to be with their families. The EOC spokesman, however, was keen to stress the *symbolic* value of granting paternity leave:

> Part of the reason it's not already law, is that we still don't think of men as parents – they're seen as workers and little else. But something like a legal right to paternity leave could really help to change attitudes; it could help to make the idea of playing a greater role in family life more *legitimate* for most men. If it's treated as 'compassionate leave', it's still seen as something which isn't all that important, something which is really all a bit of a joke. If we really want parenthood to be shared – and that's the first step in achieving real equality for women – then that's exactly the attitude we've got to change. We've got to build a society in which men are seen as fathers as well as workers.

The same spokesman was also quick to point out that 'sympathetic consideration for compassionate leave' was all very well, but what do you do if your employer gives your case 'sympathetic consideration' and then decides that he doesn't want to be particularly compassionate in the question of leave? Part of the reason that over a quarter of fathers *don't* take time off after the birth is simply that they can't, either because they can't afford the loss of money it entails or because they're afraid to lose their jobs. Admittedly some of them are also 'workaholics', but they're the sort of men whom it's hoped the 'symbolic value' of paternity leave will help in the long run.

Britain is a long way behind some other countries in terms of the deal it offers fathers. Belgium isn't generous, but Belgian fathers do have the legal right to two days' paternity leave. In Denmark it's a week, in France it's three days, and in Sweden there's a much better deal – as you might expect of one of those Scandinavian countries which Al Alvarez calls 'harbingers of the future'. Very roughly, the scheme offers both parents up to around six months 'parental leave' each, to be taken either as a block or to be split up into smaller units of weeks or months to be taken over a longer period of time in the early years of parenthood. It appears that the thinking behind the scheme was specifically to encourage fathers to take a greater share in early parenthood, and fascinatingly, it has proved difficult so far to persuade them to take up the paternity leave which is on offer. It appears that fewer than 10 per cent used anywhere near their full allowance in the first year of the scheme's operation; but the figure has grown substantially every year since.

Part of the reason for that low take-up must be what I can only call the 'employer factor'. Obviously, the conditioning I've been talking about makes it difficult for men to see themselves as primary, full-time parents, and hence to see much point in spending six months at home with a baby or small child. At the same time, there's always the fear that you'll miss out on promotion if you're absent for any length of time, or lose your job to a younger and more dynamic competitor. That sort of feeling is only fostered by most employers, who look askance at the idea of a man taking six months off to be a 'parent'. Don't forget that most employers are men, and that often we fathers have to deal with men of *our* fathers' generation in seeking time off to be with our families or paternity leave – and it's all a bit foreign and strange to them.

Interestingly enough, the EEC is actively trying to promote the idea of shared parenthood with legislation of its own. During the writing of this book draft legislation has been prepared on the subject of 'parental leave', and a directive has been issued on it to all member states, including Britain. The directive says: 'The aim of the legislation is to ensure that workers are allowed to take off at least a minimum period to look after young children and cope with emergencies in the family.' The directive stresses that this means *both* parents, and it's therefore an attempt to break the conditioning which produces the sort of pressure on women I talked about earlier, the pressure to remain primary parents whether they're working or not.

It would seem logical to me to extend the idea of parental leave to help fathers on the principle of positive discrimination. I've said that 'fatherhood classes' should take place in the evenings and at weekends to that fathers can get to them; what I'd really like to see is a society in which fathers could have the *legal* right to time off during their partner's pregnancy to attend such classes and to go along to antenatal clinics, too, as well as the right to share the burdens in taking time off for other family matters later on as the children grow up.

I also spoke to ICI, the giant multinational chemicals company, when I was researching paternity leave. Their spokesman said that the company offered 'sympathetic consideration' to men who wanted leave after their wives gave birth. 'But we're not in favour of a rigid system of paternity leave. We prefer a less formal arrangement because, obviously enough, paternity leave is a benefit which will cost the company money – and at the end of the day we've still got to run an industry.' That spokesman summed up the two main objections to paternity leave opponents of the idea usually put forward: the alleged cost, and a fear that introducing the legal right to paternity leave will bring industry to its knees overnight.

Interestingly, these are the commonest objections that used to be put forward against the idea of giving women the legal right to maternity leave. That right is paid for in this country by the government in a system administered by the Department of Employment. A woman's maternity pay is paid by her employer, who can reclaim it from the *maternity pay fund*, the money for which is raised by a levy on all of Britain's employers. It's actually done by adding a levy to the employers' national insurance contributions and works out to 0.05 per cent of the amount they pay. It's been suggested that paternity leave could be paid for by exactly the same system; all we would need to do would be to rename the fund the *parental leave fund* and double the levy to 0.1 per cent of the employers' national insurance contributions. That would raise something like £100 million, enough to give every new father in Britain (there are about

650,000 new babies born every year at the moment) two weeks' paid paternity leave at the national average salary of around £160 per week before tax. It would obviously have to be worked out in detail, and like maternity pay would have to be related to the level of a man's earning. But it would average out, and it doesn't take a genius to see that paying for a fortnight's paternity leave isn't going to push even Britain over the edge into bankruptcy, especially when you consider that in 1983 the government spent £14½ billion on defence and £32½ billion on social security. In fact I worked out that the £100 million needed to pay for fathers to have paternity leave could be raised by levying an extra national insurance contribution of 10p per head of the working population per week for a year. That's all it would cost – 10p per person per week. I've got my 10p ready – have you?

British industry, or industry anywhere in the world, isn't going to collapse, either, just because men take a fortnight off. That's a lesson that we ought to learn as individuals; your company isn't going to collapse just because you have a couple of weeks off. It's important to remember that most fathers only have two children in their lives anyway these days, so what we're talking about is allowing them to have something like four weeks' paid time off in a lifetime of work which might last as long as 40 or 45 years. I'll admit that I'd like to see a system like Sweden's in operation in this country too (and all over the world!), and although six months – a year for two children – sounds like a long time, it's nothing compared to the full length of time you're going to be spending at work. It's also important to bear in mind that few men are going to have a baby just to get two weeks off work. It might sound insane even to think of such a thing, but I've heard it said by an employer more than once.

## Financial help

It would also help if families had more financial help from the state. At almost every level, financial benefits to families in Britain are very low indeed. The maternity grant at £25 is absolutely derisory; it was set at that level in 1970 and now hardly keeps most families in disposable nappies for more than a few weeks. It was originally meant to help couples defray some of the costs incurred when they had to buy equipment and so on in the wake of losing the woman's wage. At the same time, child benefit is very low indeed, and there was even a recent suggestion that it should be taxed, though the point of taxing £6.85 which is being paid out of taxes in the first place escapes me. Both maternity grant and child benefit – and similar payments – are very much higher in some other countries, and it seems to me that we could quite easily quadruple the grant and double the benefit without causing even a small hiccough in the British economy. More money would, quite simply, help to take the pressure off young families. For fathers it might mean less overtime and more time at home.

We've got to break the mould that puts men under pressure, the mould that means fathers find themselves struggling with the demands of career pressures and the need to work overtime during the same years – *exactly* the same years, usually – that they've got small children. It seems to me that we put too much emphasis on 'making it' while we're still young. Why should you have to sacrifice your family life for your career? After all, the years of young parenthood are quite short in comparison to your working life. If you have two children quite close together, the real pressures of parenthood – those involved in babyhood and the toddler stage – could well be over in three or four years. Even if you think of the 'intense' years of parenthood as lasting up until the time both of your children are in full-time school, that could mean little more than seven or eight years when family life fills the centre of the stage.

As I tried to show in the earlier chapters, children do tend to become less of a practical problem as they get older. Of course family life is always complicated to a certain degree; of course it's important to keep your family in the centre of your personal stage always. But what I am saying is that I would like to see a society in which it was legitimate for fathers to spend more time during the years of young parenthood at home with their families than out at their jobs. In short, I'm hoping that we can build a future in which something like Al Alvarez's 'Scandinavian solution' could be made to work. I think we have to accept the fact that many mothers would prefer to spend the years when their children are small at home with them. But that they need to be able to keep a foothold in the world of work at the same time. Equally, men need to keep a foothold at home in the years during which they have to build their careers. What we need is a system in which there could be some sort of 'sliding scale' of commitment: a scale by which men and women could vary the amount of time they devoted to different areas of their lives according to their needs at particular times of life.

Of course such a system would be difficult to devise and perhaps quite complicated to put into operation – at first – but it is the only fair way of arranging such matters in the long run. Perhaps we could make a start by offering a system to fathers and mothers based on an extended form of jobsharing. If a father, for example, wanted to take a back seat in his career during the early months of his child's life, the idea would be to get someone who was unemployed to share his job. The state could then pay a proportion of the unemployed person's benefit to the jobsharing father, or simply get the company to pay him and keep paying benefit to the unemployed person taking up the jobsharing option. Many unemployed people – especially the young – would jump at the chance of such experience, if only to get them out of the round of depression and boredom that long-term unemployment often brings in its train. I can already hear the voices saying that it would never work; but like Sweden's parental leave system, it's an idea which is bound to gain momentum once people see it in operation. I'm not claiming this as a new idea I've dreamed up myself – it's one which has been around for a while. What's different about my suggestion is that it's based on the principle of positive discrimination to raise the status of fatherhood – and to make life easier for both parents.

The important thing for employers and opponents of such ideas to remember is that they're coming anyway. Unemployment is here to stay, and the age of the computer will bring with it a shorter working week and greater flexibility. We're already beginning to see massive changes in the way we work, and there are more to come. The point is that if employers treat fathers better as fathers, and make it easier for them to share family life, in the long run they're going to have happier workers. As it stands, many fathers react to the pressures of family and parenthood by becoming part of the absenteeism statistics and building up a certain amount of resentment towards the structures and prejudices which cause their problems. What I'm saying to employers is simply this: treat fathers right and they'll treat you right, too. It's a straightforward case of you scratch my back now while I'm a young dad – and I'll scratch yours better for you later on.

One last point; this may all sound like speculation, like talk

## CHANGING ATTITUDES

about a future which will never arrive, but we make the future by what we do today. If you believe in getting a better deal for dads and families, then you need to be aware of these issues and to raise them whenever you can, with your employers, with your union, with your MP. Right at the beginning of this book I quoted Betty Friedan, who wrote of a 'quiet movement' among men towards these goals. It's time to start making a noise about that movement; it's time to start working together to achieve what we all want – happier families in which no one feels a failure just for being what he or she *is*, families based on *sharing*.

# Envoi:
# The love you make

> 'I don't believe it,' she said, 'It's an obstinacy, a theory, a perversity.'
> 'Well – ' he said.
> 'You can't have two kinds of love. Why should you!'
> 'It seems as if I can't,' he said. 'Yet I wanted it.'
> 'You can't have it, because it's false, impossible,' she said.
> 'I don't believe that,' he answered.
>
> from *Women in Love* by D. H. Lawrence

I have lived, eaten, drunk and slept the ideas in this book for the last nine months, appropriately enough. And because I've been living the reality of what I've been writing about, I've often found myself discussing these ideas with all sorts of people. Their reactions, comments and arguments have been an essential part of *The Essential Father*. What they've had to say has sometimes changed my opinion, sometimes confirmed it, and sometimes – perhaps after a heated discussion – left me feeling confused. In the end, I've come to realise that a certain amount of confusion is also an essential part of this book. There are no complete solutions to the problems you'll face as a father. I've tried to indicate ways in which you can tackle almost all the difficulties you'll have to face, just as I've suggested ways in which we ought to change society to make life easier for families, but in the long run there are as many individual solutions as there are fathers and mothers and children. I hope this book will help you to find *your* particular answers.

Recently, however, several people have accused me of being an 'idealist'. 'In an *ideal world*,' they've said, with the usual faint sneer on that phrase, 'what you're talking about would be wonderful. But it isn't going to happen, is it? Men and women are fundamentally different. And men will never share parenthood as much as you obviously hope they will.' I've given the question

## ENVOI: THE LOVE YOU MAKE

of the differences between men and women a lot of thought. As you might have suspected from what I wrote earlier on about the 'charmed circle' in which mother and baby often find themselves and the role fathers can play as a 'stepping stone' into the outside world, I do believe that there are fundamental – and important – differences between men and women. I don't see how it could be any other way, and although I may have appeared to have played down these differences, I believe that the physical facts of human reproduction represent a real division between the sexes. What I *don't* believe is that those differences should be the basis of a society in which one group exploits the other, or in which both groups of human beings lose out in major areas of life because society operates in ways which deny large parts of our humanity on a selective basis. I'm saying that I want my son to grow up in a society in which he can be proud of being a man and enjoy being a father with none of the negative connotations that such pride might once have evoked. Equally, I want my daughters to be able to enjoy motherhood and avoid the problems many women have to face today, to enjoy their femininity and do whatever they want in the world of work without having to overcome unnecessary obstacles or feel guilty about it. I want my children to grow up in a world which allows – and perhaps which even helps – them to be fulfilled in every sense as people and as parents, if that's what they want.

I'm talking about creating a world in which there is a new fatherhood as part of a new way of looking at both men and women. We have to accept the fact that there are differences, and go beyond mere acceptance into a celebration of those differences. We also have to realise that just as there is a part of every woman which has been denied up to now – her more 'masculine' part, her independence and assertiveness – so the 'feminine' side of men has been repressed and distorted. What we must do is to create a society in which both men and women can develop *every* area of their personalities and lives, as far as is possible and as much as they want to.

Both sides of the great divide have things to give up too, and giving up privileges or positions of power is always very difficult. We men must relinquish at least half of the hold we have over the world of work and politics. We must make women our partners in a true sense of the word, and that doesn't mean simply thinking of them as 'surrogate males' who can fit into our working structures without those structures being changed. We need a *feminine* dimension to the way we organise work and society in general, and although it's a much over-used and criticised word, that dimension must be one of *caring*. The hard edge of masculine aggression and competition causes most of the problems we have.

Equally, women must be prepared to relinquish some of the power they have over the world of home and family. I'm not saying women don't want to, or that they have consciously excluded men from the home. I freely admit that it's men's dominance over the wider world outside the home that has led to their exclusion within it; women have taken power in the only place where it has ever really been on offer to them. Yet women have to accept the fact that men are going to be a greater part of home life; more than that, women are going to have to be encouraging and welcoming to men in the home, just as I hope men will be encouraging and welcoming to women in the world of work. Of course both sides of the great divide are afraid of giving up what they know and what they're comfortable with; it's easier to stay as we are. But that is no longer possible. Both men and women have to face up to their fears and help each other to create the new world of sharing.

I don't think that's too idealistic, if by idealistic what's meant is 'impossibly utopian'. Indeed, I think we're all on the way to that future already. Women have achieved a lot so far, and it's now time for men to start catching up with them; it's time for Mr Banks to get out that kite from the cupboard and start looking for places to fly it. I have a final word for men on this point too. You may think that much of what I've written is impossible for *you*. It isn't. In fact, you owe it to your partner and your children to try and be the essential father I've outlined, but most of all, you owe it to yourself. Don't forget that by being the essential father you'll be helping to make sure that your children grow up to break the mould, and to avoid many of the problems I've talked about in this book. And whenever you come across a problem in your experience of fatherhood, whenever you reach an obstacle that you don't think you can overcome, remember one thing above all: the more you put into parenthood, the more you're likely to get out of it – and the better off your family will be as a result. That's what makes being the essential father so worthwhile.

I've always been a Beatles fan, and I've written large sections of this book to the sounds of their music. The record player and tape deck are in my study, next to the desk on which I'm writing these words. Of the four Beatles, however, I've always been more interested in John Lennon than the other three, mostly because he was the first one to become a father. John Lennon was the son of an absent father and a mother who preferred to hand him over to her sister to be brought up rather than to do the job herself. When John's first son Julian was born, Beatlemania was just taking off, and he was quoted years later as saying that he had never been a 'proper' father to Julian because he had 'always been on tour at the time'. From biographies I've read of him, it's also apparent that John Lennon played the role of 'weekend father' to his son, a father who would arrive with presents every so often, but who couldn't cope with his son's practical needs and demands. But he broke the cycle when his second son was born. John Lennon opted to stay at home to look after baby Sean, and did so as a full-time parent and househusband for five years while Yoko looked after their business interests. He would still probably be Sean's 'primary parent' today if he hadn't been gunned down in December 1980. All very well for a rich rock star, you might say, and it's true that John Lennon didn't have to worry about earning a living at the same time as being a father, but that rich rock star was once a little boy living in a Liverpool suburb without a father. John Lennon came a long way. He found in himself the resources he needed to make a success of being a parent; he got in touch with his feminine half. If he could do it, I see no reason why the rest of us can't either.

My father never knew his father, either. My grandparents split up when my father was a small boy, and he had no memories of the man who had had a half share in creating him. My grandfather walked out of his son's life and never came back, and that small boy grew into a man who wondered often – until his dying day – if his father was still alive somewhere, as he may well have been, and may still be. I long ago decided that I would break the cycle of absent fathers breeding absent fathers with my own children. That's partly why I wrote this book; it's why it's dedicated to my father and my son, two people who will never meet. Sometimes when I pick up my son and hold him I hope that one day he will be the sort of father my father could have been to me. The last words in this book are for him, and for all the other fathers to come. They're the last words from the last record the Beatles made together, a record I've played often while I've been writing this book:

And in the end, the love you take is equal to the love you make.

# Useful addresses

There are several organisations which may well be of help to you at different times, and for different reasons, when you become parents.

**Active Birth Movement**, 47, Pilgrim's Lane, London NW3 (01-794 2354). Provides information and support for couples who want an active, natural childbirth.

**Association for Postnatal Illness**, c/o Institute of Obstetrics and Gynaecology, Queen Charlotte's Hospital, Goldhawk Road, London, W6 (01-741 5019). A self-help group and source of information for couples for whom postnatal depression is a problem.

**Association of Breastfeeding Mothers**, 129 Catford Hill, London SE6 (01-659 5151). 24-hour information service which will also put you in touch with a breastfeeding counsellor in your area.

**Community Health Foundation**, 188-194 Old Street, London EC1V 9BP (01-251 4076). Classes run and information given on preventative medicine, health and nutrition.

**Cry-sis**, c/o Zeta Thornton, 63 Putney Road, Enfield, Middlesex (01-882 4720/886 5848). National support group for the parents of babies who cry excessively.

**Families Need Fathers**, 198 High Road, London N22 (01-888 5544). Organisation for fathers without custody of their children after a divorce or separation. Local groups in some areas.

**Family Planning Association**, 27-35 Mortimer Street, London W1N 7RJ (01-636 7866). Leaflets and information on all aspects of contraception available; also, the address and phone number of your local FPA clinic.

**Foresight, The Association for Pre-Conceptual Care**, The Old Vicarage, Church Lane, Witley, Godalming, Surrey (042879 4500). Foresight aims at helping couples to have healthy babies by teaching them a programme of pre-conceptual care.

**Gingerbread**, 35 Wellington Street, London, WC2 (01-240 0953). Information and support for one-parent families.

**La Leche League** BM 3424, London WC1N 3XX (01-404 5011). Help, advice and information on breastfeeding, with personal counselling by phone or letter if necessary.

**Marriage Guidance Council**, 76A New Cavendish Street, London W1 (01-580 1087). Help and advice for couples with marital problems; can put you in touch with your local counsellor.

**Maternity Alliance**, 59-61 Camden High Street, London NW1 (01-388 6337). Campaigns for maternity rights and welfare, and also provides information on those subjects.

**Miscarriage Association**, Dolphin Cottage, 4 Ashfield Terrace, Thorpe, Wakefield, WF3 3DD, West Yorkshire (0532 82 8946). Provides advice and information for couples dealing with a miscarriage.

**National Caesarean Support Association**, 72 Perry Rise, London SE23 3QL (01-699 8399). Support and advice for couples dealing with a Caesarean birth.

**National Childbirth Trust**, 9 Queensborough Terrace, London W2 (01-221 3833). National organisation which promotes education for parenthood and to help parents to get a real choice in childbirth. The NCT operates a widespread, national network of antenatal classes, breastfeeding counsellors and postnatal support groups. A recent development is the setting up of support groups for fathers (both before and after birth). A leaflet entitled *Becoming a Father* is available from the above address.

**National Childminding Association**, 204-206 High Street, Bromley, Kent, BR1 1PP (01-464 6164).

**Organisation for Parents Under Stress** (OPUS), The Information Officer, Great Carr Farm, Kirkby Misperton, Moulton, North Yorkshire (065 38 6256). OPUS is a centre for self-help groups and helplines for parents with problems of all sorts anywhere in the country. Contact this address for help in your area.

**Parents Anonymous**, North Islington Welfare Centre, 6-9 Manor Gardens, Holloway Road, London N7 6LA (01-263 5672 – office, 01-263 8918 – Lifeline). An organisation for parents under stress. An answering machine gives you the name and phone number of the volunteer on duty. It's a 24-hour service.

**Samaritans** (London Branch), Crypt of St Stephen's Church, 39 Walbrook, London EC4 (01-283 3400/626 9000).

**Stillbirth and Neonatal Death Society (SANDS)**, Argyle House, 29-31 Euston Road, London NW1 2SC (01-833 2851). Support groups, advice, information.

# Useful books

The shelves of bookshops are weighed down by books on pregnancy, birth, family life, child development and all the problems thereof, so I won't burden you with an enormous list of erudite books to read. What I've tried to do here is to point you in the direction of some books which you will find enlightening as a father. Both you and your partner may well find my other book on this subject useful; it's called *So You Want to Have a Baby* (Julia MacRae, 1985), and it's designed to be a complete one-volume guide for couples to becoming a parent.

## Pregnancy and birth

As it says in the blurbs to her books, Sheila Kitzinger is a world authority on childbirth and allied subjects, and all her books are worth reading. I particularly recommend *The New Good Birth Guide* (Penguin, 1983), *The Experience of Childbirth* (Penguin, 1984) and *Birth at Home* (OUP, 1980).
*Why Us?* (Thorsons, 1984), by Dr Andrew Stanway, is an excellent one-volume study of infertility. Also worth looking at if you're interested in fertility and conception is *Natural Family Planning* (Allen & Unwin, 1984), by Dr Anna Flynn and Melissa Brooks.

## Babies and Early Parenthood

*The Baby Care Book* (Dorling Kindersley, 1983) by Miriam Stoppard, is one of the best and most informative books on looking after babies and young children that I've read. It's full of common sense and very easy to use.
*Babyhood* (Penguin, 1983) and *Baby and Child* (Penguin 1981) are two classics by Penelope Leach which are also worth reading, even though they more or less ignore fathers. Penelope Leach has also written *The Parents' A-Z* (Penguin, 1985), which is a comprehensive reference book covering almost everything you are likely to want to know about your children's health and development.
*Breast is Best* (Pan, 1978) by Drs Penny and Andrew Stanway is the best book available on breastfeeding, but it's still worth backing that up with Sheila Kitzinger's *The Experience of Breastfeeding* (Penguin, 1982) and Maire Messenger Davies' *The Breastfeeding Book* (Century, 1983).

## Books specifically about men and/or fatherhood

In the last few years there has been a spate of books about men. The following are just a selection of the more interesting titles.
*Fatherhood* (Allen & Unwin, 1984) by Brian Jackson, an excellent short look at what it means to be a young father today.
*Men* (Century, 1984) by Mary Ingham, a fascinating survey of attitudes and stereotypes.
*Man Enough* (Chatto & Windus, The Hogarth Press) by Yvonne Roberts, a series of very revealing interviews with men of thirty-five.
*The Hearts of Men* (Pluto Press) by Barbara Ehrenreich. This book's central theme is that the rise of feminism could be seen as a reaction to a male 'flight from commitment' to the old ethic of working to support wife and children. As you would imagine, it's a fascinating angle on an old chestnut.
*The Father Figure* (Tavistock Publications, 1982), edited by Lorna McKee and Margaret O'Brien, and *Fathers* (Junction Books, 1982), edited by Nigel Beail and Jacqueline McGuire are collections of academic research papers which are very hard going, but worth persevering with for some interesting insights.
*Fathering* (Fontana, 1981) by Ross D. Parke is another fairly heavy academic book which is also worth the struggle.
*The Second Stage* (Abacus, 1983) by Betty Friedan and *Outrageous Acts and Everyday Rebellions* (Jonathan Cape, 1984) by Barbara Steinem are two books by senior figures in the women's movement worth reading; they're full of things which apply to men – in a hopeful way.
*Men – An Investigation into the Emotional Male* (BBC Books, 1984) by Phillip Hodson.

## Sex and Marriage

*Marriage* (Fontana, 1984) by Maureen Green is a book which explores the great divide between men and women and reveals that men need to do some catching up as far as their ideas about marriage are concerned.
*Life After Marriage* (Flamingo, 1984) by A. Alvarez. It might seem defeatist to include a book which is about divorce in the section headed 'marriage', but this book gave me more insight into what makes marriages work as well as the causes of marital failure than anything else I've read.
*Sex in History* (Hamish Hamilton, 1980) By Reay Tannahill is a wonderful book tracing the history of attitudes to sexuality from time immemorial. If you want to know why you think about sex in the way you do, read Reay Tannahill's book.

## Work, Women and Single Parents

*Kitchen Sink, or Swim? Women in the Eighties – The Choices* (Penguin, 1982) by Deirdre Saunders with Jane Reed. An excellent survey of the problems facing women in their attempt to find a way of reconciling their traditional role and their need and desire for meaning outside the home and family.
*How to Survive as a Working Mother* (Penguin, 1982) by Lesley Garner, a book which should be required reading for the partners of all working mothers.
*One Parent Families* (Davis Poynter, 1975), edited by Dulyan Barber.

## Miscellaneous

*Families and How to Survive Them* (Methuen, 1983) by John Cleese and Robyn Skinner. This is an original and revealing study of families and how they work, based on Robyn Skinner's work as a family therapist. It's worth reading for insight into almost every area of family life.
*Dream Babies* (OUP, 1984) by Christina Hardyment, is a history of babycare manuals, and therefore a marvellous way of learning a very simple lesson about parenthood – which is that there are as many ways of bringing up children well as there are of skinning a cat, to use a traditional simile. Fascinating reading for the long-term battered parent.
*Babies Need Books* (Penguin, 1982) by Dorothy Butler. This is a personal hobby horse, but I feel strongly that children need good books from an early age, and Dorothy Butler's book tells you which books to use with your children, and how to do it at every stage.
*Birdy, Dad, A Midnight Clear* (All Penguin and currently available) by William Wharton, three novels by an American writer which cover much of what I've talked about in this book. *Dad* in particular is a wonderful study of the relationships between three generations of men, grandfather, father and son. As with many works of imagination, William Wharton manages to charge his books with more significance, meaning and insight into human behaviour and feeling than any number of manuals could ever hope to do.
*Home before Dark* (Weidenfeld and Nicolson, 1985) by Susan Cheever, and *My Father and Myself* (Penguin, 1984) by J. R. Ackerley are two memoirs of fathers by highly gifted writers. One tells of a deep and loving relationship between a father and daughter (although it was also difficult at times), the other of a relationship characterised by secrecy, deception and absence. Both will help you to understand just what sort of an influence a father can be on his children.